Collins

INTERNATIONAL PRIMARY ENGLISH AS A SECOND LANGUAGE

Teacher's Guide 2

HarperCollins
PUBLISHERS
200

William Collins' dream of knowledge for all began with the publication of his first book in 1819.

A self-educated mill worker, he not only enriched millions of lives, but also founded a flourishing publishing house. Today, staying true to this spirit, Collins books are packed with inspiration, innovation and practical expertise. They place you at the centre of a world of possibility and give you exactly what you need to explore it.

Collins. Freedom to teach.

An imprint of HarperCollins*Publishers*
The News Building
1 London Bridge Street
London
SE1 9GF

Browse the complete Collins catalogue at
www.collins.co.uk

10 9 8 7 6 5 4 3 2 1

978-0-00-821363-3

Daphne Paizee asserts her moral right to be identified as the author of this work.

British Library Cataloguing in Publication Data

A catalogue record for this publication is available from the British Library.

Publisher Celia Wigley
Commissioning editor Karen Jamieson
Series editor Karen Morrison
Managing editor Sarah Thomas
Editor Alexander Rutherford
Project managed by Tara Alner
Edited by Tracy Thomas
Proofread by Zoe Smith
Cover design by ink-tank and associates
Cover artwork by QBS Learning
Internal design by 2hoots publishing services and QBS Learning
Typesetting by 2hoots publishing services and QBS Learning
Illustrations by QBS Learning
Production by Lauren Crisp

Printed and bound by CPI Group (UK) Ltd, Croydon, CR0 4YY

All exam-style questions and sample answers have been written by the author. In examinations marks may be given differently.

Acknowledgements

The publishers gratefully acknowledge the permissions granted to reproduce copyright material in the book. Every effort has been made to contact the holders of copyright material, but if any have been inadvertently overlooked, the Publisher will be pleased to make the necessary arrangements at the first opportunity.

Poem on page 17, 'Come to the Carnival' by Erica Stewart, © Erica Stewart 2001 with permission from John Foster. Poem on page 42, 'Chinese New Year' by Barbara Moore, © Barbara Moore 2001. Poem on page 42, 'Diwali' by Tony Mitton first published in Sounds, published by Oxford University Press © Tony Mitton 2001 with permission from David Higham Associates Ltd. Poem on page 50, 'Skipping Rope Spell' by John Agard first published in No Hickory, No Dickory, No Dock, published by Puffin Books © John Agard with permission from Caroline Sheldon Literary Agency. Poem on page 80, 'Sounds like me', by Ian Larmont in Oxford Reading Tree: Levels 3-4: Glow-worms: Sounds Poems, compiled by John Foster © Ian Larmont 1995. Poem on page 80-81, 'My Big Band' by Tony Mitton first published in Sounds, published by OUP © Tony Mitton 1995 with permission from David Higham Associates Ltd.

HarperCollins*Publishers* Limited for extracts and artwork adapted from:

Pirates by Paul Shipton, illustrated by Kelly Waldek, text © 2005 Paul Shipton. *It Was a Cold, Dark Night* by Tim Hopgood, illustrated by Tim Hopgood, text © 2010 Tim Hopgood. *The Hare and the Tortoise* by Melanie Williamson, illustrated by Melanie Williamson, text © 2013 Melanie Williamson. *The Lion and the Mouse* by Anthony Robinson, illustrated by Ciaran Duffy, text © 2011 Anthony Robinson. *The Baby Turtle* by Andy & Angie Belcher, text © 2007 Andy & Angie Belcher. *Best Bird* by Laura Hambleton, illustrated by Laura Hambleton, text © 2011 Laura Hambleton. *Dance to the Beat* by Uz Afzal, text © 2005 Uz Afzal. *Helper Bird* by Anita Ganeri, text © 2011 Anita Ganeri. *The Magic Egg* by Vivian French, illustrated by Karen Donnelly, text © 2010 Vivian French. *The Dolphin King* by Saviour Pirotta, illustrated by Fausto Bianchi, text © 2012 Saviour Pirotta. *Rebecca at the Funfair* by Frances Ridley, illustrated by Teri Gower, text © 2005 Frances Ridley. *Sounds* by Julie Sykes, text © 2005 Julie Sykes.

Photo acknowledgements

The publishers wish to thank the following for permission to reproduce photographs. Every effort has been made to trace copyright holders and to obtain their permission for the use of copyright materials. The publishers will gladly receive any information enabling them to rectify any error or omission at the fi rst opportunity.

(t = top, c = centre, b = bottom, r = right, l = left)

Cover & p1 QBS Learning

PCM3 5a Niwat singsamarn/Shutterstock, PCM3 5b Laia Design Studio/Shutterstock, PCM8 1r Rauf Aliyev/Shutterstock, PCM8 2l Neonic Flower/Shutterstock, PCM8 3l Sudowoodo/Shutterstock, PCM8 3r Altana8/Shutterstock, PCM8 4l Viktar Dzindzikav/Shutterstock, PCM8 5l 5r 6r Noch/Shutterstock, PCM8 6l Gisele Yashar/Shutterstock, PCM9 t irin-k/Shutterstock, PCM9 tc Zhukov Oleg/Shutterstock, PCM9 bc Eric Isselee/Shutterstock, PCM9 b Pakhnyushchy/Shutterstock, PCM23 1a runzelkorn/Shutterstock, PCM23 1b Gelpi/Shutterstock, PCM23 2a Rtimages/Shutterstock, PCM23 2b Solid Web Designs LTD/Shutterstock, PCM23 3a michaeljung/Shutterstock, PCM23 3b Minerva Studio/Shutterstock, PCM23 4a Lisa F. Young/Shutterstock, PCM23 4b jassada watt_/Shutterstock, PCM23 5a 9nong/Shutterstock, PCM23 5b Tom Wang/Shutterstock, PCM27 KinokoTagawa/Shutterstock

CONTENTS

Introduction

About the *Collins Cambridge Primary English as a Second Language* course

The *Collins Cambridge Primary English as a Second Language* course is specifically written to fully meet the requirements of the Cambridge Primary English as a Second Language curriculum framework, and the material has been carefully developed to meet the needs of young English learners and teachers in a range of international contexts.

The material at each level is organised into nine topics, each divided into three related units. The activities in each unit are introduced and explored in context so that language is developed and learned in meaningful and familiar contexts related to learners' interests and what they may be learning in other school subjects.

The course materials are supplemented and enhanced by printable and downloadable resources, including photocopiable (printable) master sheets for support and extension of classroom based activities (you can find these on pages 97–126 of this Teacher's Guide) and audio recordings to model pronunciation, develop listening skills and add interest and excitement to learning.

Components of the course

For each of Stages 1–6, as detailed in the Cambridge Primary English as Second Language curriculum framework, we offer:

- a full colour, highly illustrated, magazine-style **Student's Book** with integral reading texts
- a write-in **Workbook** linked to the Student's Book and clearly referenced in the teaching guidelines
- this comprehensive **Teacher's Guide** with clear instructions for using the materials in a flexible and clearly differentiated way
- free-to-download **Audio** of key texts and listening activities.

Approach

The course is designed with flexible and interactive learning at its heart but it follows a consistent approach.

- Generally, lessons will start with a warm-up session in which the teacher leads the class into the unit either by linking back to previous learning or by engaging in some other activity to hook their attention and interest.
- This is followed by a whole class teaching session to introduce vocabulary and model language structures to be used in the unit.
- Once the basics are covered, the teacher then selects from the differentiated activity bank to suit the needs of each class. These activities can be done in small groups or pairs, but they can also be used as whole class activities if that is what the teacher wants to do.

The Teacher's Guide is the central element of the course. It provides a detailed and structured script for teaching the core vocabulary and language structures to the whole class, as well as the bank of differentiated activities (marked triangle, circle and square) which provide different levels of challenge for learners. The teacher can select from the activities in the bank, to suit the level of English among learners and to meet the needs of particular groups, or classroom contexts.

It is not intended that learners should work through all the activities in the Teacher's Guide, but rather that teachers should select according to the needs of the learners. If teachers try to complete *all* activities listed in the triangle, circle and square sections of the activity banks in the Teacher's Guide, they will find in some cases quite similar activities pitched at a slightly higher level of challenge, and this would be too repetitious, so teachers should select activities according to the need and ability level of learners. This way, the materials within this course are truly flexible and can be tailored to each class and learner.

The suggested activities relate to, and use, the magazine-style Student's Book (which contains the stimulus, or 'input', for learners, in the form of varied reading texts, scene pictures, picture-dictionary-style pages, and photographs for discussion).

The suggested activities in the activity bank also provide ideas for using the Workbook which enable learners to consolidate and apply what they have learned, and to relate what they are learning both to the environment in which they live and beyond, to other contexts.

Much of the learners' work is conducted in pairs or small groups in line with international best practice. The tasks and activities are designed to be engaging for learners and to support teachers in their assessment of learner progress and achievement.

Throughout the course, there is a wide variety of learning experiences on offer. The materials are organised so that they do not impose a rigid structure, but rather allow for a range of options linked to the learning objectives. The materials are therefore truly flexible and can be adapted to suit a range of learning contexts.

Differentiation

Differentiation is a key element of second language teaching and learning so it forms a key element of the support and teaching ideas in this Teacher's Guide.

Fluency levels are likely to vary from learner to learner. The triangle, circle and square symbols indicate what learners at varying levels might be expected to manage. The triangle indicates what can be expected of almost all learners. The circle indicates what might be expected of most learners with some support, and the square indicates what level of achievement might be expected from more able and confident learners. Levels will vary, as some learners may find some topics more interesting and/or easier. Similarly, some may excel at speaking activities rather than written ones.

Using the Teacher's Guide

The Teacher's Guide offers detailed guidance for covering each topic.

The topics are designed to cover approximately three teaching weeks. The teacher knows their class and context best, so they should feel free to vary the pace and the amount of work covered each week to suit their circumstances. The course has been designed to be totally flexible and allow for speeding up and slowing down.

At the start of each of the nine topics, a full list of learning objectives is provided. The objectives which are the main focus of the topic are underlined for planning purposes.

In addition, a summary of the grammar and language structures covered in each topic is provided for reference. This summary is for teacher information only. The structures and grammar detailed here will be taught in context and modelled for learners to use.

Each of the units has a clear structure, with:

- a list of resources
- suggestions for introducing the unit
- lead-in ideas
- ideas for introducing vocabulary and language structures to the whole class
- a differentiated activity bank for each unit. Activities are grouped in sections according to lower-, mid- and higher-level challenge (**triangle** activities for lower-level challenge; **circle** activities for mid-level challenge; **square** activities for higher-level challenge).
- suggestions for a plenary wrap-up session at the end of the unit
- ideas for informal assessment activities.

Student's Book

The Student's Book offers a colourful and attractive set of stimulus (or 'input') materials to introduce vocabulary and match the language structures being taught. The book follows a magazine-style design with strong visual appeal, for maximum enjoyment and engagement. The following features are found at all levels:

- A range of fiction and non-fiction text types, including stories, poems, play scripts, information texts and transactional texts are provided to use as a starting point for contextualised learning.
- Instruction rubrics are kept short and simple, allowing more space on the page for the visuals and the text. Traditional-style language exercises are kept off the Student's Book pages, so that it doesn't feel like a textbook.
- 'Let's talk' and 'Let's think' bubbles are included on the pages, with questions to prompt personalisation of the topic, and to introduce higher-order cognitive skills, no matter how young learners are or how fluent they are in English.

Workbook

The Workbook is clearly linked to the Student's Book pages. The activities here contain structured spaces for learners to record answers. The activities can be used as classroom tasks, for homework, or for assessment purposes. The completed Workbook tasks give the teacher an opportunity to check work and give written feedback and/or grades. Learners have a consolidated record of their work and parents can see what kind of activities learners are doing in class.

Online resources

The audio recordings for the course are available online as a free download. You can access these at Collins.co.uk. These resources can be downloaded, stored offline and used to support the activities as needed.

Handwriting

Handwriting is not taught explicitly in this course, although the following objectives are implicitly covered in the activities and supporting notes in the Teacher's Guide:

1Wa1 Hold a pen/pencil in a comfortable and efficient grip

1Wa2 Form higher and lower case letters of regular size and shape

1Wa3 Write letters and words in a straight line from left to right with regular spaces between letters and words.

We recommend that teachers choose a structured and suitable course for teaching handwriting skills at Stage 2. The *Collins Treasure House Handwriting* series is a useful resource for this, progressing from the introduction of fine motor skills, through cursive styles at the early stages, then to different handwriting styles, calligraphy and links to computer fonts at higher levels.

Personal dictionaries and journals

It is useful for learners to have a hardcover notebook that they use to make a personal dictionary and for independent writing (journaling). You can decide at which point to start these, but even emergent readers and writers can keep a journal. Make sure each learner has a book and allow them to decorate the cover as they like. They should write the letters of the alphabet (upper and lower case) at the tops of the first 26 pages. They can then write down any new words they learn to spell and draw pictures to help them remember the meanings. Insert a tab after the alphabet pages and use the rest of the book for independent writing. Research shows that encouraging emergent writing is a good way of improving literacy skills. At first, learners will draw and scribble. You can ask them to tell you about their drawing and write the words for them. They will then move to letters and letter-like symbols and you can ask them to tell you what they mean. The next development steps are often the writing of beginning sounds, or just the writing of a single letter, which to the child represents the overall prominent sound of that word (also called the 'salient sound'). For example, writing 'k' for 'like', because that's the sound that is most distinct when the child says the word. As they write more and more, their spelling and expression generally improves. There is a very good article about this in the journal *The Reading Teacher*, which you can access online, by Sonia Q. Cabell, Laura S. Tortorelli, and Hope K. Gerde (May, 2013). *How Do I Write…? Scaffolding Preschoolers' Early Writing Skills* (*The Reading Teacher, 66*(8), pp. 650-659).

Assessment in primary English

In the *Collins Cambridge Primary English as a Second Language* course, assessment is a continuous, planned process that involves collecting information regularly about learner progress and learning, in order to provide constructive feedback to both learners and parents and also to guide planning and the next teaching steps.

The Cambridge Primary English as a Second Language curriculum framework makes it clear what learners are expected to learn and achieve at each Stage. Our task as teachers is to assess whether or not learners have achieved the stated goals using clearly-focused, varied, reliable and flexible methods of assessment.

In the *Collins Cambridge Primary English as a Second Language* course, assessment is continuous and in-built. It applies the principles of international best practice and ensures that assessment:

- is ongoing and regular
- supports individual achievement
- provides feedback and encouragement to learners
- allows for integration into the activities and classroom teaching, by combining different assessment methods, including observations, questioning and formal and informal tasks
- uses strategies that cater for a variety of learner needs in the classroom (language, physical, emotional and cultural), and acknowledges that learners do not all need to be assessed at the same time, or in the same way
- allows for, and prepares learners for, more formal, summative assessment including controlled activities, tasks and tests.

In Stage 2 of the course informal assessment ideas are included within this Teacher's Guide, at the end of each unit (the **Quick check** feature). In addition, an end-of-year Review Activity is included as photocopiable masters (**PCMs**) on pages 127–132, with ideas for how to administer it on page 85. There is also an informal assessment page in the Workbook, for each topic. These can be used in the same way as all the other activities in the classroom.

More formal testing in the form of progression tests begins in Stage 3. No formal assessments (tests or examinations) are required at Stages 1 or 2.

High-frequency sight words for Stage 2

Stage 1 words to revise:

a	can't	go	like	on	to
all	come	going	look	said	up
am	dad	has	me	see	was
and	do	he	mom	she	we
are	don't	I	mother	small	want
at	father	in	my	the	went
big	for	is	no	they	yes
can	get	it	of	this	you

Stage 2 words:

about	call	have	made	or	than
after	called	help	make	our	that
again	can't	her	man	out	their
an	cat	hers	many	over	them
another	could	here	may	people	then
any	day	him	more	play	there
as	did	his	much	push	these
away	don't	home	must	pull	time
back	door	house	name	put	yesterday
ball	down	how	new	ran	your
be	first	if	next	run	what
because	from	I'm	night	saw	when
bed	girl	jump	not	school	where
been	good	last	now	sister	who
boy	got	laugh	off	so	will
brother	had	live	old	some	with
but	half	look	once	street	without
by	has	love	one	take	would

Subject words

Number words from *one* to *fifty*

Colour words: *red*, *green*, *yellow*, *blue*, etc. (Used in context and with support.)

Days of the week: *Monday*, *Tuesday*, *Wednesday*, *Thursday*, *Friday*, *Saturday*, *Sunday*

Months of the year: *January*, *February*, *March*, *April*, *May*, *June*, *July*, *August*, *September*, *October*, *November*, *December*

Instruction words

choose, copy, count, cross, find, make, match, point to, tick, write

Topic 1 Friends and neighbours

Overview

This topic allows you to revise basic vocabulary and knowledge of English while assessing the prior knowledge of learners in your class. There are opportunities to integrate language lessons with other subjects in the curriculum, such as social sciences, mathematics, art and drama. Vocabulary and concepts are developed using familiar topics and by encouraging learners to express themselves using whatever knowledge they already have.

Units in this topic

Unit A: This is me!

Unit B: Let's be friends

Unit C: Neighbours

Teaching focus

- **2Rg1** Recognise, identify and sound, with support, a limited range of language at text level
- **3Rf1** Read and follow, with support, familiar instructions for classroom activities
- **2Rg2** Begin to read, with support, very short simple fiction and non-fiction texts with confidence and enjoyment
- **2Rd1** Understand, with support, some specific information and detail in very short, simple texts on a limited range of general and curricular topics
- **2Rm1** Understand the meaning of very short, simple texts on familiar general and curricular topics by rereading them
- **2Rd2** Understand the meaning of simple short sentences on familiar general and curricular topics
- **2Wa1** Plan, write and check, with support, short sentences on familiar topics
- **2Wc1** Write, with support, short sentences which give basic personal information
- **2Wo3** Use upper and lower case letters accurately when writing names, places and short sentences during guided writing activities
- **2Ug14** Spell a growing number of familiar high-frequency words accurately during guided writing activities
- **2Wo2** Include a full stop and question mark during guided writing of short, familiar sentences
- **2Ug2** Use numbers 1–50 to count
- **2Ug3** Use adjectives, including possessive adjectives, on familiar topics to give personal information and describe things
- **2Ut2** Use *who, what, where, how many* to ask questions on familiar topics
- **2Ut3** Use impersonal *you* in the question: *How do you spell that?*
- **2Ut5** Use personal subject and object pronouns, including possessive pronouns *mine, yours* to give basic personal information and describe things
- **2Uf2** Use common simple present forms, including short answer forms and contractions, to give personal information
- **2Uf3** Use common past simple forms [regular and irregular] to describe actions and narrate simple events including short answer forms and contractions
- **2Uf5** Use common present continuous forms, including short answers and contractions, to talk about what is happening now on personal and familiar topics
- **2Ug4** Use *–ing* forms *swimming, spelling* as nouns to describe familiar and classroom activities
- **2Ut6** Use *There is/are* to make short statements and descriptions
- **2Uf6** Use *Have you [ever] been?* to talk about experiences
- **2Uf7** Use *can* to make requests and ask permission and use appropriate responses: *here you are, OK*
- **2Uf8** Use *must* to express obligation
- **2Uf9** Use *have + object + infinitive* to talk about obligations
- **2Uf10** Use *will* to talk about future intention
- **2Ug8** Use *What/How about* + noun/*-ing* to make suggestions
- **2Ug9** Use prepositions of location, position and direction: *at, behind, between, in, in front of, near, next to, on, to* on personal and familiar topics
- **2Ug10** Use prepositions of time: *on, in, at,* to talk about days and times on personal and familiar topics
- **2Ug11** Use *with* to indicate accompaniment and instrument and *for* to indicate recipient on personal and familiar topics
- **2Ld4** Understand an increased range of short, basic supported classroom instructions

- **2Ld3** Understand a growing range of short, supported questions which ask for personal information
- **2Lg3** Recognise words that are spelled out in a limited range of general and curricular topics
- **2Lg2** Identify initial, middle and final phonemes and blends
- **2S1** Make basic statements which provide personal information on a limited range of general topics
- **2S2** Ask questions to find out about an increasing range of personal information
- **2S4** Use basic vocabulary for a limited range of general and curricular topics
- **2S5** Give short, basic descriptions of people and objects
- **2S6** Contribute a growing range of suitable words, phrases, and sentences during short pair, group and whole class exchanges
- **2S7** Take turns when speaking with others in a growing range of short, basic exchanges
- **2S8** Relate very short, basic stories and events on a limited range of general and curricular topics

Language patterns

Grammar summary for teachers:

- **Verb 'to be':** This is an irregular verb used in affirmative and negative sentences and questions. It is also commonly used in contractions and short answers. (Examples: *This isn't my book. We are friends. Are you 7 years old? No I'm not.*) The different forms of the verb (*am, is, are, was, were*) are high-frequency words which learners need to be able to recognise, read and write. Do not teach the grammar; use repetition to teach this structure.
- **Verb 'can':** This is a modal or auxiliary verb. Modal verbs do not have infinitive forms or *–ing* forms. They also do not have third person singular forms that end in *–s*. The verb does have a past tense form (*could*) as well as negative forms (*cannot/can't, could not/couldn't*).
- **Questions with 'do':** The auxiliary verb *to do* is often used to ask questions and to give short (negative and positive) answers to questions. *Do you have a sister? Does he have a sister? Yes, I do. No, I don't. Yes, he does. No, he doesn't.*
- **Possessive adjectives:** These are words such as *my, your, his, her, our, their*. The words are used before nouns. *This is **my** book.*
- **Personal pronouns:** There are subject pronouns and object pronouns.

Subject pronouns	Object pronouns
I am a 6. **You** are a friend. **She** is a girl. **He** is a boy. **We** are friends. **They** are happy.	I see **her/him/them/us**.

Unit A This is me!

Resources and materials

- Student's Book pp. 4–6
- Workbook pp. 4–9
- Audio files: Audio 1; Audio 2
- Photocopiable Masters (PCMs) PCM 1; PCM 2
- Cards for learners to make their own name tags
- Prompt cards with letters of the alphabet and number words 1–20
- Sentence strips with sentences from the story in the Student's Book (pp. 4–6)
- Map of the world or of the part of the world where most of your learners come from
- Sheets of paper with a big circle drawn on them, one for each group of learners
- Boxes of 20 small counters (buttons, stones, etc.)

Key vocabulary

name, age, girl, boy, is, are, am, have, can, there, I, he, she, they, we, you, me, him, them, my, his, her, their, our, have, like

Numbers: one–twenty

nationalities of learners in the class (Japanese, Kenyan, and so on)

Lead-in ideas

- Introduce yourself to the class, using the structure: *Hello. My name is ____________. I am your teacher this year.*
- Let learners sing any familiar song, rhyme or chant about greetings or names (**Audio 1** and **2**).

Script for the lesson

Introducing vocabulary

Use the first lessons of the year to revise what should already be familiar vocabulary, such as personal pronouns (including *he, she, him, her*), numbers 1–20, common verbs (*be, can, have*) and adjectives (*big, small, colours*).

Introduce the names of different countries and the nationalities of the people who come from those countries. Start with the nationalities of learners in the class.

Encourage everyone to take part and spend some time talking about group work and how you behave in groups. For example, tell learners that they need to listen carefully when other group members are talking and that they need to give everyone a chance to contribute. Be aware that some learners may not be confident talking in groups yet, and allow for pair work where necessary as it is less stressful to talk to one person (as well as more difficult to avoid contributing).

Sounds

Revise and teach phonemes within the context of the unit. Focus on the initial and end sounds of the names of learners and countries mentioned in this unit, for example.

Revise the names of the letters of the alphabet.

Introducing structures

Revise structures that should already be familiar, such as: *What's your/my/his/her name? My/His/Her name is ________. I'm ________. Can you ________? Are you ________? Yes. No.*

Previous knowledge

Learners should already be familiar with the alphabet and with phonemes from literacy lessons in their first language and from Stage 1. They should also have some basic vocabulary in English with which to respond to questions and give personal information. Use these first lessons to identify where learners have gaps in their knowledge.

Possible areas of difficulty

Some letter sounds may be the same in other languages, but others will be different. Help learners to pronounce letter sounds correctly in English.

Some learners may not be familiar with contracted forms such as *It's*, *What's* and *I'm*, as they may have only learned the full forms of these structures. You can teach written contractions later, but encourage learners to use and respond to oral contractions, as that is the way most people speak.

Activities

Select from these activities depending on the level of challenge needed for different learners, interest levels and what you have time to include. Supplement these with additional activities of your own and/or digital activities from the online resource.

▲ **1.** Learners can make their own name tags (with first name and family name) and use these to introduce themselves to the rest of the class. Let them say something that they think is interesting about themselves. (Example: *My name is Majal. My family name is Khan. I am new. I like playing football.*)

▲ **2.** Learners can sit in groups and take turns to ask each other questions. Remind them to take turns, listen and give everyone a chance to take part. Each learner asks another learner in the group one question. The learner who answers the question then asks another learner a new question. For example:

A: *What's your name?*

B: *It's Jo.*

B: *How old are you?*

C: *I'm eight.*

C: *Are you a new student?*

D: *Yes, I am.*

D: *What's your name?*

And so on.

Listen to learners as they work and make notes about learners who are not yet able to form basic questions and give basic answers.

3. Learners work in groups. Each learner puts his or her name tag in a pile, face down, in the middle of the group. Learners take turns to pick up a card and read the name. If they can't read the name, they hold up the card for the owner to identify him or herself. Then they make sentences using possessive adjectives. (Example: *Anna Brown. Her name is Anna Brown.*)

4. Find out if learners know any telephone numbers. They may know these in their first languages. Some learners may have their own phones, or they may have a landline at home or know their parents' numbers in case of emergencies. Be sensitive to ensure that some learners do not feel left out.

   Teach learners how to say these numbers in English. For example, say: *My phone number is 062 97459 (zero six two nine seven four five nine). What's your phone number?* This is a way to revise numbers. You can also let learners practise reading the names of numbers 1–10, using the prompt cards.

5. **Link to social sciences*. Show learners a map. Use a map of the world if you have learners of many different nationalities. Use a map of your own country and its neighbours if most learners come from the area. Ask the question: *Where are you from?* Help learners to reply: *I'm from* __________ (Spain, Buenos Aires, Green River, etc.). Write the name on a card and attach the name to the map. Help learners to read the names by identifying the initial phonemes first.

6. Learners fill in personal details about themselves and then write sentences. Learners can complete activities 1 and 2 in the Workbook. Remind learners to use capital letters for the first letters of their names.

7. Revise the alphabet with learners. Then let learners revise the names of the letters by spelling their own names (example: *My name is Tamara: tee ay em ay ar ay*). Learners can also sing an alphabet song.

   Then practise putting letters in alphabetical order. Use the prompt cards for this. Work with groups. Give each group a batch of five or six cards and see which group can put their cards in order the quickest.

8. Learners can complete activities 3 and 4 in the Workbook**.** This revises alphabetical order and number words from one–ten.

9. Let learners find *Can you see me*? in the Student's Book (pages 4–6). Discuss the title and the pictures with the class or with groups. Then read the story and let learners follow and answer the questions as you read. Revise vocabulary as you work if necessary.

   Give learners the sentence strips you have made and let them match the strips to the sentences in the Student's Book. For further practise, cut up the sentence strips and let learners use the words to recreate the questions and statements.

10. Use the names of learners as well as the names of the towns and countries that they come from to revise initial phonemes. You can write letters on the board and play a game with the class. Call out a letter and see who can suggest a name that begins with that letter. Write the names under the letters as learners suggest them. Work out a system of scoring with the class before you begin.

11. Play a game such as 'Simon says' to revise simple classroom instructions. Give instructions, such as *Simon says … Open your books. Stand up. Get into a line. Go outside.* Learners can take turns to give instructions as well.

12. **Link to mathematics.* Write the numbers 11–20 on the board (or use your prompt cards) and find out if learners know the names of these numbers in English. Help them to read and say the numbers by breaking them into syllables (*four/teen*, *e/le/ven*, and so on). Then spell the numbers aloud and see if learners can recognise the number.

13. Let learners work in groups. Give each group a box with 20 stones (or buttons or other small counters) and a piece of paper with a circle or square on it. Say: *Put* ________ *[say a number between 1 and 20] in your circle.* Learners follow the instructions.

14. Learners reread *Can you see me?* in the Student's Book. Ask them to find high-frequency words in the story, for example: *I, you, see, me, my, it, is, a, he, she, can*. Ask them to count how many times they can find each word.

    Learners can then complete activities 5 and 6 in the Workbook.

15. Revise subject and object pronouns with the class. One way to do this is to have learners sit in groups. Give simple instructions and then let each learner have a turn to give an instruction as well. For example: *This is Mary. Come and sit next to her. This is Raj. Come and stand next to him. This is my bag. Put it on the table.*

    Learners complete activities 7 and 8 in the Workbook which provides practice with recognising numbers, as well as with subject and object pronouns.

16. Give learners some words to learn for spelling. Choose about six words. You could, for example, give learners some number words to learn. Write the number words on the board in a jumbled order and let learners work out how to write each word correctly by referring to the prompt cards you have made.

17. Teach learners the names of some nationalities. Teach the names of the nationalities in the class first. Help them to make sentences, such as: *I am from Spain. I am Spanish. They are from India. They are Indian. She is from Britain. She is British. He is from the UAE. He is Emirati. I am from Jamaica. I am Jamaican.*

    Then focus on names of nationalities that end in *-an, -ish* and *-ese* so that learners begin to recognise the ends of these words.

    Learners complete activities 9 and 10 in the Workbook.

18. Give learners instructions to draw pictures. This will help you to assess how much learners understand of basic structures and vocabulary. Use colour words, numbers, high-frequency words, names of familiar objects. Give them copies of **PCM 1** to draw in, or create your own sheets. For example, say:

    Draw a picture of a girl with long hair in block 1.

    Write the number eight in block 2.

    Draw a ball and colour it red and blue in block 3.

19. Learners read *Can you see me?* in the Student's Book. They then answer questions about pictures from the story in activity 11 in the Workbook, which asks them to underline the correct answer.

Wrap-up plenary

If you have learners from different countries, talk about what it is like to live in different places. Help learners to share information about where they come from. If most of the class come from the same area, talk about how everyone in the class is special. Find out about the special things that learners in the class have or do. Remind learners to listen while others are talking.

Quick check

Play 'Bingo' with high-frequency words. Give learners blank sheets of paper with space for twelve words. (You can use **PCM 2**.) Write about fifteen words on the board and let them choose twelve words to copy onto their Bingo sheets. Choose words from the high-frequency word list on page 7 of this Teacher's Guide, or use the following words:

I, you, see, me, my, it, is, a, he, she, can, they, we, am, is

Explain how the game works: You say a word aloud and learners cross out the word if it is on their Bingo card. The first person to cross out all the words on their card shouts 'Bingo'.

Unit B Let's be friends

Resources and materials

- Student's Book p. 7
- Workbook pp. 10–14
- Audio files: Audio 3; Audio 4; Audio 5; Audio 6
- Photocopiable Master (PCM) PCM 3
- Prompt cards with pronouns: *I, he, she, it, you, we, they, my, his, her, your, their, our*
- Pictures of people for learners to describe (different colour hair, long, short hair, big, small, etc.)

Key vocabulary

friends, happy, sad, kind, best, cry, smile, laugh, fun, sorry, ant, dove, bite, river, stick

Lead-in ideas

- Let learners sing any familiar song about friendship.
- Discuss what friends do to help each other. Ask: *How do friends make you feel?* Revise or teach vocabulary, such as: *happy, sad, cry, laugh, smile, fun.*
- Play or read the poem *My Friends* (**Audio 3**). Discuss what it means. Learners can then recite it in groups.

Script for the lesson

Introducing vocabulary

Revise or teach adjectives that learners can use to describe their feelings towards friends.

You can pre-teach any vocabulary that you think will be unfamiliar before reading stories with the class.

Sounds

Let learners identify words that rhyme in poems. This develops an awareness of the phonemes with which words end.

Use familiar words in context to revise initial, middle and end phonemes and the sounds that they make.

Introducing structures

Revise structures that should already be familiar, such as the use of subject, object and possessive pronouns and the present simple tense of familiar verbs (such as: *have, live, help, like, go*). You can also revise structures such as: *There is ______/There are______, I like ________/___ing/I don't like ______/_____ing.* Teach simple requests and responses (*Can I have _____? OK. Here you are.*) in context as you revise the names of classroom objects. Teach the word *with* to show accompaniment. It is introduced in **Audio 3** and **4**.

Learners may have come across some contractions. Start to teach more in the lessons that follow. Use stories and natural conversation for this.

Previous knowledge

Learners will have some knowledge of basic structures and vocabulary in English.

Possible areas of difficulty

Learners will be at different stages in their acquisition of literacy skills as well as in their acquisition of English. Some learners may be reading with confidence and others not, for example. The differentiated activity suggestions in this Teacher's Guide will help to address this.

Some learners may start to say *This is for me* instead of *This is mine*. Correct them gently and move on if they do this.

Activities

Select from these activities depending on the level of challenge needed for different learners, interest levels and what you have time to include. Supplement these with additional activities of your own and/or digital activities from the online resource.

▲ **1.** Revise classroom objects and then teach learners a simple conversation to practise in pairs. Each pair of learners will need a selection of small classroom objects. One partner makes a request and the other replies. For example:

A: *Can I have the eraser, please?*

B: *OK. Here you are!*

A: *Can I have the blue book please?*

B: *Here you are.*

▲ **2.** Teach the structure: *This is for you*. You can do this during a class activity, for example if you are handing out reading books or other items to the class or to learners in a group. Make it quite clear that you are giving learners something. Say: *Jo, this book is for Debbie. This book is for you and Ali*. Or you can give an item to one learner to pass on to another learner. Say: *Jo, this is for Peter. Can you please give it to him?*

▲ **3.** Revise end sounds in rhymes and poems. Play the poem *My Friends* (**Audio 3**). Learners identify the words that rhyme (*kind/find, sad/bad, me/be/see*). Then read another poem or familiar song and let learners identify more rhyming words. Short poems like *Friends at School* (**Audio 4**) are useful for this activity.

▲ **4.** Teach the class to undertand and use the word *with* to mean 'accompaniment'.

Play the poems *My Friends* (**Audio 3**) and *Friends at School* (**Audio 4**) again. Then say the poems and leave out the word *with*. Let the class complete the poems orally. Write *with* on the board and let the class make simple sentences with the word.

You can build this into general class instructions. For example, if learners are to work in pairs, say: *Malik, you work with Jo. Andy, go with Mara. Anne, come with me.* Or let learners choose a partner by saying: *[name], please work with me.*

▲ **5.** In this activity learners revise asking questions to find out personal information. They ask questions beginning with *Do you like + noun* or *verb + -ing?* They give appropriate answers using the short answers *Yes, I do./No, I don't.*

Teach a simple conversation in which two people ask and answer questions. Demonstrate the interview with a learner who is fairly fluent. Then let learners work with partners to practise asking and answering questions.

A: *Do you like (swimming/fishing/chocolate/stories)?*

B: *Yes, I do./No, I don't.*

Then let each learner tell the class (or group) what they have found out. For example:

This is my friend, [name].

He/She likes ________________.

He/She also likes ______________.

He/She doesn't like _____________.

▲ **6.** Play a game to revise subject and object pronouns and possessive adjectives. Put the prompt cards with the pronouns face down on a table in front of a group of learners. Let each learner come up in turn and pick a card. The learner reads the pronoun on the card and then makes a sentence with the pronoun. The rest of the group decide if it is a good sentence (that is, grammatically correct) or not. You will need to facilitate this and offer support to any learners who find it difficult. Gently correct learners if they are wrong. If the sentence is correct, the learner gets a point.

▲ **7.** Learners complete activities 1 and 2 in the Workbook, which gives them an opportunity to complete a few sentences with personal information about a friend, using familiar structures.

▲ **8.** Show learners the pictures you have collected of different people. Make a short sentence to describe each person. For example: *She has black/brown/blonde hair. He is big/small/thin/fat. She has blue/brown/green eyes. He is young/old.* Revise and teach appropriate adjectives as you do this. Write the adjectives on the board.

Then play a game. Put all the pictures face up and let learners take turns to describe one of the people in the pictures. The other learners guess which person is being described. Remind them again if necessary to listen to each other's descriptions and to give everyone a chance to speak.

▲ **9.** Learners complete activities 3 and 4 in the Workbook.

▲ **10.** Give each learner a copy of **PCM 3**. Learners listen to sentences and tick the picture that matches the description that you read. Describe one of the people in each pair of pictures. For example:

1. *He is old*. OR *She is old.*
2. *She has long hair.* OR *She has short hair.*
3. *She is young*. OR *He is young.*
4. *It is round*. OR *They are round.*
5. *She likes cake.* OR *She likes apples.*
6. *They like playing football.* OR *He likes playing football.*

This sheet could also be used for assessment.

▲ **11.** Learners find the story *A Friend Helps* on page 7 of the Student's Book.

You can pre-teach the meanings of the words: *ant, dove* and *trap.* Discuss the pictures and ask learners what they think the story is about. Then play the full story (**Audio 5**). Play the story again, or read the text yourself this time. Note that the story is told in the present tense, so revise this tense before teaching the past tense.

Ask learners simple questions about the story to help them identify the characters, the setting and the sequence of events. For example:

Why does Ant go to the river?

What happens to him?

Who helps him?

What does Dove do?

How does Ant help Dove?

Whose foot does Ant bite?

What is the boy doing?

● **12.** Learners listen to the story *A Friend Helps* on page 7 of the Student's Book (**Audio 5**) again. They work in pairs to retell the story. Then they complete activities 5, 6 and 7 in the Workbook, in which they rewrite sentences from the story in the correct order.

* *Link to drama*. Learners can then work in groups of three (ant, dove, boy) to act the story. Help them to collect small props, like a small branch for the Ant to climb onto and a small box that they can use as a trap.

● **13.** Do some spelling activities with the class. Write some familiar words on the board and leave out the first, middle or last letters of the words. Let learners suggest how to complete the words. Use high-frequency words and words from familiar stories or poems. For example:

__nt (ant), *__oy* (boy), *__ove* (dove), *__iver* (river), *__riend* (friend), *____ee* (tree), *sch____l* (school), *pl____* (play), *s__y* (say).

● **14.** Learners complete activities 8 and 9 in the Workbook. They rearrange words to make simple sentences.

■ **15.** **Link to drama*. Learners reread the story *A Friend Helps* in the Student's Book (page 7). Let learners work in groups and make up their own stories about how friends can help each other. They can make up animal stories or stories about real people. Help them brainstorm a few ideas first. Read them another appropriate story about friends who help each other. Let them practise their stories and act them for the rest of the class. Take time to discuss the best stories.

■ **16.** Play the story *The Stupid Goats and the Clever Goats* (**Audio 6**), to the class twice. Then ask a few questions to help learners identify the main ideas in the story. For example:

What did the goats want to do?

How many goats crossed the bridge?

How many goats fell in the water?

Which goats were stupid?

Which goats were clever?

■ **17.** Learners listen to the story *The Stupid Goats and the Clever Goats* (**Audio 6**) again. Then they complete activities 10, 11 and 12 in the Workbook.

■ **18.** **Link to art.* Learners create a collage about a friend. They can draw pictures, take photographs, write sentences about their friends. They can also include pictures of things that their friends like. Some learners may also want to include symbols or emoticons like hearts or linked hands. Allow time for learners to talk about their collages. If they feel comfortable talking in front of the whole class, encourage them to do so. If they don't yet feel comfortable doing this, let them do this in groups.

■ **19.** Learners could also draw a picture or make up a rhyme for a friend. When learners have completed this, let them present their work to a friend using the structure *This is for you.*

Wrap-up plenary

Let learners talk about their friends or try and tell their favourite stories about friends.

Quick check

1. Learners can read adjectives and pronouns that you have written on prompt cards. You can also make duplicates of the cards and let learners play games in which they match the words.

2. Write a few familiar sentences from the unit on the board. Then erase one word in each sentence. Ask learners to complete the sentences orally. Then erase two words in each sentence and repeat the activity.

Unit C Neighbours

Resources and materials

- Student's Book p. 8
- Workbook pp. 15–19
- Audio file: Audio 7
- Photocopiable Master (PCM) PCM 2
- Pictures of streets where people live and work (with details such as shops, street names, numbers on buildings, for incidental reading) and a picture of a steel band
- Prompt cards with number words: *eleven, twelve, thirteen, fourteen, fifteen, sixteen, seventeen, eighteen*
- Prompt cards with prepositions: *at, behind, between, in, in front of, near, next to, on, to*

Key vocabulary

street, live, number, side, house, apartment, office, shop, restaurant, left, right, big, small, floors/storeys, carnival

Numbers: eleven, twelve, thirteen, fourteen, fifteen, sixteen, seventeen, eighteen

Prepositions of location, position and direction: at, behind, between, in, in front of, near, next to, on, to

Lead-in ideas

- If you can, take the class out on a field trip to a street nearby where people live and work. Help learners to use English words to name places on the street, shops and office or apartment blocks, as well as the numbers on houses and other buildings. If you have support and a safe area to work, give learners the opportunity to take photographs or to make a few drawings.
- If you are unable to take the class out, find pictures of streets with elements mentioned above. Maps and pictures of streets are widely available on the internet too, if this is available. Try to choose some pictures that give 'bird's eye' views of streets to help learners begin to understand how maps work.

Script for the lesson

Introducing vocabulary

Introduce vocabulary in context, if possible by visiting places with which learners are familiar. See the list of key words, but introduce any other words that you think would be useful in describing streets in your community. (For example, if there are many hotels or factories in the area, teach these names.)

Teach the number words eleven to twenty.

Revise and teach prepositions of location, position and direction: *at, behind, between, in, in front of, near, next to, on, to.*

Sounds

Use familiar words in context to revise initial, middle and end phonemes.

Help learners to see the patterns in the end phonemes of number words (*-teen*). This will help them when they need to distinguish between numbers such as *fourteen* and *forty*, for example.

Introducing structures

Continue to revise basic structures such as *There is ______/There are ________. It has ____________.*

Teach the possessive pronouns *mine* and *yours* to help learners to give basic personal information and describe things where they live.

Previous knowledge

Most learners will be familiar with the numbers 11–20 in their first language, but they may not be able to pronounce or read the English number words. These names are high-frequency words that are not all easy to decode. Seeing them often will help learners to recognise them.

Possible areas of difficulty

Some learners may struggle to understand prepositions of location, position and direction. Work with these learners in small groups. Use a box (or a desk) as a prop. Give learners instructions to carry out. For example, say:

Sit in the box.

Stand next to the box.

Hide behind the box.

Put a book on the box.

Place your foot in front of the box.

Point to the left side of the box.

Activities

Select from these activities depending on the level of challenge needed for different learners, interest levels and what you have time to include. Supplement these with additional activities of your own and/or digital activities from the online resource.

▲ **1.** Introduce the word *neighbours* to the class. Talk about who our neighbours are. Prompt learners to talk about people who live on the same street, in the same community and in the same buildings (apartment block/flat). Ask questions with *Who/What/Where/How many*. For example, say: *Where do you live? What do you live in – a house or an apartment? What is the name of the street/apartment? Who lives with you? Who lives in the house/apartment next to you? How many people live ____________?*

Learners then work in pairs and ask each other questions about their own neighbourhood. Make sure they are forming questions correctly and that they understand which answers are expected.

2. Revise the number words for numbers 11–20. Use the prompt cards. Read each name and display the words or write them on the board. Learners can then complete activities 1 and 2 in the Workbook.

3. Play a listening game with numbers. Give each learner a sheet with the numbers 11–20 written in a random order. For example:

12	14	16	11	17
20	18	13	19	15

Put the prompt cards with the number words in a pile face down. Learners take turns to pick up a card and say the name. Everyone then circles the number on their sheet of paper.

Alternatively, give learners a blank sheet with 10 blocks on it. Call out numbers in a random order and let learners write the numbers as you say them. Make sure they know to work in rows across the blocks.

4. **Link to mathematics*. Help learners to recognise the initial phonemes in number words. Write the numbers on the board. Ask questions such as: *Which numbers begin with 's'? Which number begins with 'eh'? Do the numbers twelve and twenty begin with the same sounds? Which other number that you know begins with 'th'? (three)*

Then help learners to see the spelling pattern in the ends of some of the number words (*-teen*). You could explain that 'teen' means 'ten', so fourteen is 'four plus ten'. This will help them to distinguish these numbers from other numbers such as forty.

5. Let learners find page 8 in the Student's Book and read the title: *On the street where I live.* Discuss the questions in the Student's Book. Teach new vocabulary as necessary. This may be a good time to check that learners understand the words *left* and *right* and understand the difference between them. Teach prepositions such as *between, in front of, next to, on* and *behind*.

6. Learners work in pairs and make sentences to describe page 8 in the Student's Book, using the structures *There is* ___________ and *There are* ___________.

7. Use prompt cards to revise and teach prepositions of location, position and direction: *at, behind, between, in, in front of, near, next to, on, to.* You could hold up one card at a time, ask learners to read the card and then respond to it by acting (total physical response). For example, learners could go behind a table, next to a friend, near the door, and so on. You may wish to do this outside on the playground.

8. Play **Audio 7**, which is a short story about a street party in a neighbourhood. Play the audio a second time or read the story yourself. Then ask learners some questions to see if they have understood the main ideas. For example, ask:

Where do the children live?

What do they want to do?

Who do they ask?

What do they make for the party?

9. Revise questions with the question words *Who, What, Where, How many*. Then let learners complete activities 3 and 4 in the Workbook.

10. **Link to mathematics*. Do some simple number problems with the class. Give learners simple oral problems to solve, involving numbers from 1–20. For example, say:

There are 16 people on the street. Five people go away. How many are there now?

How many people live in New Apartments? There are four apartments in the block. There are four people in apartment number one, six people in number two, two people in number three and four people in number four.

11. Learners complete the word search activities 5 and 6 in the Workbook.

12. Teach the possessive pronouns *mine* and *yours*, using real classroom objects, or pictures of homes if they are available.

Learners work in pairs. They take photographs or draw maps of the streets where they live. They should label their pictures. Then they make sentences with possessive pronouns and adjectives to describe their pictures. (*This house/apartment is mine. Is that yours? This is my neighbour.*)

13. Show the class the prompt cards with prepositions and let them make sentences with each preposition, orally. Then let them complete activity 7 in the Workbook.

14. Learners role-play a simple conversation about talking to a neighbour on the street. This will help them to practise the present tenses and contractions. For example:

A: *Hello,* ___________. *How are you?*

B: *I'm fine thanks. And you?*

A: *I'm also fine. Can you help me please?*

B: *Yes, of course. What do you need?*

A: *I need some milk.*

B: *I'll get some. Here you are!*

A: *Thanks! I'm planting some vegetable seeds.*

B: *Can I see?*

A: *Yes, of course. Come with me.*

15. **Link to art*. Talk more about the things that people do on a street and introduce the idea of a carnival. Refer to real events in your community or country as far as possible. Talk about food, dancing, music and having fun.

Let learners paint pictures of these events and then describe their pictures, practising the present continuous tense. For example: *We are dancing. We are eating nice food.*

16. Read the poem *Come to the Carnival*.

Poem: *Come to the Carnival*

Come to the Carnival.
Hear the steel bands play.
Come to the Carnival.
It's Carnival Day today.
Dress up like a peacock.
Dress up like a king.
Dress up like a monkey.
Clap your hands and sing.
Dance like a princess.
Tumble like a clown.
Stamp your feet to the beat,
Jump up and down.
Come to the Carnival.
Hear the steel bands play.
Come to the Carnival.
It's Carnival Day today.

Read the poem again. Show them a picture of a steel band if they do not know what these are. Discuss the poem to make sure that learners understand it. Then teach them the words and let them recite the poem, with actions.

17. Learners complete activities 8, 9 and 10 of the Workbook.

18. Learners work in groups and make up number puzzles to ask each other.

Wrap-up plenary

Discuss what it means to be a good neighbour. Let learners talk in their first language if necessary at first. Then help them to say a few sentences in English to describe being a good neighbour. For example: *My neighbours help me. Our neighbours visit us. The neighbours are kind. The neighbours don't make a lot of noise.*

Quick check

1. Let the class play 'Bingo' with prepositions and other words from this unit. Give learners blank sheets of paper with space for 12 words/phrases. (You can use **PCM 2**.) Write approximately 15 words or phrases on the board and let them choose 12 of them to copy onto their Bingo sheets. For example: *at, behind, between, in, in front of, near, next to, on, to, left, right, street, live, neighbour.*
2. Let learners play a game with the number word prompt cards. Put the words face down on a table. Each learner chooses one card, reads the number on the card and then writes the number on the board. The other learners say if the learner has written the correct number or not. Work out a system of scoring with the class or group before they begin the game.

Assessment

You can complete an oral assessment of the work done in this topic by asking learners to draw a picture. Use a few prepositions in your instructions, for example say: *Draw a house on the street. Draw a tree next to the house*, and so on.

Learners can also complete Progress check activities 1, 2, 3 and 4 in the Workbook as a simple assessment.

You could allocate marks for these activities and record these as part of continuous assessment.

Topic 2 Homes

Overview

In this topic the focus is on sharing information about homes of different kinds using familiar vocabulary and structures to build confidence and then introducing new structures and vocabulary to develop language skills.

There are opportunities to integrate activities with other curricula, such as social sciences, natural sciences and drama.

Units in this topic

Unit A: My home

Unit B: Palaces, bridges and pirate ships

Unit C: Holes, hives and caves

Teaching focus

- **2Rg1** Recognise, identify and sound, with support, a limited range of language at text level
- **2Rg2** Begin to read, with support, very short simple fiction and non-fiction texts with confidence and enjoyment
- **2Rd1** Understand, with support, some specific information and detail in very short, simple texts on a limited range of general and curricular topics
- **2Rm1** Understand the meaning of very short, simple texts on familiar general and curricular topics by rereading them
- **2Rd2** Understand the meaning of simple short sentences on familiar general and curricular topics
- **2Wa1** Plan, write and check, with support, short sentences on familiar topics
- **2Wo3** Use upper and lower case letters accurately when writing names, places and short sentences during guided writing activities
- **2Ug14** Spell a growing number of familiar high-frequency words accurately during guided writing activities
- **2Wo2** Include a full stop and question mark during guided writing of short, familiar sentences
- **2Ug1** Use singular nouns, plural nouns – including some common irregular plural forms – and uncountable nouns, genitive 's/s' to name and label things
- **2Ug3** Use adjectives, including possessive adjectives, on familiar topics to give personal information and describe things
- **2Ut1** Use determiners *a, the, some, any, this, these, that* to refer to familiar objects
- **2Ut2** Use *who, what, where, how many* to ask questions on familiar topics
- **2Ut3** Use impersonal *you* in the question: *How do you spell that?*
- **2Ut4** Use demonstrative pronouns *this, these, that, those* and object pronoun *one* in short statements and responses
- **2Ut5** Use personal subject and object pronouns, including possessive pronouns *mine, yours* to give basic personal information and describe things
- **2Uf2** Use common simple present forms, including short answer forms and contractions, to give personal information
  2Uf3 Use common past simple forms [regular and irregular] to describe actions and narrate simple events including short answer forms and contractions
- **2Ut6** Use *there is/are* to make short statements and descriptions
- **2Uf6** Use *Have you [ever] been?* to talk about experiences
- **2Ug9** Use prepositions of location, position and direction: *at, behind, between, in, in front of, near, next to, on, to* on personal and familiar topics
- **2Ug10** Use prepositions of time: *on, in, at,* to talk about days and times on personal and familiar topics
- **2Ug11** Use *with* to indicate accompaniment and instrument and *for* to indicate recipient on personal and familiar topics
- **2Ld4** Understand an increased range of short, basic supported classroom instructions
- **2Ld3** Understand a growing range of short, supported questions which ask for personal information
- **2Ld5** Understand an increasing range of short supported questions on general and curricular topics
- **2Lg1** Understand short supported narratives on an increasing range of general and curricular topics
- **2Lg2** Identify initial, middle and final phonemes and blends
- **2S2** Ask questions to find out about an increasing range of personal information
- **2S3** Describe basic present and past actions on a limited range of general and curricular topics

- **2S4** Use basic vocabulary for a limited range of general and curricular topics
- **2S5** Give short, basic descriptions of people and objects
- **2S6** Contribute a growing range of suitable words, phrases, and sentences during short pair, group and whole class exchanges
- **2S7** Take turns when speaking with others in a growing range of short, basic exchanges
- **2S8** Relate very short, basic stories and events on a limited range of general and curricular topics

Language patterns

Grammar summary for teachers:

- **Determiners:** These are words that we use with a noun to make it clear whether the noun refers to something specific or to something in general.

  The following determiners are specific: *the, this, these, those*

  *This is **the** house where I live.*

  *Please pass me **that** book.*

  The following determiners are general: *a, some, any*

  *He lives in **a** house on New Street.* (We don't know which house it is.)

  *I have **some** money in my wallet.* (But I don't know how much.)

  Possessive adjectives (such as *my, his*) are also determiners that refer to specific things.
- **Demonstrative pronouns:** These are words such as *this, that, these* and *those*. The same words are used as demonstrative adjectives but they are used to replace nouns, rather than describe them in sentences. Examples:

  Pronouns: ***This** is my home. **That** is the fox's home.*

  Adjectives: ***This** book is mine. **That** house is Mr Brown's.*
- **Possessive 's (genitives):** 's and s' are used to show possession (except with *it*). Examples:

  *This is the **rabbit's** home.* (singular)

  *This is the **rabbits'** home.* (plural)

Unit A My home

Resources and materials

- Student's Book p. 9
- Workbook pp. 22–26
- Audio files: Audio 8; Audio 9; Audio 10
- Photocopiable Masters (PCMs) PCM 4; PCM 5
- Square pieces of paper (one per learner)
- Additional pictures of houses and different rooms in houses

Key vocabulary

room, door, floor, roof, ceiling, wall, window, front, back, inside, outside, bedroom, bathroom, kitchen, living room, garage, garden

Lead-in ideas

Teach the class a song about houses, for example *The House That Jack Built* (**Audio 8**). This is a shortened and adapted version of the traditional song. You can change the names and the animals in this song and you can add lines to the song too.

Script for the lesson

Introducing vocabulary

Revise and teach vocabulary relating to the different parts of houses. You should also introduce words/concepts, such as *the back*, *the front*, *inside* and *outside*, as these are commonly used when talking about homes. Although furniture is not the main focus in this unit, you can also revise the names of items of furniture if you think this is necessary.

Sounds

Revise consonant and vowel digraphs in context, in words such as: *floor, door, room, roof, front, bathroom, kitchen.*

Introducing structures

Learners may already be using some determiners in their speaking and writing, for example *a, the, this* and *that*. In this unit the focus is on getting learners to use these determiners correctly, to refer to general or specific things. This is easier taught through practising simple conversations and exposure, rather than through grammatical explanations at this stage.

Previous knowledge

Learners should know some of the key vocabulary in this unit already, in their first language and in English.

Possible areas of difficulty

Some learners may not yet be familiar with reading simple floor plans and diagrams, so you may need to spend some time explaining what these are and what they represent.

Activities

Select from these activities depending on the level of challenge needed for different learners, interest levels and what you have time to include. Supplement these with additional activities of your own and/or digital activities from the online resource.

▲ **1.** Show learners the pictures you have collected of different houses. Let learners use the language they know to describe the pictures. Help them to name the main rooms in the house (examples: *bedroom, bathroom, living room, kitchen*) as well as parts of houses (*roof, door, floor, wall, window*). Teach the words *inside* and *outside*, *back* and *front.* If your pictures have gardens with *fences* and *gates*, then teach those words as well.

▲ **2.** Read the short poem *My house* on page 9 of the Student's Book or let learners try and read the poem in pairs. Teach the word *ceiling*. Ask learners to identify the rhyming words and then to recite the poem.

▲ **3.** Talk about singular and plural nouns. Write the poem from Student's Book page 9 on the board and underline the plural nouns.

My house has…

blue walls

white windows

brown floors

and red doors!

Ask: *What does the –s at the ends of the words tell us?* Ask learners to give the singular form of each word.

Then write sentences on the board and ask learners to complete them orally. Learners will need to pay attention to the adjectives and the verbs in the sentences to decide if the nouns should be singular or plural. For example:

The house has one ______________.

The house has six ______________.

The ______________ *in the living room is brown.*

The ______________ *of the house are red.*

Learners can then complete activities 1, 2 and 3 in the Workbook. Alternatively, they can do this later on, in activity 7.

▲ **4.** Learners discuss the floor plan on page 9 of the Student's Book. Explain what it shows. Let learners read the labels on the plan. Then ask them to point to various places on the plan. Ask questions such as:

Where is the bathroom?

Where is the front door?

Is this the inside or the outside of the house?

How many rooms are there?

How many windows are there?

▲ **5.** Learners label the picture of the house in activity 4 and complete activities 5 and 6 in the Workbook.

▲ **6.** Play the story *Fixing Our House* (**Audio 9**) twice, or read the text. Then ask learners oral questions to see if they have understood the main ideas. Learners do not have to understand every word in the story. Focus on understanding the gist or main ideas. Ask the following questions:

What happened to the house?

Why?

What are the neighbours doing?

What are the family painting?

What colour are the walls inside the house?

Are they painting walls inside or outside the house?

▲ **7.** Write some sentences on the board with the determiners: *a, the, some, any, the, this, these, those*, as well as sentences with possessive adjectives (*my, his, her*). Underline the determiners in the sentences. Then read each sentence with the class and ask them questions to help them understand the exact meanings of the words and whether the words refer to specific or general things. For example:

(*Do we know whose house it is?*)

This is my house. (yes)

She lives in a house in New Street. (no)

He lives in this house. (yes)

(Do we know which shoes they are talking about?)

These are my shoes. (yes)

I like that pair of shoes. (yes)

She doesn't have any shoes. (no)

Then let learners use some of the determiners to make their own sentences. Learners can then complete activities 1, 2 and 3 in the Workbook (if not done already in Activity 3) to practise using some determiners as well as singular and plural forms. You may want to learners complete the conversations in activity 3 orally first.

● **8.** Read the poem on page 9 of the Student's Book again. Then let learners work in pairs and write their own poems in the same style. Some learners may be able to get words to rhyme at the ends of lines, but it doesn't matter if they don't.

● **9.** Let learners open their Workbooks at activity 7 (which is the same as the plan on page 9 of the Student's Book). Play *A walk around the house* (**Audio 10**) in which a person called Ben walks through different rooms in the house, or read the text. Let learners trace the path through the house as they listen to the text.

When they have completed the path let learners work in pairs and tell their partners where Ben went.

10. Learners work in pairs and pretend that they are taking someone on a tour of a house. They walk around and point out the different rooms and places, using familiar structures. They can also start to use the demonstrative pronoun *one*. Do a demonstration with one or two learners first, for example:

A: *This is the living room.*

B: *I like the chairs.*

A: *Yes, that one is my favourite.*

B: *What's this?*

A: *That is the back door.*

This is the kitchen.

B: *Where's your bedroom?*

A: *It's this one.*

11. Learners complete activity 8 in the Workbook. They make up sentences and questions with given words.

12. Teach or revise positive and negative instructions. Take the class outside and give them some instructions. Revise the names of places around the school as you do this. For example, say:

Walk to the door.

Go out into the yard.

Don't run!

Sit down on the benches near the window.

Don't sit on the ground.

13. Let learners play alliteration games with the adjectives and nouns they have used in this unit. Write nouns on the board, for example:

bedroom, garden, kitchen, living room, roof, wall, bathroom

Then ask learners to think of words that describe the nouns and that start with the same letter (or sound). For example:

blue bedroom

green garden

clean kitchen

large living room

big bathroom

Circle the repeated letters, or highlight them in some way.

If learners enjoy this, help them to make up short tongue-twisters with these key words. For example: *A big ball bouncing in the blue bedroom.*

14. **Link to art*. Give learners copies of **P** and a square piece of paper. They follow instructions on the sheet to fold a paper h Before they begin the activity discuss the instructions. Demonstrate what a crease (fold)

15. Learners can draw a simple floor plan of their own homes. Don't expect the drawings to be accurate, although learners should be able to explain what they have drawn. When the drawings are complete, learners work in pairs and describe their houses to their partners. They can take their partner on a 'tour' of the house or apartment.

16. Learners work out the answers to the clues and complete the crossword puzzle in activity 9 in the Workbook.

Wrap-up plenary

Talk about homes and why they are important: safety, shelter, a place to sleep, eat, work and play.

Quick check

Play a game with the class. This game is based on the game 'battleships'. Give learners **PCM 5**. Learners draw parts of houses on their grids, as follows:

1 block for a door and a window (x6)

2 blocks for a bathroom (x1)

3 blocks for a kitchen (x1)

4 blocks for a bedroom (x2)

5 blocks for a living room (x1)

Call out numbers (for example, C4, B8, and so on). Learners place a cross on the corresponding block on their sheets. For example:

	A	B	C	D	E	F
1						
2				X	X	
3				X		
4						
5						
6				X		
7		X				X
8		X				
9						
10						

The first learner to have crosses in all blocks in all the rooms has a complete house and wins the game.

aces, bridges and pirate ships

naterials

-12

- Audio file: Audio 11
- Photocopiable Master (PCM) PCM 6
- Collect additional pictures of places where people live, including alternative homes like riverboats, informal housing, palaces
- Sentence strips with the words from the story *Pirates*
- Globe or map of the world

Key vocabulary

palace, castle, ship, bridge, grass, beach, hill, cave, pirate, king, queen, prince, princess, giant, leader, protect

Lead-in ideas

In this unit learners are introduced to the homes of characters in traditional and fairy stories. You could start by reading or telling the class a well-known story about a giant or a princess who lived in a palace or castle. Use examples from your own cultural community or stories such as *Snow White, Cinderella, Rapunzel, The Princess and the Frog, The Princess and the Pea, Princess Savriti, The Selfish Giant, The Dragon King's Daughter*.

Script for the lesson

Introducing vocabulary

Use the pictures that support the texts in the Student's Book to introduce the vocabulary in this unit. Introduce any other words that you think may be useful.

Sounds

Revise consonant digraphs (*sh, ch, th, ck*) in the context of the texts in this unit. Help learners to recognise these as initial, middle and end parts of words.

Make learners aware of and help them to pronounce *-ed* at the end of regular past tenses verbs. (Learners don't need to distinguish between the different sounds made by *–ed* yet.)

Introducing structures

The stories in this unit are told in the simple past tense. High-frequency irregular past tense words (such as *went, fell*) are introduced alongside regular simple past tense verbs with *-ed* endings (such as *walked, wanted*). Help learners to understand that these words refer to actions that happened in the past by introducing time markers such as *yesterday* or *a long time ago* in example sentences. Focus on recognising this tense and using it orally, rather than on writing the tense at this stage.

Previous knowledge

Learners will probably have heard and may already be using some words in the simple past tense.

Possible areas of difficulty

Learners may at first confuse the past and present tenses when they are speaking. Just correct them kindly and move on. Don't spend too much time trying to explain the difference at this stage.

Activities

Select from these activities depending on the level of challenge needed for different learners, interest levels and what you have time to include. Supplement these with additional activities of your own and/or digital activities from the online resource.

▲ **1.** Learners find the picture story *The Three Goats* in the Student's Book on page 10. Talk about the pictures. Teach the word *giant* if you think this will not be familiar. Ask learners what they think the story is about. Then play **Audio 11** while learners follow in their books. Ask a few questions to test comprehension.

▲ **2.** Play learners the story *The Three Goats* (**Audio 11**). Discuss the names of the characters in the story. Learners then complete activity 3 in the Workbook.

▲ **3.** Give learners a copy of **PCM 6**. They cut up the pictures and put them in the correct order. Then they use the pictures to retell the story.

▲ **4.** Teach learners some past tense verbs. Explain briefly that when we talk about things that happened before now (*yesterday, long ago*) we often use different words. Give them some examples:

Yesterday I went to the park. I walked down the street. I talked to my friends.

Let learners work in groups and tell their group what they did the previous day. Let groups report back some of the ideas to the rest of the class afterwards. Write some of the best examples on the board and underline the past tense verbs to build awareness. This may be a good time to teach learners that a verb is a word that describes an action.

▲ **5.** Learners can complete activities 1 and 2 in the Workbook to practice some past tense verbs.

▲ **6.** Learners find the story *Pirates* in the Student's Book on page 11. Do some of the usual pre-reading activities. Find out what learners know about pirates. Ask them what a pirate ship looks like. Then read the story and let learners follow as you read. Then point to each picture and ask some questions to make sure that learners can describe what is happening in all the pictures. For example, ask: *How many pirates are there?*

Where did they go? What's this/What are these? - a crab, a crocodile, a map, some monkeys, a hill, a cave.

7. Revise consonant digraphs (*sh, ch, th, ck*). Help learners to recognise these as initial, middle and end parts of words. Write words such as *ship shop, chip, the, this, that, duck, luck, wish, fish* on the board. Then erase the digraphs and let learners complete the words.

8. **Link to social sciences*. Learners find the non-fiction text *Palaces and castles* in the Student's Book on page 12. Start with some pre-reading activities. Ask learners if this page is a story or if it is about real places. Ask learners to choose a picture and then focus on that picture. Read the text and talk about the picture. Talk about what the building is, who lives or works there, where the building is. Refer to a map of the world. Some learners in the class may know some of these places. Choose two or three pictures to discuss in this way and leave the other pictures for another lesson.

9. Have learners listen to the story *The Three Goats* (**Audio 11**). Then they complete activities 4 and 5 in the Workbook, which are based on this story.

10. **Link to drama*. Learners reread the story *Pirates* in the Student's Book on page 11. Write some words from the story on the board and ask learners to point to the words in the story.

    Then let learners work in groups and act the story. One learner in the group can narrate the story while the others act the story, or learners can make up their own conversation for the story. For example:

    Let's go to the beach.
    Where's the map?
    Ouch! There are crabs on the beach.
    Let's go across the river.
    This way!
    Help! There's a crocodile!

11. Learners complete activities 6 and 7 in the Workbook after they have reread the story *Pirates*.

12. Learners find the non-fiction text *Palaces and castles* in the Student's Book on page 12. Read the text with learners. Help them to describe the places using adjectives that they know (*big, small, old, tall, square, round*).

    Then let them complete activities 8 and 9 in the Workbook.

13. Learners listen to the story *The Three Goats* (**Audio 11**). Then they work in groups to retell and act the story. Encourage learners to expand the story and to change the characters if they want to. One learner in the group can narrate the story while the others act the story, or learners can make up their own conversation for the story. Learners should use the past tense to narrate the story.

14. Learners can work in groups and make up their own pirate maps after rereading the story *Pirates*. They can pretend that there is treasure buried somewhere on an island. They can draw a map to show where the treasure is. They should also write short instructions to go with their maps. Give learners some examples:

    Start on the beach.
    Look for three trees.
    Go to the trees.
    Go across the river.
    Be careful! There is a crocodile in the river.

    Help with vocabulary as necessary. Learners can use activities 10 and 11 in the Workbook to write their maps and instructions neatly. Give them paper to make rough maps first.

15. Learners reread the text *Palaces and castles* in the Student's Book on page 12. Then let them choose a palace or castle that interests them. Help them to spell the name of the place correctly. They should research this castle (online or in a library). Then they complete activities 12 and 13 in the Workbook. They draw or paste a picture of the place and complete a guided writing activity.

Wrap-up plenary

Let learners talk about their favourite stories. Some learners could act the stories they made up in groups, or tell other stories. Learners could also watch a film about a story and then talk about it afterwards.

Ask learners why people enjoy stories. Prompt them to say things such as: *They make us laugh. They make us dream. They are interesting. We learn from stories.*

Quick check

1. Use the sentence strips from the stories in this unit. Learners use them to retell the stories.
2. Learners can act some of the characters from the stories in this unit. The other learners guess who they are and what they are doing.

Unit C Holes, hives and caves

Resources and materials

- Student's Book pp. 13–15
- Workbook pp. 34–37
- Audio files: Audio 12; Audio 13
- Photocopiable Master (PCM) PCM 2
- Additional pictures of animal homes
- Additional stories, films or non-fiction texts about animal homes
- Paper for animal pictures and sentences (one sheet per pair)

Key vocabulary

Animals: lion, zebra, penguin, bat, meerkat, bee, monkey, bird, snake, owl, hedgehog, rabbit

group, cave, hole, beehive, ground, land, barn, night, wind, blow, winter, sleep

Lead-in ideas

- Let learners sing any familiar song or recite familiar rhymes/chants about animals.
- You could also teach a new song, such as *The Little Blue Bird* (**Audio 12**). You can add your own verses to this song.

Script for the lesson

Introducing vocabulary

Focus on introducing the names of a variety of animals and talking about places where these animals live, in a general way (*on land, under the ground*) and using specific words in some cases, such as *beehives, caves*.

Sounds

Revise initial and middle phonemes using the vocabulary in the Student's Book texts.

Introducing structures

The texts in the Student's Book provide a context for revising the following: possessive adjectives, the simple past tense, pronouns, prepositions and plurals.

Although learners will have come across the genitive (possessive with *'s*) in stories, you could teach it more formally in this unit and let learners start to use it in their writing as well. They will do more of this in the next topic as well.

Previous knowledge

Learners may know the names of some animals in English or in their first language. Use pictures to help them make connections between the names in different languages.

Possible areas of difficulty

The possessive *'s* (genitive) is tricky and is often confused with contractions and plural forms. At this stage, focus on getting learners to use the genitive in oral sentences and to recognise what it can mean in written sentences.

Activities

Select from these activities depending on the level of challenge needed for different learners, interest levels and what you have time to include. Supplement these with additional activities of your own and/or digital activities from the online resource.

▲ **1.** **Link to science*. Find out what learners know about the habitats of domestic and wild animals. Talk about animals that are common in your community or country. Ask learners where the animals live and what they eat. Introduce some key vocabulary in short phrases, such as: *under the ground, in the grass, in caves, in holes, in hives*.

▲ **2.** Let learners find the non-fiction text about animal homes *Who lives there?* in the Student's Book (page 13). Talk about the pictures and let learners say what they know about each one. Then read the text with groups of learners. Help them to decode words and to work out meanings of words by looking for clues in the pictures and by rereading the text.

The nouns that name animals in this text are all in the plural. Ask learners to give the singular forms, for example *There is one* ___________.

▲ **3.** Learners complete activities 1, 2 and 3 in the Workbook. They will need to refer to the text on page 13 of the Student's Book to do this.

▲ **4.** Revise the simple present, especially the third person forms. Write a simple substitution table on the board and let learners make oral sentences, choosing the correct forms of verbs to match the subjects. For example:

Bears	live lives	in holes.
Baby meerkats		in this tree.
The brown monkey		in our house.
Lions and zebras		in caves.
My baby cat		on the land.

▲ **5.** Write some common nouns on the board or on prompt cards. (For example: *tree, baby monkey, snake, spider, bird.*) Work with groups of learners. Each learner chooses a word and makes a sentence with the word.

Then give a simple dictation. Read words off the board without pointing to the word you are reading. Let learners write down the word as you say it.

6. Write the words *cave, hole, web* and *nest* on the board. Then make sentences which describe whose home each one is, using the possessive *'s* (genitive). Start with sentences that have singular subjects, for example, say:

   A web is a spider's home.

   A cave is a bat's home.

   A hole is a meerkat's home.

   A nest is a bird's home.

   Let learners repeat the sentences after you. You can also write them on the board so that learners begin to recognise the structure.

7. Let learners find the story, *It Was a Cold, Dark, Night* in the Student's Book (pages 14–15). Give them a few minutes to read the title and look at the pictures. Then ask what they think the story is about. Teach the word *hedgehog*.

   Play the audio version of the story (**Audio 13**). Read the story aloud while learners follow in their books. Much of the language in this story will be familiar to learners. There are nouns, pronouns, prepositions, adjectives and verbs in the story that have been introduced in Stages 1 and 2 already.

   Learners can then complete activities 4 and 5 in the Workbook.

8. Let learners draw pictures about animal homes as you describe them. Give each learner a sheet of paper divided into four boxes and numbered 1–4. For example:

1	2
3	4

   Then read out these instructions (or any other similar instructions):

   Draw a bird's nest in block 2. Draw three eggs in the nest.

   Draw a beehive in block 1. There are eleven bees flying around the beehive.

   Draw a spider's web in block 3. Draw a big spider in the middle of the web.

   Draw some bats in a cave in block 4.

9. Learners read the text *Who lives there?* in the Student's Book (page 13). They can work in pairs and ask each other questions about the text. For example:

   Who lives here?

   Which animal lives here?

   Is this a nest?

   What is this?

   Where do bees live?

   Learners can then complete activities 6 and 7 in the Workbook.

10. Learners work in groups and play a game. Each group makes up five riddles about animals for other groups to solve. They can write the riddles on pieces of paper and put them in a box. The other group chooses a riddle from the box and attempts to solve it. Discuss the rules and scoring with the groups before they begin. Here is an example of a riddle:

    This is a small animal.

    It is brown and yellow.

    It has wings.

    It lives in a hive. (a bee)

11. Learners listen to **Audio 13** *It Was a Cold, Dark Night* again. Then they read the text alone or in pairs. The text is in the Student's Book (pages 14–15). Learners can then work in pairs and retell the story to each other.

12. Learners complete activities 8 and 9 in the Workbook. They need to know the story *It Was a Cold, Dark Night* in order to complete this page.

13. Focus on the pronouns and possessive adjectives in the story *It Was a Cold, Dark Night.* Write some sentences up on the board and underline the pronouns and possessive adjectives. For example:

    *Ned, the hedgehog, was looking for a home. **He** looked down a little hole.*

    *The rabbits said, "This is **our** home! Look next door."*

    Ask learners who the pronouns refer to, for example: *Who is **he**?* (Ned the hedgehog). *Who is **our**?* (the rabbits). Go through the story pointing out how the pronouns are connected to the nouns in the text.

14. Learners read the text *Who lives there?* in the Student's Book (page 13) again. Then they work in pairs and find out about the home of another animal. They can use prior knowledge and do some research in the library or online. Help them to choose suitable animals.

    Learners find a picture of the animal home (or draw a picture). They write one or two sentences about the home. Help them to do this in rough first. They should check that they have used capital letters and full stops. Then give each pair a sheet of paper with a space to draw or paste a picture at the top and a few lines for writing at the bottom of the sheet. They paste their pictures and write their sentences on the sheet. Display these in class for other learners to read.

15. Learners can work in groups and make up their own plays about an animal looking for a home.

Wrap-up plenary

Talk again about why homes are important for people and for animals.

Quick check

1. Write vocabulary words from this topic on the board. Give learners Bingo sheets (**PCM 2**) and let them choose words to complete their sheets. Then play 'Bingo' in the usual way.
2. Learners can play a memory game that also practices vocabulary and structures. Working in groups, the first learner in the group makes a sentence. The other learners in the group take turns to repeat the sentence and add to it. Check the first sentence to make sure it is grammatically correct. For example:

   I went to the forest and I saw a fox.

   I went to the forest and I saw a fox and a lion

   I went to the forest and I saw a fox, a lion and a hedgehog.

   And so on.

   There is an owl in the tree.

   There is an owl and a monkey in the tree.

   There is an owl, a monkey and a snake in the tree.

   And so on.

Assessment

You can complete an oral assessment of the work done in this topic by:

- asking learners to describe the actions in pictures (use the Student's Book)
- giving learners instructions to do simple actions (*hop, run, jump, walk,* etc.)
- using the prompt cards with letters of the alphabet to check knowledge of sounds (initial sounds) made by phonemes.

Learners can also complete Progress check activities 1, 2, 3 and 4 in the Workbook as a simple assessment.

You could allocate marks for these activities and record these as part of continuous assessment.

Topic 3 Wild animals

Overview

In this topic the focus is on naming and describing wild animals. There are narrative and non-fiction texts for learners to read, listen to, discuss and enjoy. In the narratives the focus is on introducing common regular and irregular verbs in the simple past tense, which is a natural tense for narrative stories. Learners will continue to practise the simple present tense when reading non-fiction texts. Genitives, uncountable nouns and further conjunctions are some of the new structures that are introduced. There are opportunities to integrate activities with natural sciences, drama and mathematics in this topic.

Units in this topic

Unit A: Big, furry and fast

Unit B: Animal stories

Unit C: Baby animals

Teaching focus

- **2Rg1** Recognise, identify and sound, with support, a limited range of language at text level
- **2Rg2** Begin to read, with support, very short simple fiction and non-fiction texts with confidence and enjoyment
- **2Rd1** Understand, with support, some specific information and detail in very short, simple texts on a limited range of general and curricular topics
- **2Rm1** Understand the meaning of very short, simple texts on familiar general and curricular topics by rereading them
- **2Rd2** Understand the meaning of simple short sentences on familiar general and curricular topics
- **2Ug15** Use, with more infrequent support, a simple picture dictionary
- **2Wa1** Plan, write and check, with support, short sentences on familiar topics
- **2Ug14** Spell a growing number of familiar high-frequency words accurately during guided writing activities
- **2Wo2** Include a full stop and question mark during guided writing of short, familiar sentences
- **2Ug1** Use singular nouns, plural nouns – including some common irregular plural forms – and uncountable nouns, genitive 's/s' to name and label things
- **2Ug2** Use numbers 1–50 to count
- **2Ug3** Use adjectives, including possessive adjectives, on familiar topics to give personal information and describe things
- **2Ut2** Use *who, what, where, how many* to ask questions on familiar topics
- **2Ut3** Use impersonal *you* in the question: *How do you spell that?*
- **2Uf2** Use common simple present forms, including short answer forms and contractions, to give personal information
- **2Uf3** Use common past simple forms [regular and irregular] to describe actions and narrate simple events including short answer forms and contractions
- **2Ut6** Use *there is/are* to make short statements and descriptions
- **2Uf6** Use *Have you [ever] been?* to talk about experiences
- **2Ug5** Use adverbs of time and place *now, today, over, there,* to indicate when and where
- **2Ug6** Use common *–ly* adverbs to describe actions
- **2Ug7** Use the adverb *too* to add information
- **2Ut8** Use conjunctions *and, or, but* to link words and phrases
- **2Ld4** Understand an increased range of short, basic supported classroom instructions
- **2Ld3** Understand a growing range of short, supported questions which ask for personal information
- **2Ld5** Understand an increasing range of short supported questions on general and curricular topics
- **2Lg1** Understand short supported narratives on an increasing range of general and curricular topics
- **2Lg2** Identify initial, middle and final phonemes and blends
- **2S3** Describe basic present and past actions on a limited range of general and curricular topics
- **2S4** Use basic vocabulary for a limited range of general and curricular topics
- **2S5** Give short, basic descriptions of people and objects
- **2S6** Contribute a growing range of suitable words, phrases, and sentences during short pair, group and whole class exchanges
- **2S7** Take turns when speaking with others in a growing range of short, basic exchanges
- **2S8** Relate very short, basic stories and events on a limited range of general and curricular topics

Language patterns

Grammar summary for teachers:

- **Conjunctions:** Conjunctions are words that connect or link words, phrases or sentences. In Stage 2 the focus is on the coordinating conjunctions *and, but* and *or* and how these words link words, phrases and sentences. For example:

  We saw lions ***and*** *zebras at the park.* (*and* links two nouns)

  Does the owl live here ***or*** *in that tree over there?* (*or* links two adverbial phrases)

  I like apples ***but*** *I don't like bananas.* (*but* links two sentences)

  Coordinating conjunctions are usually used between the words or phrases that they join, not at the beginning or ends of sentences, although sometimes it is possible to start with *but* to obtain a certain meaning of effect in literary writing.
- **Uncountable nouns:** Uncountable nouns describe things that cannot be counted or separated, for example, *fur* or *rice*. We do not use the determiners *a* or *an* with these words, nor do we use numbers. Uncountable nouns are usually used in the singular form (example: *food, wool*), although there are cases when plurals are possible (example: *There are many different* ***foods*** *to eat*). Sometimes uncountable nouns do not have singular forms, for example, *news*.

  We can use determiners, such as *some, my, a lot of*, or *this* with uncountable nouns. For example:

  There are six ***monkeys*** *in the tree.* (*monkeys*: countable noun)

  A bear has thick ***fur.*** (*fur*: uncountable noun)

  This is my ***food.*** (*food*: uncountable noun)
- **Adverbs of time and place:** Adverbs of time describe when an action takes place, for example, *yesterday, now* or *today*.

  Adverbs of place describe where something happens, for example, *over there, here.*

Unit A Big, furry and fast

Resources and materials

- Student's Book pp. 16–17
- Workbook pp. 40–45
- Audio file: Audio 14
- Photocopiable Master (PCM) PCM 7
- Pictures of animals which show their body covering (skin, hair, fur, scales, feathers, shell)
- Prompt cards with irregular verbs in both present simple and past simple tenses

Key vocabulary

Nouns: skin, feather, fur, shell, scales, wool, race, carrot

Animals: duck, bear, tortoise, crab, snake, sheep, goat, hare

Verbs: have, play/played, walk/walked, is/was, eat/ate, sleep/slept, run/ran, win/won

Connectors: and but

Adverbs: slow/slowly, fast, now, there, too

Lead-in ideas

- Display a picture of an animal on the board and hold a class brainstorming session in which learners call out words that describe the animal. Write the words around the picture, then have learners practise saying those words. Repeat the activity with pictures of other animals.
- Take learners outside. Call out an animal name and have learners behave like that animal. (Be aware that in some communities, there might be a different level of sensitivity around certain animals.)

Script for the lesson

Introducing vocabulary

Use the pictures in the texts in the Student's Book, as well as pictures you have collected, to introduce the vocabulary in this unit. You can pre-teach some words and let learners try and work out the meaning of other words from clues in the pictures.

Sounds

Revise initial middle and end sounds in context. For example, you could focus on consonant digraphs and blends, such as *ck, sk, sc, sn, sl, pl* and vowel digraphs, such as *oa* and *ea* in words which occur in the texts in the Student's Book.

Introducing structures

The simple present tense is used in the non-fiction text in the Student's Book to provide continued practice. You can focus on the simple past tense again when learners read the story *The Hare and the Tortoise*. This text has several common but irregular simple past tense verbs. Learners will need to recognise these as sight words.

Connectors such as *and, or* and *but* are introduced in the texts and can be practised in conversation activities.

Previous knowledge

Learners will be familiar with some animal names in English and in their first language.

Possible areas of difficulty

Irregular forms of simple past tense verbs will need some practice. These need to be learned as sight words, so display the words around the classroom – on the board, on labelled pictures, on prompt cards – to help learners remember the words.

Activities

Select from these activities depending on the level of challenge needed for different learners, interest levels and what you have time to include. Supplement these with additional activities of your own and/or digital activities from the online resource.

1. ******Link to science*. Talk about body coverings with the class. Teach the word *skin* if learners don't yet know it and discuss why we have skin on our bodies (to protect our bodies, to hold parts of the body together, to keep the correct temperature). Then talk about other animals and find out what learners know about their body coverings. Start with familiar animals (such as cats, goats or cows, for example). Start to introduce new vocabulary as you do this.

2. Let learners find the non-fiction text *Different coats* in the Student's Book on page 16. Start with some pre-reading activities. For example, let learners read the title and suggest what the text is about. Ask them if it is a story or if there is information about animals on the page. Let them look at the photographs and suggest what the text is about.

   Then read the text with the class. Help learners to decode and work out the meanings of words as you do this. Talk about what each skin covering feels like, for example: *soft, hard, thin, thick.*

   Discuss why animals have skin, fur, feathers, wool and scales. Which are warmer? Which protect the animal?

   Learners complete the matching activity 1 in the Workbook.

3. Learners find the story *The Hare and the Tortoise* in the Student's Book on page 17. Let learners read the title of the story and suggest what it is about. Then play the extended version of the story (**Audio 14**). Play (or read) the story twice, while learners look at the pictures in the Student's Book. The story introduces some common verbs with irregular past tense forms, simple conjunctions and some adverbs of place, time and manner.

   Then give learners a copy of **PCM 7**. Learners cut out the pictures and sequence them. Then they use the pictures to retell the story using whatever language they can. Encourage them to use the past tense verbs from the story – write some key verbs in the past tense on the board to help learners to do this.

4. Use the prompt cards with irregular verbs. Let learners see how many of the verbs they can find in the story of *The Hare and the Tortoise*. Make some oral sentences using the verbs in the present tense and the past tense to help learners to make the connection.

   The hare runs fast.
   Yesterday the hare ran fast.
   The hare eats a carrot.
   Yesterday the hare ate a carrot.

   Then let learners use the cards to match the two different forms of the verbs. Then ask them to make their own oral sentences with the verbs.

5. Revise initial, middle and end sounds in context. For example, write the following words on the board and underline the digraphs. Let learners look at the two texts in the Student's Book on pages 16 and 17. They look for another word with the same letters. They read the two words aloud. For example:

   luck (*duck*)

   weather (*feather*)

   ship (*sheep, shell*)

   You can do the same with initial blends. For example:

   skip (*skin*)

   crib (*crab*)

   sneeze (*snake*)

   scare (*scale*)

   The text *Different coats* also has examples of words with vowel digraphs that you could practise. Write the words on the board and let learners say the words aloud. Prompt them to suggest other words that have the same sounds (and that are spelled in the same way). For example:

   ea: bear, feather + wear

   oa: goat + oats, soap, boat

   oo: wool + cool, stool, pool

   ee: sheep + meet, feet

   Learners do activities 2, 3 and 4 of the Workbook.

6. Learners can work in groups and play a telephone game. Learners whisper a sentence to each other in turn. They see how well they have listened when the last learner says the sentence aloud. Choose sentences about the texts learners have read in the Student's Book for this activity. Whisper the first sentence to one learner in the group and then let them continue.

7. Introduce the connectors *and*, *or* and *but*. Write some example sentences on the board. Then help learners to make similar sentences using other nouns and verbs. Do not expect learners to be able to join two sentences at this stage.

   Tortoises and crabs have shells.
   Owls and penguins have feathers.

   Do you like birds or goats?
   Do you like lions or tigers?

The hare ran fast <u>*but*</u> *the tortoise won the race.*
Tortoises are slow <u>*but*</u> *they are clever.*

8. Learners read the text *Different coats* in the Student's Book on page 16 by themselves. Then they complete the sentences in activity 5 in the Workbook.

9. Teach learners how to form negative sentences with *don't.* Give them some examples:

   Sheep don't have shells. They have wool.

   Hares don't have feathers. They have hair/fur.

   Then let them practise making up more sentences in pairs. They can write their sentences as well.

10. Focus on the uncountable nouns in the text *Different coats.* Explain briefly that some nouns do not have an *–s* (a plural form). Say:

    We say: A bird has feathers. A sheep has wool. (*not wools*).

    This is because we can count feathers but we can't count the wool on the sheep.

    (Learners will get more practise recognising and using uncountable nouns in Topic 4.)

11. Learners reread the story *The Hare and the Tortoise* in the Student's Book on page 17, alone or in pairs. Then they retell the story to their partners. After that let them work in pairs and act the story. They can use conversation from the extended story or their own conversation as they do this. Encourage them to talk as much as possible. You may want to play **Audio 14** again to remind them of the conversation.

12. Write some sentences from the stories in this unit on the board. Then erase one or two words in each sentence. Choose high-frequency words or words that you think learners should be able to spell. Let learners complete the sentences orally. Then let them write the complete sentences.

13. Learners complete activities 6 and 7 in the Workbook.

14. **Link to mathematics*. Do a survey with the class to find the animals they like. Draw up a list of eight to ten wild animals (some of them familiar, others less so). Write the names on the board in a table. For example:

bear	fox	owl	penguin	lion	elephant	bat	bee

    Then ask: *Who likes bears?* Learners raise their hands. Count the number of hands raised and fill in the number. Do this with each animal. Then ask learners to make sentences about the results of the survey. This practises numbers and plural nouns. For example:

    Ten learners like bears.

    Sixteen learners like penguins.

15. Learners read the text *Different coats* in the Student's Book on page 16 again. They can then refer to the page as they complete the puzzle in activity 8 in the Workbook.

16. Learners work in pairs and do some research about two other animals that interest them, or animals that are common in your community or country. Give learners some suggestions. They find out what body covering the animals have. They draw a picture and write a sentence about the animals. Once learners have finished, display their pictures and sentences for other learners to read.

17. Write some sentences in the simple past tense on the board. Ask learners to repeat the sentences, starting with the word *Yesterday*. Remind them that this means that they will need to change one of the words in the sentence. For example:

    I win the race. (Yesterday I *won* the race.)

    She sleeps in the afternoon. (Yesterday she *slept* in the afternoon.)

    They go to school. (Yesterday they *went* to school.)

18. Learners read the text *The Hare and the Tortoise* in the Student's Book on page 17 again. They can then complete the story in activity 9 in the Workbook.

19. Talk about what we can learn from animal stories like *The Hare and the Tortoise*. Ask learners if they know any other stories that teach us things.

Wrap-up plenary

Ask learners to tell you about what they have learned in this unit. Accept all reasonable suggestions.

Quick check

1. Write some animal names that have been introduced in this unit in a jumble and let learners write the names correctly. For example:

   erah (hare), *toisetor* (tortoise), *low* (owl) *bare* (bear) *toag* (goat), *akesn* (snake)

2. Let learners tell the story of *The Hare and the Tortoise* in groups. One learner starts the story with one sentence. The next learner adds another sentence, and so on, around the group until the story is told. Remind them to give others time to speak and not to interrupt.

Unit B Animal stories

Resources and materials

- Student's Book pp. 18–19
- Workbook pp. 46–51
- Audio files: Audio 15; Audio 16; Audio 17; Audio 18; Audio 19
- Photocopiable Masters (PCMs) PCM 8; PCM 9
- Additional animal stories, particularly stories from the cultural groups of learners in your class and from your country
- Pictures of ants and grasshoppers (to support an oral story)
- Counters (per learner, optional)
- Paper for writing poems

Key vocabulary

Nouns: lion, mouse, eyes, net

Pronouns: you, his, me, he

Verbs: open, sleep, see/saw, let go, go away, thank, was, bite/bit, save/saved

Adverbs: too

Conjunctions: but

Lead-in ideas

- Let learners sing or recite any familiar rhymes, songs or poems about animals.
- Teach a new rhyme and let learners add their own verses. For example, *Two Little Bears* (**Audio 15**).

Script for the lesson

Introducing vocabulary

Use the pictures in the text in the Student's Book to introduce the vocabulary in this unit. You can pre-teach some words and let learners try and work out the meaning of other words from clues in the pictures.

Sounds

You can teach and revise vowel digraphs in context in this unit. For example, you can teach *ou* in words such as *mouse, house, shout* and *ee* in words such as *bee, sleep, free, me.*

Introducing structures

Continue the focus on the simple past tense when learners read the story *The Lion and the Mouse.* This text has several common but irregular simple past tense verbs which learners will need to recognise as sight words.

Connectors such as *and, or* and *but* can be practised in conversation activities. The structures are also built into in the extended stories.

Revise genitives (possessive *'s*) in context.

Previous knowledge

Learners should be familiar with animal stories in their first language. Encourage and help them to tell or talk about these stories in English too.

Possible areas of difficulty

Irregular forms of simple past tense verbs will need some practice. As these need to be learned as sight words, display the words around the classroom – on the board, on labelled pictures, on prompt cards – to help learners remember the words.

Activities

Select from these activities depending on the level of challenge needed for different learners, interest levels and what you have time to include. Supplement these with additional activities of your own and/or digital activities from the online resource.

▲ **1.** Revise names of wild animals. You can play a game. For example, you can say: *I am thinking of an animal whose name begins with 'm'.* Learners then suggest all the names that they know that begin with *m*. Write the nouns on the board in a random order. Do this with several letters until you have about 15 names on the board.

Then ask learners to spell some of the names aloud. After that let them read out the names that begin with the same letters. You can also ask learners to put some of the names in alphabetical order (focus on the first letters only).

Learners can work in pairs and practise spelling the names aloud. One learner can spell a name while the other learner writes the name down.

▲ **2.** **Link to mathematics*. This activity practices listening skills (numbers 1–20 and the names of common animals). Give each learner a copy of **PCM 8.** Read the following descriptions aloud. Learners listen and tick the pictures that correspond to your oral descriptions.

1. *twelve snakes*
2. *seventeen bees*
3. *fifteen ants*
4. *eleven spiders*
5. *one lion*
6. *thirteen hares*

▲ **3.** Tell the class a familiar animal story which is in the oral storytelling tradition of your country or the culture of learners in the class. Ask them a few questions about the main characters. Then let them describe the animals (size, body coverings, noises they make, etc.). Encourage learners to share their knowledge of stories like this.

You can also let them tell stories in their first language. Summarise the stories briefly in English afterwards.

4. Learners find the story *The Lion and the Mouse* in the Student's Book on pages 18–19. Discuss the pictures and let learners predict what the story is about in the usual way. Then play the audio (**Audio 16**) while learners follow in their books. The audio story is an extended one, which provides richer language and more detail than the text in the Student's Book. Play the audio a second time, or read the story yourself, stopping to ask questions as you do this.

   Learners can then complete activities 1 and 2 in the Workbook.

5. Teach or revise some vowel digraphs using words from the stories learners have read, for example *ou* and *ee*. Write these words on the board:

   mouse

   sleep

   Then read out a list of words and ask learners to say whether the words have *ou* or *ee* in them. Here is a list of words you could read:

   house, shout, our, blouse, louse, bee, free, me, tea, knee, sea

6. Play a game to revise instructions and develop listening skills. Give each learner a copy of **PCM 9**. Give learners instructions about how to move the animals on each grid. Learners draw on the grids to show that they understand the instructions. You could also give them counters. They place a counter on the animal picture to start and then move their counters.

   Example instructions:

   - *Find the ladybird. Move it to the right, then go up one block. Then go three blocks to the left. Then go up one block. Which block is the ladybird in now?*
   - *Find the hare. Move it two blocks down. Then move one block to the right, then up two blocks, then one block left. Where is the hare?* (Where it started!)

7. In this activity, learners listen to a story without picture support. The story is about some ants and a grasshopper (**Audio 17**). To prepare learners for this activity, show them pictures of ants and grasshoppers and find out what they know about them. Prompt learners to talk about the fact that ants live and work in groups and that they are always busy. Some learners may know that grasshoppers can destroy plants and crops as well, because they eat everything. You should also re-teach the words *summer* and *winter.*

   Play the audio twice. Then ask learners a few questions to see if they understand the main ideas of the story. For example, ask:

   What did the grasshopper do in summer?

   What did the ants do?

   Was the grasshopper happy or sad in summer? Why?

   Was the grasshopper happy or sad in winter? Why?

8. Play the story *The Lion and the Mouse* (**Audio 16**) to the class. Learners work in pairs and can retell the story to their partners before completing activities 4, 5 and 6 in the Workbook.

   Learners could also work in groups to act the story.

9. Do some phonemic awareness activities with words from the story *The Lion and the Mouse* or *The Hare and the Tortoise*. For example, write the words *mouse, lion, hare* and *tortoise* on the board. Let learners try and think of adjectives that start with the same letters which describe these nouns, for example: *lazy lion, mini/mighty mouse, horrible/happy hare, tiny tortoise.*

   Learners can then make short sentences to practise putting the adjectives in different places in sentences. For example:

   The lion is lazy. He is a lazy lion.

   The hare is happy. The happy hare eats carrots.

10. Write the poem *Spiders* (**Audio 18**) on the board or on a poster. Find out what learners know about spiders. They may know about them in their first language. Prompt them to say:

    They are small animals. They live in webs. They make (*spin*) *webs.*

    Play the poem *Spiders* (**Audio 18**). Then read the poem aloud yourself. Ask the class to tell you what the poem is about. For example, ask:

    What does the person who wrote the poem like? (This person is "I" in the poem.)

    Why does he or she like this animal?

    What can the animal do?

    What does the animal have?

    Let learners work in groups of four to recite the poem. Each person in the group can recite two lines

11. Play the audio of the story *The Ants and the Grasshopper* (**Audio 17**) again. Then let learners complete activities 7 and 8 in the Workbook.

12. Focus on the way words and phrases are joined by the conjunctions *and* and *but*. One way of doing this is to let learners match parts of sentences. Use some of the sentences from the stories learners have read or listened to. Cut the sentences up and let learners match the parts. For example:

It was warm	and he sang.
The grasshopper hopped	goats have wool.
Sheep and	but he won the race.
The hare was fast	and chewed the net.
Tortoise was slow	and sunny.
Mouse chewed	and the tortoise was slow.

13. Learners can work in groups and make up animal riddles for the others in the group (or for other groups) to guess. For example:

    This is a small animal. It likes to sing and hop. It eats a lot. Its name begins with 'gr'.

14. Learners complete writing activity 9 in the Workbook.

15. Let learners practise saying sentences with genitives (possessive 's). Read the sentences and let learners repeat them after you. Some learners find it difficult to pronounce this genitive form. They will practise writing these forms later in the year. For example:

The mouse jumped on the lion's back.

The grasshopper's tummy was empty.

Hare's carrot is big.

This is Anna's bag.

16. Work with small groups of learners. Write a poem with the group, using the poem *Spiders* as a model. This is not a rhyming poem, which makes it easier for learners at this stage.

Write this frame on the board:

I like __________________.

Do you know why?

Because they are __________________

And I am __________________

Because they can __________________

And I can't __________________

Because they have __________________

And I have __________________.

____

I like them.

This is why.

Then ask for suggestions about how to complete the poem. Discuss and decide with the group what works best. Then write the completed poem on the board. Learners can copy the poem into their exercise books and then practise reciting the poem they have helped to write in their groups. Display all the poems written in this way in the classroom for others to read.

17. Let learners listen to another story about wild animals. Read or tell any story that you think will be familiar to learners (for example, *The Ugly Duckling, Goldilocks and the Three Bears*) or you can play *The Bear and the Bees* (**Audio 19**). Play the audio twice, or tell or read the story twice, before you ask simple questions to find out if learners have understood the main ideas of the story.

18. Let learners listen to the story *The Bear and the Bees* again. Then they can complete activities 10 and 11 in their Workbooks.

19. Learners write the story *The Ants and the Grasshopper* using pictures and key words as prompts, in activities 12 and 13 in the Workbook.

Wrap-up plenary

Tell learners another animal story with a moral lesson and discuss it.

Quick check

**Link to drama*. Let learners work in small groups. Each group chooses a story they have read or heard in this unit. They act the story for the rest of the class. The class has to guess the name of the story.

Unit C Baby animals

Resources and materials

- Student's Book pp. 20–21
- Workbook pp. 52–57
- Audio file: Audio 20
- Photographs or films about baby animals
- Picture dictionaries
- Pictures of baby animals, including a tiger cub, an ostrich and an ostrich egg
- Small booklets of blank paper, 6–8 pages long (one per learner)
- Sheets of A4 paper, folded in half (one per learner)

Key vocabulary

Nouns: baby, lion, hair, ears, paws, claws, tail, whiskers, mane, mother, eggs

Verbs: be, have, lay, cover, hatch, run, eat, grow, live

If you want to extend the vocabulary in the unit, teach the names of the baby animals: cub, kitten, puppy, and so on.

Lead-in ideas

Play a film/video about baby animals for the class, if this is available.

Script for the lesson

Introducing vocabulary

Introduce the names of common parts of the body of familiar animals. Use the pictures in the Student's Book, or any other pictures you may have, to do this.

Sounds

Teach and revise vowel digraphs in context. For example, *aw* (*paw, claw*) and *ai/ay, a-e* (*tail, mane, lay, baby, same*).

Introducing structures

Teach learners to recognise and start to use the genitive (possessive 's) in simple sentences in context. Teach only the singular forms at this stage.

Previous knowledge

Learners should be familiar with most of the animals that are introduced in this unit.

Possible areas of difficulty

Pronunciation of the possessive 's can be tricky to pronounce, so let learners practise saying sentences aloud wherever possible.

Activities

Select from these activities depending on the level of challenge needed for different learners, interest levels and what you have time to include. Supplement these with additional activities of your own and/or digital activities from the online resource.

▲ **1.** Show learners the pictures of baby animals you have collected and let learners try and name the animals. If you feel learners are ready to learn the names of baby animals, you can introduce the more common names such as *cub, puppy, kitten, lamb*, even though the main focus of the topic is on wild and not domestic animals.

▲ **2.** Let learners find the labelled photographs in *Lions* on page 20 of the Student's Book. Discuss the photographs and help learners to read the labels.

Learners can then colour in and label the pictures in activities 1 and 2 in the Workbook.

▲ **3.** **Link to science*. Write the following table on the board and let the class discuss and complete the points of comparison. Learners can copy the tables into their exercise books once you have agreed on how to complete the table. You can add further points of comparison if you think the class is ready to do this.

People	Lions
feet, hands	
nails	
no tail	
hair, skin	
two legs	
beards/moustaches	
can: talk, sing, sleep, play	

▲ **4.** Teach and revise vowel digraphs in context. Write the following words on the board. Read them aloud. Tell learners to look for words on page 20 of the Student's Book that have the same 'aw' and 'ai' sounds. They should read all the labels aloud to understand this as the spelling is not necessarily the same.

claw (*paw*) (also: *door, floor*)

tail (*mane*) (hair does not have the same sound, but *same, lay* and *baby* do)

Then help learners to think of other words that sound the same. Say the words aloud and write them on the board too. This will help to build awareness of the fact that sounds can be written in different ways.

▲ **5.** Let learners listen to a well-known story, *Goldilocks and the Three Bears* (**Audio 20**). The story revises many familiar words – names of rooms in a house, numbers, adjectives – and structures – simple present and past tenses. You may wish to re-teach the past tense verbs *lay down* and *broke*. Play **Audio 20** at least twice, or read the story yourself the second time. Then ask simple questions about the main characters and the events in the story. For example, ask:

How many bears are there in the story?
Who are the bears?
What do they do first?
What do they do next?
Whose house is it?

▲ **6.** Write the following table on the board. Make sure learners have access to picture dictionaries (or the internet). Read each word on the table. Learners identify the initial letter and you write it on the table. Then let learners use that first letter clue as a starting point to finding the word in their dictionaries. They should look for a picture to help them understand what the word means.

Word	First letter	Answer the question
hippo		Where does a hippo live?
fox		Is this a big animal or a small animal?
hyena		What colour fur does this animal have?
badger		Where does this animal live? In trees or under the ground?
cub		What do you call this animal's mother or father?

(Note: The words in some beginner picture dictionaries are arranged in themes, rather than simply in alphabetical order, so you will need to check this first. Learners may have to find a page about wild animals rather than just looking at the beginning letter. You may also need to adjust the suggested words and questions given on the table above to match the dictionary that your learners are using.)

▲ **7.** Learners can complete activities 3 and 4 in the Workbook. They look at the picture and complete the table.

● **8.** Learners open the Student's Book on page 20. Point to the pictures and say sentences using genitives, for example:

This is the lion's tail.
The lion's paws are big.
This is the lion's mane.

Let learners work in pairs and make similar sentences. Learners can complete activities 5 and 6 in the Workbook.

● **9.** Play a question game with learners to practise asking questions. You can call this *10 questions*.

Think of a familiar animal but don't tell learners the name of the animal. Then tell them they can ask you ten questions about the animal to get clues about the animal. You will only answer *Yes* or *No*. Give learners some examples of the sort of questions they could ask, for example:

Is the animal big?

Does the animal have feathers?

Is the animal black and white?

Is it a panda?

Learners can't ask questions like *Is the animal big or small?* because you can only answer *Yes* or *No*. If they ask questions like this, tell them to try again.

The learner who guesses the name of the animal wins a point and gets the next turn to think about another animal and answer questions.

10. Learners write simple descriptions of animals using the writing frames in activity 7 in the Workbook.

11. Learners find the page about the life of *Baby turtles* in the Student's Book on page 21. Discuss the page with learners first. Ask them *Is this a story or is this information? What is the information about? What do the arrows mean?*

Then read and discuss the chart with the class or with groups. Explain anything that learners do not understand but encourage them to use clues from the pictures to work out what words mean as well.

12. Learners can work in groups and compile booklets about baby animals using all the information they have learned in this topic. Give each group a list of three or four animals. Write some notes on the board about what learners should do and discuss this with them before they begin. For example:

- *Read the stories in the Student's Book again.*
- *Make simple word spiders with information about each animal.* (Give them an example.)
- *Draw or find pictures of each animal.*
- *Write at least two sentences about each animal.*
- *Plan your booklet. Write a contents page.*

Let learners do their planning and research first. Then give them small booklets that you have made up with six to eight pages each. Number the pages for learners or let them number the pages before they start. The contents page can be page 1.

Write a contents frame on the first page to prompt learners to do this. For example:

Contents	
Name	**Page**

13. **Link to drama*. Show learners a picture of an ostrich and an ostrich egg. Explain that an ostrich egg is very big. A baby ostrich hatches out of an egg. Let learners work in groups and make up a story about a baby ostrich hatching out of an egg. Brainstorm some ideas with the group first or make up a short story yourself which can inspire learners.

14. Show learners a picture of a tiger cub. Talk about features of the tiger cub such as colours, patterns and body parts. Write the key words on the board and have learners say them. Learners complete activities 8 and 9 in the Workbook.

15. Let learners look at the chart about baby turtles on page 21 of the Student's Book again before they complete activities 10, 11 and 12 in the Workbook.

16. **Link to science*. Talk about how baby animals are born and how animals protect and care for their babies. Ask questions such as: *Do they hatch out of eggs? What do the babies eat? Who looks after them?*

Wrap-up plenary

Let the groups read and share the booklets they have made about baby animals.

Quick check

Let learners play a drawing game in pairs. Give each learner a sheet of paper folded in half. One learner draws the head of an animal on the front of the folded sheet, with the head facing the edge of the paper and the neck line just crossing the fold. The learner must NOT say which animal he or she is drawing. You will need to show learners where to draw for this to work. The learner turns the sheet over so that the other learner cannot see what he or she has drawn, except the end of the neck line. The second learner draws the body of an animal. Then learners open the sheet of paper and look at the 'animal' they have drawn. Encourage learners to describe their animals.

Assessment

You can complete an oral assessment of the work done in this topic by asking learners to retell one of the stories in the unit, using pictures as prompts.

Learners can also complete Progress check activities 1, 2, 3 and 4 in the Workbook as a simple assessment.

You could allocate marks for these activities and record these as part of continuous assessment.

Topic 4 Super food

Overview

In this topic the focus is on sharing information about foods of different kinds using familiar vocabulary and structures to build confidence and then introducing new structures and vocabulary to develop language skills.

There are opportunities to integrate activities with other curricula such as natural sciences, health education, drama and mathematics.

Units in this topic

Unit A: Crunch munch

Unit B: Let's cook

Unit C: Food from different places

Teaching focus

- **2Rg1** Recognise, identify and sound, with support, a limited range of language at text level
- **2Rf1** Read and follow, with support, familiar instructions for classroom activities
- **2Rg2** Begin to read, with support, very short simple fiction and non-fiction texts with confidence and enjoyment
- **2Rm2** Understand the main points of very short, simple texts on some familiar general and curricular topics by using contextual clues
- **2Rd1** Understand, with support, some specific information and detail in very short, simple texts on a limited range of general and curricular topics
- **2Rm1** Understand the meaning of very short, simple texts on familiar general and curricular topics by rereading them
- **2Rd2** Understand the meaning of simple short sentences on familiar general and curricular topics
- **2Wa1** Plan, write and check, with support, short sentences on familiar topics
- **2Ug14** Spell a growing number of familiar high-frequency words accurately during guided writing activities
- **2Wo2** Include a full stop and question mark during guided writing of short, familiar sentences
- **2Ug1** Use singular nouns, plural nouns – including some common irregular plural forms – and uncountable nouns, genitive 's/s' to name and label things
- **2Ug3** Use adjectives, including possessive adjectives, on familiar topics to give personal information and describe things
- **2Ut1** Use determiners *a, the, some, any, this, these, that* to refer to familiar objects
- **2Ut2** Use *who, what, where, how many* to ask questions on familiar topics
- **2Ut3** Use impersonal *you* in the question: *How do you spell that?*
- **2Uf1** Use imperative forms [positive and negative] to give short instructions
- **2Uf2** Use common simple present forms, including short answer forms and contractions, to give personal information
- **2Uf3** Use common past simple forms [regular and irregular] to describe actions and narrate simple events including short answer forms and contractions
- **2Uf5** Use common present continuous forms, including short answers and contractions, to talk about what is happening now on personal and familiar topics
- **2Ug4** Use *–ing* forms *swimming, spelling* as nouns to describe familiar and classroom activities
- **2Ug13** Use *Would you like to …* to invite and use appropriate responses *yes please, no thanks*
- **2Ug12** Use declarative *what [a/an]* + adjective + noun to show feelings
- **2Ld3** Understand a growing range of short, supported questions which ask for personal information
- **2Ld5** Understand an increasing range of short supported questions on general and curricular topics
- **2Lg1** Understand short supported narratives on an increasing range of general and curricular topics
- **2Lg3** Recognise words that are spelled out in a limited range of general and curricular topics
- **2Lg2** Identify initial, middle and final phonemes and blends
- **2S2** Ask questions to find out about an increasing range of personal information
- **2S4** Use basic vocabulary for a limited range of general and curricular topics
- **2S5** Give short, basic descriptions of people and objects
- **2S6** Contribute a growing range of suitable words, phrases, and sentences during short pair, group and whole class exchanges
- **2S7** Take turns when speaking with others in a growing range of short, basic exchanges
- **2S8** Relate very short, basic stories and events on a limited range of general and curricular topics

Language patterns

Grammar summary for teachers:

Present continuous tense: We use this tense to describe actions that are happening at the present. *I **am** reading a book. They **are** cooking supper.*

The tense is formed with the relevant part of the verb *to be* + the present participle (which is the infinitive form of the verb + *-ing*). Special spelling rules apply when adding *–ing* to the ends of verbs that end in *–e* or words that end in a short vowel followed by a consonant. For example:

*I **write** every day. I **am writing** a poem now.*

*He runs to school every day. He **is running** to school now.*

The tense should not be used to describe actions that occur regularly, for example:

*I **go** to school every day.* (Not: *I **am going** to school every day.*)

Unit A Crunch munch

Resources and materials

- Student's Book pp. 22–24
- Workbook pp. 60–66
- Audio files: Audio 21; Audio 22
- Photocopiable Masters (PCMs) PCM 10; PCM 11
- Pictures of different fruits, vegetables and other foods, such as noodles, bread, rice, meat, cheese, jam
- Blank prompt cards to write words on
- Some real fruits (to teach adjectives such as sweet, juicy, sour), empty packets and boxes
- 1–6 spinner (PCM 11) and counters

Key vocabulary

Common foods: fruit, vegetables, water, bread, milk, rice, pancakes (or flat breads), pasta (noodles), meat, fish, cheese, jam

Mealtimes: breakfast, lunch, supper/dinner, snack

Adjectives: healthy, tasty, crunchy, juicy, sweet, sour, half

Lead-in ideas

- Teach learners a short, new poem with some alliteration in it. For example, the rhyme *Five Fat Peas* (**Audio 21**) in which learners can use their hands as pea pods and clap them together when the pod pops.
- Teach a short tongue-twister (**Audio 22**).

Script for the lesson

Introducing vocabulary

Revise and teach the names of common foods mentioned in texts in this unit. You should also teach the names of popular local foods. Sometimes the names of these foods do not have names in English, so let learners use the names that they know.

Sounds

Revise end phonemes in adjectives such as *crunchy, tasty* and *juicy.*

Help learners to break longer new words up into syllables in order to read and pronounce them (examples: *to*ma+to, co*co+nut*).

Introducing structures

Let learners practise using the simple present and simple past tenses in this unit using new verbs such as *find, cut, put*.

Learners can also practise making and answering questions that begin with *What*.

You can also introduce the structure *What a/an + adjective + noun* to express feelings about different foods. (The structure is in **Audio 22**, **24** and **26**.)

Previous knowledge

Learners will be familiar with the names of some foods. Help them to relate the names they know in their first language to English names (if these exist).

Possible areas of difficulty

Some learners may struggle to read the texts. Help them to use context clues and their knowledge of phonics to read the words and understand the texts.

Activities

Select from these activities depending on the level of challenge needed for different learners, interest levels and what you have time to include. Supplement these with additional activities of your own and/or digital activities from the online resource.

▲ **1.** Ask learners what their favourite foods are. Write the names on the board. Then use the pictures you have collected to revise and teach the names of other common foods.

Put the pictures on a table and ask each learner to come up and choose a picture. They choose a picture of a food that they can name and describe. (Examples: *This is a coconut. I love coconuts! It is hard. There is milk inside.*)

Learners read the names of the food and copy them under the appropriate pictures in activities 1 and 2 in the Workbook.

2. If learners are familiar with mangoes, pretend you are eating a mango and it is very messy. Ask learners to guess what you are doing. Teach the words *messy* and *juicy.*

Then read *Mangoes are messy!* on page 22 of the Student's Book. Make sure learners understand any new vocabulary in the poem. Then let them learn and recite the poem in groups of four. Each learner in the group can recite one line, or they can recite the whole poem together.

3. Use the adjectives from *Mangoes are messy*! to teach and revise end phonemes in adjectives. Ask learners to find the words that rhyme in the poem (*crunchy, milky, tasty* and *messy*). Ask them why the words rhyme and help them identify the final end phoneme *–y*. Write the words on the board and then prompt learners to think of more words that end like this. For example: *happy, funny, silly, pretty, fruity, salty*. Then help the class to make sentences about different foods with some of the adjectives on your list. (Examples: *Oranges are juicy. I like juicy oranges. Apples are crunchy.*)

You could also turn this into a game again. Write the adjectives on slips of paper or prompt cards. Put the cards face down on a table and let learners select cards in turn. They read the word and make a sentence with it. If the sentence is good they score a point and have another turn. If they can't make a sentence, they can ask a friend to help them, but then they only score half a point. (You can discuss and make up rules with the class before you play this.)

4. Read the story *Raj Has a Good Idea* on page 23 of the Student's Book. Write the title on the board and let learners read the title. They can then find the story in the Student's Book.

(Note: You can revise and teach number words from 20 upwards each time learners need to find or read something in the Student's Book. Say the number and let learners find the page. Alternatively, write the numeral on the board and let learners say the number word.)

Discuss the pictures in the usual way and prompt learners to say what they think the story is about. Then read the text with groups of learners. Ask a few oral questions as you work, for example: *What does Ada have? What does Raj do? What does Raj put in the bottle?*

Discuss the idea of planting seeds and growing your own food. Ask questions such as: *Why should people do that? Can we grow all the foods that we like to eat?*

5. Write the following sentences from the story *Raj Has a Good Idea* on the board, but leave out the determiner. Read the sentences with the class and ask them to suggest which word is missing in each sentence.

Ada found ______________ (a) *plastic bottle.*

Raj had ______________ (an) *idea.*

Raj cut ______________ (the) *bottle in half.*

Do you have ______________ (any) *soil?*

Write the suggestions on the board and then let learners check in the Student's Book to see if they were correct.

6. Learners find the non-fiction text *What's inside?* on page 24 of the Student's Book. Make sure learners understand what the word *inside* means. Read each question with learners and help them to find the answers in the pictures and labels. Ask learners which of the foods in the pictures they like and don't like. Ask them to try and describe the foods using adjectives that they know.

Learners can name them in activity 3 in the Workbook.

7. Teach learners a few more adjectives with which to describe foods. For example, *sweet* and *sour.* You could even bring a few fruits like lemons and bananas to class and let learners taste the fruits to help them understand the meanings of the words.

Let learners play a quick guessing game in groups. One learner describes a food and the others guess what it is. Learners can use whatever words they know to describe the food. For example: *It is round and sweet and juicy. It is orange and it has a big seed* (mango). *It is cold and sweet and delicious. You can have chocolate or vanilla or strawberry* (ice cream).

8. Let learners read or recite the poem *Mangoes are messy!* (page 22 of the Student's Book) again. Then work with the class or groups of learners and write another similar poem together. One way of doing this is to write the whole poem on the board and then to start rubbing out the names of the fruits. Learners suggest different fruits. Then rub out the adjectives and let learners suggest different adjectives.

9. Find out if the class know what noodles are. Show learners a picture of some noodles (or an (empty) packet of noodles). If learners eat noodles, ask what they eat with them and how they eat them. Ask them if noodles are easy to eat, or if they are messy, like mangoes.

Then read the poem *Eating noodles* on page 22 of the Student's Book. Explain that this is a poem that has a shape. The words in the poem look like some noodles. Read the words of the poem with the class and help them to understand it.

10. Use the poems on page 22 of the Student's Book to revise some initial sounds. Give learners a word and ask them to find another word that begins with the same sound or initial letters in the poems. For example:

shout (shirt)

strong (stringy, strips)
ten (tongue, tomato, turn)
twenty (twist)
cabbage (carrots, coconut)

11. **Link to mathematics and science.* Give each learner a copy of **PCM 10**. Explain that the pie chart shows a plate of healthy foods. The plate is divided into sections to show us how much of each kind of food we should eat.

Let learners name all the foods they can see on the plate. Teach the words *half* and *quarter* by relating these to the fractions ½ and ¼. Then help learners to discuss healthy meals.

12. Revise or teach the words *breakfast, lunch* and *supper/dinner*. Ask learners what they eat at each meal and at what time they eat the meal. (This is revision from Stage 1.) Write words on the board as you talk because learners will need these words to complete the activity in their Workbook. Spell out the words and see if learners can recognise the words.

Learners can then complete activities 4 and 5 in the Workbook.

13. Learners read or reread the non-fiction text *What's inside?* on page 24 of the Student's Book. They can also work in pairs and ask each other questions about the text. Help them to pronounce the contraction *what's* correctly.

14. Talk about the parts of plants that we can eat. Examples could include: the nut inside some shells, the roots of some plants (carrots), the leaves of plants (spinach), and so on. You can also use this opportunity to discuss the idea that some plants are poisonous or that some people are allergic to some foods such as nuts, for example.

15. Learners complete activities 6 and 7 in the Workbook.

16. Reread the poem *Eating noodles* on page 22 of the Student's Book. Then work with groups of learners and help them to create a simple shape poem that reflects the shape of some food. You could make another noodles poem or you could use any other suitable shape, for example: circle like the shape of a plate of food, an orange or an apple; a bunch of grapes; a carrot; grains of rice (with one word in each grain).

17. **Link to science.* Read the story *Raj Has a Good Idea* on page 23 of the Student's Book.

Learners then work in groups and grow their own seeds in cut-off plastic bottles. They should observe their seeds and seedlings every day and record what they see. They can follow the instructions in activity 8 in the Workbook and record their observations in activity 9.

Wrap-up plenary

Talk about healthy meals again.

Quick check

Have learners complete the instructions and play the snakes and ladders game in activities 10 and 11 in the Workbook. To complete the game, learners must fill in types of food on the lines. Encourage them to write healthy foods on the blocks at the bottom of the ladders and unhealthy foods in the blocks at the top of the snakes.

They can either play in pairs or small groups, taking turns to use a different learner's book each time they start a new game. Each learner needs a counter (stone, shell, coin). Each group needs a 1–6 spinner (use **PCM 11**). Discuss how to play the game.

Instructions:

Put all your counters on Start.
Take turns to spin the spinner and move your counter.
If you land on a snake's head, go down the snake.
If you land at the bottom of a ladder, go up the ladder.

Unit B Let's cook

Resources and materials

- Student's Book pp. 25–27
- Workbook pp. 67–73
- Audio files: Audio 23; Audio 24; Audio 25
- Ingredients to make a simple recipe with the class (for example, a fruit salad, a sandwich), poster with name of the dish you will make as well as a list of ingredients
- Prompt cards with key verbs: wash, peel, cut, boil, mix, turn, beat, put
- A cup, teaspoon and a tablespoon and some sugar, rice or salt to demonstrate quantities

Key vocabulary

Verbs: mix, add, beat, warm, out, turn, let, cook, cut, wash, peel, boil, try

Nouns: names of fruits + additional common foods (see Unit A)

flour, milk, sugar, eggs, salt, butter, oil, yoghurt, jam, cup, teaspoon, tablespoon

Adverbs: easy, too

Lead-in ideas

Teach learners a rhyme or chant about preparing food. For example, *Let's Make Fruit Salad* (**Audio 23**). You can add the names of any popular local fruits to extend this chant.

Script for the lesson

Introducing vocabulary

In this unit, you can extend vocabulary by using common verbs to explain food preparation. Let learners name more food types as well, including foods with which they are familiar at home.

Sounds

Revise phonemes and sounds in context. In this unit, for example, there are opportunities to revise vowel digraphs such as *ou* (*flour, our, hour*), *ow* (*bowl*), *oi* (*oil, boil, soil*) and *oo* (*spoon, cook, food*).

Introducing structures

Recipes provide a context to revise the simple present tense and the use of imperatives. The story *Jam and Yoghurt Are Easy to Make* in this unit provides opportunities to revise questions and to read the present continuous tense after you have introduced this orally.

Previous knowledge

Learners should understand simple sentences in the imperative and the present simple tense. They will also know the names of many foods in the first language. They should know some basic ways of measuring quantities from mathematics.

Possible areas of difficulty

Many uncountable nouns can also be used as countable nouns when they are used in different ways. For example:

We put some oil in the pan. (uncountable)

We use different oils for different types of food. (countable)

Learners might find this confusing. You can begin by just teaching these words as uncountable nouns. They will learn the difference later.

Activities

Select from these activities depending on the level of challenge needed for different learners, interest levels and what you have time to include. Supplement these with additional activities of your own and/or digital activities from the online resource.

▲ **1.** Demonstrate how to make a dish. For example, you could make a fruit salad. Write the name of the dish and a list of the ingredients clearly on the board or on a poster, as learners will need this information to complete a page in their Workbooks afterwards.

Let the class watch and listen as you explain what you are doing in the present continuous tense. For example, say: *I'm washing the fruit, I'm peeling the fruit, I'm cutting the fruit.* This introduces the present continuous tense in a natural and informal way. When you have completed the salad ask learners to explain how you made the salad. Ask questions such as: *What did I do first? And then what did I do?* Let learners answer in the simple past tense. (*You washed the fruit.*)

You could demonstrate how to make a simple sandwich or something similar in the same way.

When you have finished this let learners complete activities 1, 2, 3 and 4 in their Workbooks.

▲ **2.** Tell learners to find page 25 in the Student's Book and to read the title of the text (*Pancakes*). Ask them what they think the page is about. Then read the list of ingredients with the group or class. Show learners the cup, teaspoon and tablespoon you have brought to class. Use the rice, sugar or salt you have brought to demonstrate how much a teaspoonful, a tablespoonful and a cupful is. Make piles on a sheet of paper to illustrate. Make sure learners know what ½ is.

Then read the instructions. Help learners to decode words, using context clues and their knowledge of phonemes.

If you have the facility at your school, you could also take learners into the kitchen and demonstrate making pancakes.

Learners can then complete activity 5 in the Workbook.

▲ **3.** Use the prompt cards to revise imperatives. Hold up each verb in turn and let learners read the card and act what the verb means to show that they understand. You could also place the cards face down on a table and tell learners to come up one at a time, choose a card, read it and act the instruction.

▲ **4.** Play **Audio 24**. The text is an informal recipe presented on a radio talk show. Play this text a few times, or read it again to the class. Then make a summary together. Have a writing frame ready on the board or on a sheet of paper, as follows:

How to make a milkshake

What you need:

*

*

*

*

What you do:

1.

2.

3.

4.

5.

Complete this writing frame with the class or with groups. Ask questions prompting them to give you the information that you need to complete the recipe.

5. Let learners find the story *Jam and Yoghurt are Easy to Make* in the Student's Book on pages 26–27. Do some pre-reading activities in the usual way and then read the story with the class or a group. Ask questions as you do this, for example: *What does the girl like? What can Aunty make?* Talk about the last picture and help learners describe it. For example, you could say: *The children make a big mess. They are funny*silly+messy. Aunty is cross.*

   Teach the structure *What a/an + adjective + noun* if you have not yet done so. Discuss what it means in the story. Ask: *How does Aunty feel?* Then write a few more examples on the board and ask the class to explain how people feel when they make statements like this. For example:

   What a tasty soup!

   What a long trip.

   What an exciting story!

   What a long walk.

6. Give oral explanations of the contractions in the story *Jam and Yoghurt Are Easy to Make.* Write the contractions on the board in a column. Learners find the contractions in the story and read the whole sentence in which each one occurs. Then explain that these words are written in the way that we speak. The apostrophe shows that a letter is missing. Write the full forms next to each contraction so that learners can see the connection. Then read both forms aloud so that they can hear the difference.

short forms	full forms
don't	do not
it's	it is
I'm	I am
that's	that is

7. Give an oral demonstration of how to use the present continuous tense. You can use pictures or real actions to do this. For example:

   Walk to the door and ask *What am I doing?*

   Point to a picture in a story and ask *What is she/he doing? What are they doing?*

   Learners can work in pairs to practise making oral questions in the same way.

8. Use familiar words, words in the *Pancake* recipe and in the story *Jam and Yoghurt Are Easy to Make* to teach learners to recognise some medial phonemes. Write the following words on the board and underline the vowels in each:

   flour <u>our</u> h<u>our</u> s<u>our</u> cl<u>ou</u>d l<u>ou</u>d

   oil b<u>oi</u>l s<u>oi</u>l

   sp<u>oo</u>n c<u>oo</u>k f<u>oo</u>d fl<u>oo</u>r d<u>oo</u>r

   Deal with one group of words at a time. Ask learners which letters are the same in each word. Then read the words with the class and ask if they all sound the same. When you get to the words with *oo*, help learners to listen to the words and then to group them into words that sound the same (*door/floor, spoon*food+cook*).

9. Write the following words on the board. (They are uncountable nouns.)

   flour milk sugar oil butter water

   Ask learners to make sentences with the nouns. For example: *We put flour in the bowl*. Help them to understand that we can't add *–s* to these words to make them plural because we can't count them. We can use other words with these words to describe quantities, though. For example:

   a cup of sugar

   2 cups of sugar

   Draw some simple pictures on the board (or use real measuring tools) of the following to practise describing quantities correctly. For example:

   3 teaspoons of (*sugar/salt*)

   4 cups of flour

   2 bottles of oil

   2 glasses of water

   Learners complete activities 6 and 7 in the Workbook.

10. Learners read the recipe for *Pancakes* on page 25 of the Student's Book in pairs. Then they complete activities 8 and 9 in the Workbook.

11. Learners reread the story *Jam and Yoghurt Are Easy to Make* in the Student's Book on pages 26–27. Then they complete activities 10 and 11 in the Workbook.

12. Learners work in groups of three. Teach them a simple conversation based on the story *Jam and Yoghurt Are Easy to Make.* For example:

    A: *I love* ____________.

    B: *So do I./I don't.*

    A: *How do you make* ______________?

    B: *I don't know. Let's ask* ____________.

    A: *OK.*

    B: ____________ *How do you make* ____________?

    C: *It's easy. I'll show you.*

    A and B: *Thanks!*

13. Learners work in groups. They play a chain game in which they describe what they need to make a fruit salad (or any other popular dish – a curry, for example). The first learner makes a sentence. The next learner repeats the sentence, and adds another ingredient. The third learner repeats what the second learner said, and adds a third ingredient. For example:

    We need some bananas.

    We need some bananas and a pineapple.

We need some bananas, a pineapple and a passion fruit.

And so on.

14. Learners reread the recipe for *Pancakes* in the Student's Book on page 25. Then they copy and complete the instructions in the correct order in activity 12 in the Workbook.

15. **Link to drama*. Learners work in small groups and pretend they are presenting a radio programme about food. They introduce themselves and then give a short easy recipe to their 'listeners'. For example, they can explain how to make a good sandwich or wrap, or their favourite soup or vegetable. Some learners may know how to make ice cream or cookies too. Let learners talk about things they know and enjoy. Help with vocabulary as necessary.

16. Learners reread the story *Jam and Yoghurt Are Easy to Make* in the Student's Book on pages 26–27 and then complete activities 13, 14 and 15 in the Workbook.

17. Read or play learners a well-known story that involves cooking, for example *The Gingerbread Man* or *One Rice Thousand Gold*. (The *Rice and Gold* story on **Audio 25** is a version of this traditional Chinese story.) Ask learners questions to help them understand the main ideas and the sequence of events.

Wrap-up plenary

Talk about favourite foods and recipes. Let learners try and explain why they like certain foods, using the vocabulary they have learned.

Quick check

1. Ask learners to tell you what you need to make familiar recipes. They can do this orally, or if you think they are ready to do this, they can make their own written lists of ingredients. Let them compare their lists with other learners afterwards.
2. Learners work in groups and take turns to explain how to make a familiar dish. Each learner adds one instruction (one sentence) to the oral recipe.

Unit C Food from different places

Resources and materials

- Student's Book p. 28
- Workbook pp. 74–77
- Audio files: Audio 26; Audio 27
- Pictures which show foods eaten on special celebration days
- Globe or map of the world

Key vocabulary

stew, beans, sausages, onions, garlic, chilli, ginger, rice, peas, pizza, olives, bread, celebration, special, sweets

Lead-in ideas

Teach learners a poem or song about a well-known celebration at which people eat special foods. You can choose international or local celebrations. For example, read the poems *Chinese New Year and Diwali.*

Poem: Chinese New Year
On the Chinese blossom tree,
Lucky bags for you and me!
Red and gold, what can they hide?
Let's find out, we'll look inside.
Silver coins, delicious sweets;
Lucky bags bring New Year treats!

Poem: Diwali
Fetch the candles.
Make it bright.
This is *our* festival
of light.
The goddess is coming
with luck and treats.
There's going to be laughter,
fireworks and sweets.
Family and friends
are together tonight.
For this is Diwali,
our festival of light.

Script for the lesson

Introducing vocabulary

In this unit, you can continue to extend vocabulary about food by talking about foods for special occasions. Let learners name foods with which they are familiar at home.

Sounds

Revise phonemes and sounds in context. In this unit, for example, there are opportunities to revise vowel digraphs such as *ea/ee* (*peas, beans, cheese*), *ew* (*stew*).

Introducing structures

Introduce the polite request *Would you like some __________?* with positive and negative answers in this unit, by means of simple conversations.

Revise singular and plural forms including plurals that end in *–es* and *–ies* (*dishes, tomatoes, countries*).

Previous knowledge

Learners should already be familiar with the present simple tense and some of the vocabulary in this unit.

Possible areas of difficulty

Some learners may struggle to retell a story in the correct sequence. Write the main points of the story on separate strips of paper. Discuss the points and make sure learners understand the meaning. Jumble the strips then have learners arrange the strips in the correct order. They can then read the main points in order.

Activities

Select from these activities depending on the level of challenge needed for different learners, interest levels and what you have time to include. Supplement these with additional activities of your own and/or digital activities from the online resource.

1. Have a class discussion about the food that people eat on special days and celebrations. If some learners in the class are taking part in a celebration at this time, focus on that. Talk about what food people eat, what the ingredients are and when the food is served and eaten.

If you have pictures, show the class and describe what the pictures show.

2. Let learners find page 28 in the Student's Book, *Food from different places*. Give them a few minutes to look at the photographs on the pages. Ask them if they recognise any of the dishes. If they do, ask them to describe what it is. Then help learners to read the text, using the photographs for support and to help them work out meaning.

3. **Link to social sciences*. Write down some of the names of dishes that have been discussed in class. Make a table on the board and then talk about the country of origin. For example:

Dish or food	Country
rice and peas	Jamaica
pizza	Italy
feijoada	Brazil
kimchi	Korea

Let learners work in pairs to find the names of the countries on a map or globe.

4. Learners complete activities 1 and 2 in the Workbook.

5. Use familiar words to teach learners to recognise some medial phonemes. Write the following words on the board and underline phonemes in each.

peas beans cheese bread

stew new few blue you

Talk about which letters are the same in each word. Then read the words with the class and ask if they all sound the same.

6. Write the following plural words on the board and help learners to pronounce the end sounds correctly.

onions beans pears

sausages oranges

tomatoes potatoes mangoes

countries

Explain that these words are all plurals because they refer to more than one of each. Then ask learners what word they would use if they wanted to talk about one item. Discuss how the words change. You could do this in a table. Choose about ten words that form plurals in different ways for this activity. For example:

one	more than one	how the word changes
onion	onions	add *s*
bean		
orange		
tomato	tomatoes	add *es*
potato		
country	countries	change *y* to *ies*
baby		

7. Tell the class that they are going to listen to a story. The story is called *Stone Soup* (**Audio 26**). Ask them what they think the story is about. Accept all their suggestions but don't tell them the answer. You can pre-teach the words *drought, soup, stone* and *stranger.* Then play the audio at least twice. You can also read the story aloud to the class. Discuss the story. Make a list of the ingredients on the board.

Learners can then complete activities 3, 4 and 5 in the Workbook.

8. Talk about the story, *Stone Soup*. Ask questions such as: *How did the stranger help the people in the village? Did he put any food into the pot? Why did people give him food to put in his pot?*

9. Teach the class a short conversation to practise making a polite request with a polite response, using the structures *Would you like … ? Would you like to …? Yes, please. No, thanks.* Demonstrate with some learners first and then let learners work in pairs. For example:

A: *Would you like some soup?*

B: *Yes, please.*

A: *Would you like some meat?*

B: *Yes, please.*

A: *Would you like to taste the [pizza]?*

B: *No, thanks.*

10. Learners reread the text on page 28 in the Student's Book in pairs. They can ask and answer questions about the text. For example:

What is ___________ *[kimchi]?*

It is ___________ *[a cabbage stew].*

What can you put ___________ *[on a pizza]?*

You put ___________ *[tomatoes and cheese].*

11. Tell learners to imagine that they are going to make all the dishes on page 28 of the Student's Book. Let them make a list of all the things they think they will need. They can look for the answers on page 28 and then add their own ideas (for example: salt and pepper, other meats and vegetables, spices).

12. Play the *Stone Soup* story (**Audio 26**) again or read it to the class yourself this time. Help learners to retell the story in sequence. Then let them act the story in groups of about eight. Encourage them to use conversation from the story when they act.

13. Learners complete activities 6, 7, 8 and 9 in the Workbook. They must be familiar with the story *Stone Soup* before they attempt this page.

14. **Link to mathematics.* Draw a chart on the board. Insert the names of some of the foods that have been discussed in class. For example:

Food	Tally	Total
pizza		
soup		
rice and peas		
milkshake		
sweets		

Do a survey in the class to find out which of these foods learners like best. Ask learners to each choose one food. Run through the options and let learners put up their hands to show which one they have chosen. Record the results in the form of tally marks. Let learners tell you what the totals are for each food. Ask questions about the chart. Use the language that learners will be exposed to in their mathematics lessons. For example: *How many learners like pizza? How many learners like sweets?*

Then let learners make a block graph or pictogram with the results.

15. Write the poem *Stone Soup* (**Audio 27**) on the board or on a poster for the class to read. Play the audio while learners follow the words. Then let learners read the poem with you. Explain anything that is not clear to them.

Ask them to find the rhyming words in the poem. For example, ask: *What rhymes with pot*oil+too*bone+done?* Ask if the words are spelled the same.

Then read the poem again and let learners clap the syllables in each line, to get a feel for the rhythm of the poem.

Finally, let them learn and recite the poem in groups.

16. Think about the story *Stone Soup* again. Then think about the food that you eat when you celebrate something special. Ask: *Does everyone share the food? Is it good to share food? What else can you share?*

17. Learners can complete the puzzle in activity 10 in the Workbook.

Wrap-up plenary

If possible, arrange for learners to taste some of the foods mentioned in this topic. Some parents may be able to help. Learners can name foods, talk about ingredients and taste and vote for their favourite foods.

If it is not possible to bring real foods to class, talk about foods that people eat on special occasions in more detail. Ask learners if they know why we eat certain foods at certain times. (Be aware that some learners might not be able to eat certain foods due to cultural or health reasons.)

Quick check

1. Learners work in pairs and interview each other about their favourite foods and foods that they eat on special occasions.
2. Write the names of ingredients on prompt cards. These should be any familiar ingredients taught in this topic. Place the cards face down and let learners take turns to choose a card. They read the name of the ingredients and then name a dish that is made with them. For example: *beans = peas and rice, bean stew = feijoada.* (Work out a system of scoring before you begin the game.)

Assessment

You can complete an oral assessment of the work done in this topic by asking learners to retell one of the stories in the unit or to describe a familiar dish, using pictures as prompts.

Learners can also complete Progress check activities 1, 2, 3 and 4 in the Workbook as a simple assessment.

You could allocate marks for these activities and record these as part of continuous assessment.

Topic 5 Do your best!

Overview

In this topic the focus is on sharing ideas and thoughts about doing one's best, about playing games and about entering competitions. Learners revise familiar words and structures and learn new structures and vocabulary which they can use for communicating. There are opportunities to integrate activities with other curricula such as drama, art and mathematics.

Units in this topic

Unit A: Everyone can do it

Unit B: Let's move!

Unit C: Competitions

Teaching focus

- **2Rg1** Recognise, identify and sound, with support, a limited range of language at text level
- **2Rf1** Read and follow, with support, familiar instructions for classroom activities
- **2Rg2** Begin to read, with support, very short simple fiction and non-fiction texts with confidence and enjoyment
- **2Rd1** Understand, with support, some specific information and detail in very short, simple texts on a limited range of general and curricular topics
- **2Rm1** Understand the meaning of very short, simple texts on familiar general and curricular topics by rereading them
- **2Rd2** Understand the meaning of simple short sentences on familiar general and curricular topics
- **2Wa1** Plan, write and check, with support, short sentences on familiar topics
- **2Wc2** Write short familiar instructions with support from their peers
- **2Ug14** Spell a growing number of familiar high-frequency words accurately during guided writing activities
- **2Wo2** Include a full stop and question mark during guided writing of short, familiar sentences
- **2Ug2** Use numbers 1–50 to count
- **2Ut2** Use *who, what, where, how many* to ask questions on familiar topics
- **2Ut3** Use impersonal *you* in the question: *How do you spell that?*
- **2Ut5** Use personal subject and object pronouns, including possessive pronouns *mine, yours* to give basic personal information and describe things
- **2Uf1** Use imperative forms [positive and negative] to give short instructions
- **2Uf2** Use common simple present forms, including short answer forms and contractions, to give personal information
- **2Uf3** Use common past simple forms [regular and irregular] to describe actions and narrate simple events including short answer forms and contractions
- **2Uf5** Use common present continuous forms, including short answers and contractions, to talk about what is happening now on personal and familiar topics
- **2Ug4** Use *–ing* forms *swimming, spelling* as nouns to describe familiar and classroom activities
- **2Ut6** Use *there is/are* to make short statements and descriptions
- **2Uf6** Use *Have you [ever] been?* to talk about experiences
- **2Uf7** Use *can* to make requests and ask permission and use appropriate responses *here you are, OK*
- **2Uf8** Use *must* to express obligation
- **2Uf9** Use *have + object + infinitive* to talk about obligations
- **2Uf10** Use *will* to talk about future intention
- **2Ug8** Use *What/How about* + noun/*-ing* to make suggestions
- **2Uf4** Use *when* clauses to describe simple present and past actions on personal and familiar topics
- **2Ut7** Use *so do I* to give short answers
- **2Ld4** Understand an increased range of short, basic supported classroom instructions
- **2Ld5** Understand an increasing range of short supported questions on general and curricular topics
- **2Lg1** Understand short supported narratives on an increasing range of general and curricular topics
- **2Lg2** Identify initial, middle and final phonemes and blends
- **2S4** Use basic vocabulary for a limited range of general and curricular topics
- **2S5** Give short, basic descriptions of people and objects

- **2S6** Contribute a growing range of suitable words, phrases, and sentences during short pair, group and whole class exchanges
- **2S7** Take turns when speaking with others in a growing range of short, basic exchanges
- **2S8** Relate very short, basic stories and events on a limited range of general and curricular topics

Language patterns

Grammar summary for teachers:

Contractions: These are words like *I'm* (I am), *you're* (you are), *he's* (he is), *don't* (do not), *you're* (you are) that are written in the way that we speak. The apostrophe shows that a letter is missing. Contractions should not be used in formal writing.

Unit A Everyone can do it

Resources and materials

- Student's Book pp. 29–31
- Workbook pp. 80–84
- Audio files: Audio 28; Audio 29
- Photocopiable Masters (PCMs) PCM 2; PCM 11; PCM 12; PCM 13; PCM 14
- Prompt cards with number words twenty – thirty, forty, fifty
- Number chart with the numbers and number words 1–50
- Small objects to count (up to 50) for example buttons, stones

Key vocabulary

best, good at something, wrong, path, block

Numbers: twenty to fifty

Verbs: fly, dive, hoot, run, talk, hide, slide, take, throw, move, fall, jump, get lost

Lead-in ideas

Teach learners a simple chant about being positive about doing things. For example, *I Can Do It* (**Audio 28**).

Script for the lesson

Introducing vocabulary

Introduce the new verbs in this unit in context when learners read and play the board game.

Sounds

Revise phonemes and sounds in context. In this unit, for example, there are opportunities to revise long *i* vowel sounds in words such as *slide, ice, mice*.

Introducing structures

In this unit, you can revise the modal verb *can* (to mean ability) as well as imperatives, if you think learners need additional practice. You can also teach further contractions as they occur in reading and listening texts. Some activities in the unit also use *-ing* forms as nouns to describe what people are good at. (Example*: I am good at swimming.*) Introduce the question *What about ________ing?* in these activities.

Previous knowledge

Learners will already be familiar with some contractions and imperatives. They should also know how to use *can* and *can't* to describe ability.

Activities

Select from these activities depending on the level of challenge needed for different learners, interest levels and what you have time to include. Supplement these with additional activities of your own and/or digital activities from the online resource.

1. Have a short discussion with the class about things learners can and can't do. This will help to prepare them for a later discussion about things they are good at doing.

   Revise the words *can* and *can't* as ways of expressing ability. Explain that *can't* is a short form of the word *cannot.* You could write these words on the board and then make lists of words during the discussion. For example:

can	*can't*
read play football run fast make pancakes climb a tree	swim play chess make ice cream plait my hair

   Then look at the list you made under the heading *can't* and discuss how you can change these so all of these things go in the *can* list. Allow learners to use their first language if necessary and then translate key words.

2. Learners find the story *Best Bird* on page 29 of the Student's Book. Say the number 29 and write it on the board. Let learners read the title and look at the pictures to predict what the story is about. Let them try and name the birds in the story. Then write these names on the board: *owl, duck, parrot, ostrich, penguin.*

   Let learners read the story in pairs if they can. Walk around and check that they are on track. Help them decode words and look for meaning clues in the pictures.

3. Learners read the story *Best Bird* again and then complete activities 1, 2 and 3 in the Workbook.

4. Revise the sounds made by the letter *i* using words from the story *Best Bird*. Write the following words on the board. Then read each word aloud. Ask learners to identify the words that have the same sound as *I*.

   I hide   dive   slide   ice   bird

   Point out the spelling patterns (*i* + *consonant* + *-e*). Ask learners if they know other words like that. Build a few familiar words together, for example: *bike, like, hive, nice, rice, mice, mine.*

   You can also point out that the letter *i* sounds different in the word *bird* because there is an *r* after the *i* and because there is no *e* at the end of the word.

5. Have a discussion with groups or with the class. This time, ask the question *What are you good at?* Give a few examples to introduce the structure *verb + -ing* form. *I am good at singing. He is good at dancing. Maryam is good at skipping*. Then make a simple chart on the board with some of the suggestions learners have made, for example:

Things we are good at	Tally	Total
singing		
dancing		
playing		
reading		
acting		
cooking		

   Do a survey in class. Ask learners to each choose one activity they think they are good at. Go through the options and let learners put up their hands to show which one they have chosen. Record the results in the form of tally marks. Let learners tell you what the totals are to practise saying numbers.

   Ask questions about the chart. As you do this use the structures *Are you good at ______ing? What about ______ing?* For example: *How many learners are good at dancing? And what about singing? Are there more learners who are good at singing or at dancing? What are most learners good at?*

   Learners can also work in pairs and ask each other questions about the chart. Or, teach them a short conversation. For example:

   A: *You're good at ________ [singing].*

   B: *Yes, and so are you. But what about ____________ [dancing]? Are you good at that?*

   A: *No! I'm not good at ______ [dancing]. But I'm good at _________ [cooking]! What about you?*

   B: *I'm ________ [good/not good] at _______ing.*

6. **Link to mathematics*. Learners read the graph and answer the questions in activity 4 in the Workbook. You may want to do this activity orally with learners before they write their answers.

7. * *Link to mathematics*. Teach learners the number words for numbers 21–30. You can also teach *forty* and *fifty*. Use the prompt cards you have made. If you feel that learners need additional practice, give them copies of **PCM 12.** They cut out the numbers (numerals) and the number words, match them and put them in order. Encourage them to say the numbers aloud.

   Counting should be a regular classroom activity in order to help learners to become familiar with both the numbers and number words 1–50. Make a chart for the classroom with these numbers and number words and refer to the chart often. Count books, pencils and any other available objects. Make piles of small objects and ask learners to estimate the number of objects in each pile and then to count each pile.

8. Let learners listen to a short story for the main ideas. You can tell them a story about someone who overcame difficulties and later did well, or you can play the story *The Best Runner* (**Audio 29**). Play the audio at least twice or read/tell the story yourself. Ask a few simple questions afterwards to check that learners have understood the main ideas. For example, ask:

   Who is good at running?

   What about playing football? Was he good at that?

   Where is he from?

   Was he good at cricket?

9. Learners reread the story *Best Bird* on page 29 of the Student's Book by themselves. Then they complete activities 5, 6 and 7 in the Workbook.

10. Let learners play a game in which they match numbers and number words and practise saying the numbers aloud. You can use the prompt cards that you made for this unit. Include prompt cards for numbers 1–19 in addition, if you think learners need more practice.

   Learners can play in groups. Put the cards face down on a table and let each learner pick a card and read the number word on the card. Then they must say the numbers that come before and after that number to score a point. The others in the group check if the numbers are correct. Work out a scoring system with the groups before they begin.

11. Learners find the game *The cross-country race* on pages 30–31 of the Student's Book. Explain what a cross-country race is. Ask: *What are the pages about?* Let them explain that it is a game. Ask: *What do you have to do? How do you play? What do you need?*

   Then let learners read the numbers on the board aloud. Point to the first instruction and say: *Find number 3*. Read the instruction. Help learners to use the pictures as clues to work out the meanings of each instruction. Work through all the instructions with the class or with groups.

   Then play the game with groups of learners.

12. *Link to mathematics*. Write the following sentences on the board or on a poster. Explain to the class that these are the results of a survey that was made in another school. You are going to read the results and then make a bar graph to show the information. Learners who answered these questions were allowed to choose more than one answer.

What we are good at and enjoy doing

There are 28 learners in the class.

Ten learners are good at running.

All learners enjoy watching cricket.

Six learners are good at swimming.

12 learners enjoy dancing.

Half of learners are good at mathematics.

Draw a blank bar graph on the board and help learners to extract information to complete the graph. Ask questions to prompt learners as you work. Start by labelling the graph with numbers *0–30* (*y*-axis) and *running*, *watching cricket*, *swimming*, *dancing*, *mathematics* (*x*-axis). Then fill in each bar the number of learners. Alternatively, you can make a copy of **PCM 13** and guide learners to fill in the missing information.

13. Learners read the information and complete another graph in activity 8 in the Workbook.

14. Let learners make up simple rhymes with words that end in *-ice* (*mice, rice, nice*) or *–ive* (*hive, dive, five*) or *-ike* (*like, bike, hike*). Write some writing frames on the board. You could write rhyming words on prompt cards or on the board for learners to use. For example:

I like rice.

It's very ________________.

This is her new bike.

It's the one I ________________.

Is that a beehive?

Yes, I can see ________________.

Do you like to hike?

No, I like to ride my ________________.

15. Learners can play the game *The cross-country race* on pages 30–31 of the Student's Book in groups without your support this time. They can spin a spinner (**PCM 11**) as they play.

16. Help learners make a simple summary of the things they did during *The cross-country race* game. Prompt learners to look at the instruction on the board game in their books to find ideas.

They can practise using the simple past tense. Do this orally. For example:

- *What did you do? We spun the spinner.*
- *We moved our counters.*
- *I ran fast.*
- *I fell over a tree.*
- *You got lost.*
- *I stopped to drink some water.*
- *He took the wrong path.*
- *She fell into some water.*
- *I lost a shoe!*
- *I finished first.*

Let learners complete activities 9 and 10 in the Workbook.

17. Give pairs of learners a copy of **PCM 14**, which is a blank of a board game. They can use it to create their own board game. They need to number the blocks and write some instructions. Let them try and play the game afterwards to see if it works.

18. Give learners some simple oral mathematics problems to solve, using numbers from 20–30. For example, ask:

- *There are twenty-five runners on the field. Three runners fall. How many are left in the race?*
- *Six children started to play a game. Then eleven more children came to play with them. How many children played the game?*

19. Talk about the rules that we follow when we play games and sports. Ask questions such as: *Why do we have to have rules? What happens when we don't follow the rules?*

You could also raise the issue of cheating. Explain what cheating is in learners' first language. Then discuss why people cheat. (Because they want to win.)

Wrap-up plenary

Let learners have a second chance to say what they are good at doing. Then let them be honest and say what they are not good at.

Quick check

Use the prompt cards to revise number words. Learners can play a game as before. You could also let them make a Bingo game with number words. (See **PCM 2**).

Unit B Let's move!

Resources and materials

- Student's Book pp. 32–33
- Workbook pp. 85–89
- Audio file: Audio 30
- Photocopiable Master (PCM) PCM 11
- Some appropriate dance music with an easy beat to play in class (and for learners to respond to)
- Blank strips of paper for writing instructions (six per group)
- Sentence strips with instructions for a short dance routine (*Clap your hands, Jump to the left, Stamp your feet*, and so on)

Key vocabulary

dance, sing, beat, music

Verbs: dance, listen, move, clap, skip, stamp, shake, stop, keep

Lead-in ideas

- Teach learners an action rhyme or poem that involves numbers 1–50.
- Take the class outside or into an open space and let them do some simple exercises while they count. Count to 5, then give an instruction. Then count from 6–10 and give another instruction. The instructions don't have to rhyme. For example:

  Let's count and move!

  1–2–3–4–5

  Jump up and down.

  6–7–8–9–10

  Swing your arms to the ground.

  11–12–13–14–15

  Stretch up high.

  16–17–18–19–20

  Touch your toes.

  21–22–23–24–25

  Hop on one leg.

  26–27–28–29–30.

  Clap your hands.

  31–32–33–34–35

  And so on, up to 50.

  (Alternatively, count in 2s or 5s: *2–4–6–8–10–12–14–16–18–20–22–24–26–28–30–32–34–36–38–40–42–44–46–48–50; 5–10–15–20–25–30–35–40–45–50*)

Script for the lesson

Introducing vocabulary

Several verbs that describe actions are introduced in this unit. You can teach these through total physical response activities. Give learners instructions and let them respond to the instructions.

Sounds

Revise phonemes and sounds in context. In this unit, for example, there are opportunities to revise long 'ee' vowel sounds in words such as *hear, keep, feet.* You can also continue to teach and revise words with *vowel + consonant + -e*. This time, teach words with *a-e* spelling patterns, for example: *shake, wave.* Initial phonemes (digraphs and blends) such as *sk, st, cl, sh* and *th* can also be revised.

Introducing structures

Revise imperatives and then teach learners new verbs to use in this form. Use verbs from the story text that is provided with this unit.

Use conversations to teach the use of the impersonal *you* in questions such as *How do you do that?* Encourage and help learners to use short answers such as *So do I, Yes, I do/No I do not* in conversations and discussions.

There are also opportunities to revise the present continuous tense in this unit. Learners can show that they understand verbs by acting them and asking other learners to guess what they are doing. Learners can also begin to recognise the present continuous forms of verbs in simple written activities.

Previous knowledge

Learners should already be familiar with some common imperative forms used for giving instructions.

Possible areas of difficulty

Quite a few of the activities in this unit involve physical actions. If there are learners in the class with limited mobility, adapt the activities so that they can also join in. For example, a learner who cannot skip may be able to sit and hold a skipping rope.

Activities

Select from these activities depending on the level of challenge needed for different learners, interest levels and what you have time to include. Supplement these with additional activities of your own and/or digital activities from the online resource.

▲ **1.** Take the class outside or into a hall and play a game to get them moving around and following instructions. You can play 'Simon says', for example. Use numbers in the instructions to revise these at the same time. Here are some instructions that you could give the class:

Simon says hop on one leg.

Simon says jump in the air three times.

Simon says take 13 steps forwards.

Now take ten steps back.

If learners enjoy this, let some of them take turns to give similar instructions.

2. Read the poem *Skipping Rope Spell.*

Poem: Skipping Rope Spell

Turn rope turn
don't trip my feet.
Turn rope turn
for my skipping feet.
Turn rope turn
turn round and round.
Turn in the air
turn on the ground.
One for your high
one for your low.
Turn rope turn
not too fast, not too slow.
Turn rope turn
turn to the north
turn to the south.
But, please, rope, please,
don't make me out.

Read the poem again. Talk about skipping and explain any parts of the poem that you think learners may not understand.

Then invite the class to do actions as they listen. They could perhaps do this in groups of five, with some learners pretending to hold the rope and others pretending to skip. Learners turning the rope should vary the way in which they are turning the rope. You may need to demonstrate this with a learner who is good at skipping first.

As learners do the actions, let them join in and say the line that is repeated (*Turn rope turn*).

Make it quite clear that boys also skip. You may want to mention that top athletes do skipping as part of their training programmes.

3. Ask learners to tell you about games or sports or dances that they like to play or do. Then ask them to show you how to do something. For example:

Learner: *I like hip-hop dancing.*

Teacher: *How do you do that? Can you show us?*

Then teach the class a simple conversation to practise asking questions with the impersonal *you* in questions and the reply *So do I*. For example:

A: *I like skipping.*

B: *So do I! How do you spell that?*

A: *It's easy. s-k-i-p-p-i-n-g.*

B: *How do you do that? Can you show me?*

A: *Yes! Come!*

4. Let learners find the text *Dance to the Beat* in the Student's Book on pages 32–33. Discuss the title and the pictures in the usual way. Ask learners if they can dance like the children in the pictures. Write these words on the board and ask learners to read them and spell them.

skip stamp wave clap shake stop

Ask them to show you what each word means. Then ask: *How do you spell that?* Let learners spell the words aloud.

Read the sentences in the text as the class follow in their book before they complete activities 1, 2 and 3 in the Workbook.

5. Play the conversation *I like it when...* (**Audio 30**) in which learners describe what they enjoy doing. Ask a few questions afterwards, such as: *What do the children enjoy? Do they all enjoy dancing? What about singing? What do they like most?* Then let learners work in groups of three or four and discuss which games and movements they enjoy. Prompt them to use the following structures:

Do you like/enjoy ________ing?
I like it when…
So do I.
Yes, I do./No, I don't.

6. Revise the present continuous tense. Let learners use some of the new verbs they have learned, but this time using a different tense. Write the following words on the board:

dancing singing skipping stamping waving clapping shaking

Learners work in groups. They choose a word from the board and do the action. The rest of the group guess what they are doing. As learners do the action they ask and answer questions, for example:

What am I doing?

Are you waving?

Yes, I am./No, I am not.

7. Read or reread the text *Dance to the Beat* in the Student's Book on pages 32–33 with groups of learners. Learners can then complete activities 4, 5 and 6 in the Workbook.

8. Play a game in which learners complete familiar words. You can do this on a larger sheet of paper or on the board first. Draw a grid such as the one in Activity 7 in the Workbook. Write one word on each square, but leave out one or two letters in each word. You could, for example, choose a set of words with initial blends (such as <u>cl</u>ap <u>st</u>op <u>sk</u>ip), or consonant digraphs (such as <u>sh</u>ake <u>th</u>en), vowel digraphs (such as h<u>ea</u>d f<u>ee</u>t) or other words with common spelling patterns such as *vowel + consonant + -e* (*wave, like, have*). You could also use words from a familiar story that you think learners should learn to spell.

Learners work in groups. Toss a coin to see which group starts first. That group completes the word in square 1. Give a limited time in which to do this. If they get the word correct, they score a point. If that group gets it wrong, give the next group a chance. Alternatively let each group spin a spinner (use **PCM 11**). They move forward, according to the number on the spinner and then complete the word in the block. Adapt this if you work on a board.

Learners complete activity 7 in the Workbook.

9. Learners complete activities 8 and 9 in the Workbook to revise using verbs in different tenses.

10. Read the poem *Skipping Rope Spell* again. Write these words on the board and let learners listen for the rhyming words:

    round (ground), *low* (slow), *north* (south)

    Then help learners to memorise and recite the poem.

11. Prepare a set of sentence strips with short instructions about how to do a dance or exercise. For example:
    Clap your hands.
    Move to the left.
    Stamp your feet.
    Move to the right.
    Jump up and down.
    Wave good-bye!

    Teach the class this routine by showing them the sentence strips and doing the actions.

    Then tell them that they are going to work in groups and make up their own dances, using the verbs they have learned. Let them work out the steps first and practise. Then let the group write down their instructions. This should be limited to five or six short instructions. Give each group five blank strips of paper on which to write their instructions in big, clear letters. Remind them to use capital letters and full stops.

12. Learners work alone and write a short entry in their journal about a dance that they taught to another group or a dance that they have learned. Let them write freely without a frame this time. Let each learner read aloud what they have written to you. Don't correct spelling or grammar for this activity, but ask questions. Learners should be able to read what they have written.

13. Work with groups of learners and write a shape poem together. For example, you could write a poem in the shape of a skipping rope or a drum. Draw the outline shape on the board or on a sheet of paper. Then brainstorm ideas with the group and agree on what to write in the poem. It doesn't matter which words or sentences learners suggest as long as they are related to the drawing in some way. The words do not need to rhyme.

14. Learners can then work alone and write their own shape poems in activity 10 in the Workbook.

15. Let learners reread the story *Dance to the Beat* in the Student's Book on pages 32–33 in pairs.

16. Talk about why it is important to move around. Prompt learners to talk about exercising their bodies and about having fun with friends.

Wrap-up plenary

Learners talk about their favourite ways of moving around. They can also demonstrate the dance routines that they made up.

Quick check

Use the sentence strips that you made to give learners instructions and check that they understand them.

Unit C Competitions

Resources and materials

- Student's Book pp. 34–36
- Workbook pp. 90–93
- Audio files: Audio 31; Audio 32; Audio 33
- Photocopiable Masters (PCMs) PCM 15; PCM 16
- Prompt cards with the names of months of the year
- Calendar

Key vocabulary

competition, something, paper, right, newspaper, fun, welcome, everyone, online, enter, win, mine, yours

Months: January, February, March, April, May, June, July, August, September, October, November, December

Lead-in ideas

Teach a rhyme that revises numbers as well as months of the year, for example *Thirty Days Has September* (**Audio 31**).

Script for the lesson

Introducing vocabulary

Introduce new vocabulary within the context of the texts in the Student's Book.

Sounds

Using words from the texts, you could focus on words that begin with *c* or *c + another consonant*: *class, child, competition.*

You can also teach and revise vowel digraphs (*ee*/*ea*) in words such as *see, each, free, dream*.

Introducing structures

In this unit, you can revise contractions and the use of the possessive *'s* (genitive) in context. You can also revise the use of the word *can* in short conversations, this time letting learners use it to ask for permission to do things.

The word *will* is used in the story *What Will They Make?* to help learners to understand how the word is used to talk about future actions.

Previous knowledge

Learners should be familiar with some of the months of the year in English or in their first language. They should also start to recognise contractions in sentences.

Possible areas of difficulty

The names of months in a learner's first language may be similar to the English names, which will help learners to make the connections, but it may also lead them to confusing the two names. The names may also be spelled in the same way but pronounced differently (examples: *April/Avril/Aprile/Abril*).

Activities

Select from these activities depending on the level of challenge needed for different learners, interest levels and what you have time to include. Supplement these with additional activities of your own and/or digital activities from the online resource.

1. Use your prompt cards and a calendar to teach or revise the names of the months of the year. Help learners to pronounce the names correctly. They will also need to learn to read these words as sight words, so make sure the words are used and displayed frequently in the class.

2. Ask learners about their birthdays. Ask: *When is your birthday?* Let them reply: *My birthday is in* ______________.

   If you haven't already done this, you can compile a birthday calendar for the year with the names of all learners in the class. Put up a large sheet of paper on the wall with the names of the months and let learners fill in their own names.

3. Teach the word *competition* and talk about competitions that your class may have entered, or will enter, this year.

   Then let learners listen to a radio announcement about a competition (**Audio 32**). This text will also help learners to prepare for the story they will read in the Student's Book *What Will They Make?*

   Ask learners a few questions to check that they have understood the main ideas: *What month is it? What do you have to do to enter this competition? Can you make something small? On what day will we know who the winner is?*

4. Learners can complete activities 1, 2 and 3 in the Workbook.

5. Introduce and teach the word *will* to express the future. You can teach adverbs of time such as *tomorrow* and *next week/month* at the same time. You can also revise the names of days of the week as you do this. Start with some statements and questions. For example, say:
   Today is Friday. What day will it be tomorrow?
   We are at school today. Will there be school tomorrow?
   It is sunny today. Will it be sunny tomorrow?

   Let learners respond as best they can. Prompt them to use the word *will* in their answers.

   Learners can then work in groups and make sentences about what they will do the next day (or at the weekend).

6. Learners find the story *What Will They Make?* on pages 34–35 of the Student's Book. Read the title and let learners say what they think the story is about, after they have looked at the pictures.

   Then read the story with learners. Help them to decode and work out meaning using context clues. Ask oral questions to help learners try and predict as they read. For example, ask: *Look at the picture. What do you think Rui is making?* Explain to learners that *'ll* is the short form of *will*. We use this when we speak. (*You'll see.*)

   When you have finished reading the story, discuss it briefly. Help learners to make the link between this story and the radio announcement that they listened to (if they haven't done so by themselves).

   Let learners practise reading the story in pairs.

7. Teach a simple conversation to help learners use the word *can* to ask permission. To keep this in context, let learners imagine that they are going to enter a competition. They need to make something out of paper. They will need to borrow the things that they need to do this. This type of conversation will also help learners revise possessive pronouns and short answers.

   A: *I need some glue. Can I use yours?*

   B: *Yes. Here you are.*

   A: *I need a pair of scissors. Can I use yours?*

   B: *Sorry! Anna has mine.*

8. Practise identifying initial middle and end phonemes and blends and digraphs using words from the story *What Will They Make?* Write these words on the board and ask learners to find words with similar letters in the story. Underline the target letters.

chicken (child)	*bee (see)*
clap (class)	*fox (box)*
beach (each)	*cake (make)*

   You can extend this by asking learners to look at other stories to find more words with these same spelling patterns.

9. Learners find the fun walk poster on page 36 of the Student's Book. Help learners to read and discuss the poster. Explain what words such as *online* and *welcome* mean. Ask a few oral questions to check comprehension. For example:
   When is the fun walk?
   At what time does it begin?
   What time must you be there?
   Where does it start?
   Do you have to pay?
   How can you enter the competition?

10. **Link to mathematics*. Give learners a copy of **PCM 15**. Let them read the calendar and answer the questions.

11. Learners read the story *What Will They Make?* on pages 34–35 of the Student's Book again in pairs. Then let learners work in groups and act the story, using the conversation they have read.

12. Learners can complete activities 4 and 5 in the Workbook to revise contractions and possessives (genitive and possessive adjectives). You may wish to revise possessive adjectives and the possessive *'s* with the class before they do this. Write a few sentences on the board and help them to choose the correct words to complete the sentences.

13. Revise the use of the impersonal *you* by letting learners work in pairs to ask each other questions. They can pretend they are characters from the story *What Will They Make?*

    A: *Hi Rui. What are you making?*

    B: *I'm making a box.*

    A: *How do you do that?*

    B: *It's easy. I'll show you.*

14. **Link to art*. Give learners copies of **PCM 16**. Help learners to read and follow the instructions to make a ladybird. You can display the ladybirds in the class, as they fit into the next topic *Wings*.

15. Learners find the fun walk poster on page 36 of the Student's Book. Talk about the poster using the structure *Have you ever ____________?* to find out if learners in the class have ever taken part in a competition like this. Ask questions such as:

    Have you ever been on a fun walk? Where did you go? How far did you walk?

    Have you ever won a competition? What did you win?

    Then let the class work in groups and ask each other questions with the same structure.

16. Learners fill in the entry form in activity 6 in the Workbook. Discuss the form orally with the class before they write their answers.

17. Let learners listen to another radio announcement, *The kite flying competition* (**Audio 33**). Make sure learners know what a *kite* is. Then ask learners a few questions to check that they have understood the main ideas: *On what day does the competition take place? What do you have to do to enter this competition? What time does it start? Where must you go?*

18. Learners reread the story *What Will They Make?* on pages 34–35 of the Student's Book. Then they write a simple report about what the children in the story did, using the simple past tense. They can complete activities 7, 8 and 9 in the Workbook to do this.

19. Learners work in groups and make a poster to advertise a competition. Discuss the poster in the Student's Book to make learners aware of the type of information that they need to include. Then give them a list of competitions to choose from. You could also let them listen to an announcement about the kite flying competition (**Audio 33**) and let them make posters to advertise that.

    The groups can display their posters and talk about them afterwards.

20. Learners can write a journal entry about a competition that they entered. Prompt them to write about why they entered and how they felt. Let them write freely without a frame. Read what each learner has written but don't correct spelling or grammar. You can ask questions. Learners should be able to read what they have written.

Wrap-up plenary

Talk about competitions that are happening in your own community or country at present. Discuss who can enter the competitions. Then discuss why people enter competitions (to have fun, to win prizes).

Quick check

1. Use the prompt cards to revise the names of months of the year.
2. Play a game.
   - Say sentences which include some of the key vocabulary and structures introduced. Sometimes use the words and structures correctly, and at other times use them incorrectly.
   - If the sentence is correct, learners repeat the sentence.
   - If the sentence is incorrect, learners say nothing.

   Examples:

   What will you make? (learners repeat)

   My birthday is in Otober. (learners keep quiet)

   What day have it be tomorrow? (learners keep quiet)

   I need some glue. Can I use yours? (learners repeat)

   I'll making a box. (learners keep quiet)

   I'm making a bowl. (learners repeat)

   I'm make an animal. (learners keep quiet)

   I will entering the competition tomorrow. (learners keep quiet)

Assessment

You can complete an oral assessment of the work done in this topic by asking learners to tell you about one of the competitions in the unit, using pictures in the Student's Book as prompts.

Learners can also complete Progress check activities 1, 2, 3 and 4 in the Workbook as a simple assessment.

You could allocate marks for these activities and record these as part of continuous assessment.

Topic 6 Wings and things

Overview

In this topic, the focus is on sharing information about animals and machines that can fly, building on familiar vocabulary and structures to build confidence and then introducing new vocabulary to develop language skills.

There are opportunities to integrate activities with other curricula such as natural sciences, art, mathematics and drama.

Units in this topic

Unit A: Bugs

Unit B: Birds

Unit C: Flying machines

Teaching focus

- **2Rg1** Recognise, identify and sound, with support, a limited range of language at text level
- **2Rg2** Begin to read, with support, very short simple fiction and non-fiction texts with confidence and enjoyment
- **2Rm2** Understand the main points of very short, simple texts on some familiar general and curricular topics by using contextual clues
- **2Rd1** Understand, with support, some specific information and detail in very short, simple texts on a limited range of general and curricular topics
- **2Rm1** Understand the meaning of very short, simple texts on familiar general and curricular topics by rereading them
- **2Rd2** Understand the meaning of simple short sentences on familiar general and curricular topics
- **2Ug15** Use, with more infrequent support, a simple picture dictionary
- **2Wa1** Plan, write and check, with support, short sentences on familiar topics
- **2Wo1** Link with support words or phrases using basic coordinating connectors
- **2Ug14** Spell a growing number of familiar high-frequency words accurately during guided writing activities
- **2Wo2** Include a full stop and question mark during guided writing of short, familiar sentences
- **2Ug1** Use singular nouns, plural nouns – including some common irregular plural forms – and uncountable nouns, genitive 's/s' to name and label things
- **2Ug2** Use numbers 1–50 to count
- **2Ug3** Use adjectives, including possessive adjectives, on familiar topics to give personal information and describe things
- **2Ut1** Use determiners *a, the, some, any, this, these, that* to refer to familiar objects
- **2Ut2** Use *who, what, where, how many* to ask questions on familiar topics
- **2Ut3** Use impersonal *you* in the question: *How do you spell that?*
- **2Ut4** Use demonstrative pronouns *this, these, that, those* and object pronoun *one* in short statements and responses
- **2Uf2** Use common simple present forms, including short answer forms and contractions, to give personal information
- **2Uf3** Use common past simple forms [regular and irregular] to describe actions and narrate simple events including short answer forms and contractions
- **2Uf5** Use common present continuous forms, including short answers and contractions, to talk about what is happening now on personal and familiar topics
- **2Ug4** Use *–ing* forms *swimming, spelling* as nouns to describe familiar and classroom activities
- **2Ut6** Use *there is/are* to make short statements and descriptions
- **2Uf6** Use *Have you [ever] been?* to talk about experiences
- **2Ug9** Use prepositions of location, position and direction: *at, behind, between, in, in front of, near, next to, on, to* on personal and familiar topics
- **2Ug10** Use prepositions of time: *on, in, at,* to talk about days and times on personal and familiar topics
- **2Ug11** Use *with* to indicate accompaniment and instrument and *for* to indicate recipient on personal and familiar topics
- **2Ut8** Use conjunctions *and, or, but* to link words and phrases
- **2Uf4** Use *when* clauses to describe simple present and past actions on personal and familiar topics
- **2Ut7** Use *so do I* to give short answers
- **2Ld5** Understand an increasing range of short supported questions on general and curricular topics
- **2Lm1** Understand the main points of short, supported talk on an increasing range of general and curricular topics

- **2Ld1** Understand some specific information and detail of short, supported talk on an increasing range of general and curricular topics
- **2Ld2** Use contextual clues to predict content and meaning in short supported talk on an increasing range of general and curricular topics
- **2Lg1** Understand short supported narratives on an increasing range of general and curricular topics
- **2Lg3** Recognise words that are spelled out in a limited range of general and curricular topics
- **2Lg2** Identify initial, middle and final phonemes and blends
- **2S3** Describe basic present and past actions on a limited range of general and curricular topics
- **2S4** Use basic vocabulary for a limited range of general and curricular topics
- **2S5** Give short, basic descriptions of people and objects
- **2S6** Contribute a growing range of suitable words, phrases, and sentences during short pair, group and whole class exchanges
- **2S7** Take turns when speaking with others in a growing range of short, basic exchanges
- **2S8** Relate very short, basic stories and events on a limited range of general and curricular topics

Language patterns

Grammar summary for teachers:

There are no new structures to be taught in this topic. Instead, structures that have already been introduced will be revised and practised.

Unit A Bugs

Resources and materials

- Student's Book pp. 37–38
- Workbook pp. 96–99
- Audio files: Audio 34; Audio 35; Audio 36
- Photocopiable Master (PCM) PCM 17
- Films and pictures of insects and other bugs
- Picture dictionaries

Key vocabulary

insect, bird, body, wing, antenna, eye, egg, spider, worm, butterfly, ant, beetle, moth, bee, mosquito, ladybird

Lead-in ideas

- If possible, take learners outside to look at some real bugs or small animals, such as ants, spiders or beetles. Don't let learners touch these small animals. They can observe and describe what they look like (*small, brown, black*) and what they are doing (*climbing up a wall, carrying food, making a web*).
- Show the class a film about insects and discuss what the animals look like, what noise they make and some of the things that they do.
- Teach learners a simple action rhyme about an insect or other mini-beast (bug), using for example **Audio 34** and **Audio 35.**

Script for the lesson

Introducing vocabulary

Introduce new vocabulary within the context of the texts in the Student's Book.

Sounds

Using words from the texts, you could focus on words with vowel digraphs *ou, ow* and *ai* in words such as *out/spout/down, rain/again*. You can also teach and revise vowel digraphs (*ee/ea*) in words such as *beak, beetle, bee.* There are initial blends, such as *cl, dr, sp, fl, sm*, which could also be revised.

Introducing structures

In this unit, you can revise the simple present tense, which is used in non-fiction texts. Revise familiar adjectives, including colour words and numbers, as you help learners to describe different insects and other small animals. You can also teach and revise singular and plural nouns (such as names of animals). Demonstrative pronouns (*this, these, that, those, one*) can be revised along with determiners (*some, a, the*) when describing insects as well. (*This is a black beetle. That is a red one.*)

Previous knowledge

Learners may remember something about bees and spiders from Topic 2 when they read and talked about animal homes.

Activities

Select from these activities depending on the level of challenge needed for different learners, interest levels and what you have time to include. Supplement these with additional activities of your own and/or digital activities from the online resource.

▲ **1.** Hold up a few of the pictures you have collected and explain to learners that they are called bugs. You can also introduce the word *mini-beasts* (which means small animals and includes insects as well as non-insects such as spiders, ticks and worms). Tell learners to look in their picture dictionaries and find the names of ten bugs. They can do this in pairs. Let them report back with ideas. Write these suggestions on the board and then read them with the class.

Then ask the class to describe the bugs in their dictionaries. Ask questions to prompt, for example: *What colour are they? Do they have wings? How many legs can you see? What do their bodies look like?*

If there are learners who do not have picture dictionaries, make a copy of **PCM 17** for learners to refer to.

2. Learners find the poem *The incy wincy spider* on page 37 of the Student's Book. Write the title on the board and tell the class that it is on page 37.

   Let learners listen to the poem as you read it aloud twice. Explain what a *water spout* is. Then teach the poem and add actions with your hands as you speak.

3. Refer to the poem *The incy wincy spider.* Write these words on the board, underline letters as shown and tell learners to look for words in the same sounds.
   walked (*climbed*, *washed*, *dried*) (There is a difference in sounds but at this level don't worry about this.)
   out (*spout*, *down*) (Point out that the spelling is different.)
   drain (*rain*, *again*)

   Then erase the letters and let learners suggest how to complete each word.

4. Read aloud the poem *The bird* on page 37 of the Student's Book. Tell learners to listen and act to show that they understand what the poem means. Read the poem a few times.

5. Let learners find the non-fiction text *Most insects have wings* on page 38 of the Student's Book. Let learners identify the insects on the page by reading the labels under the pictures. Then teach or revise the names of key body parts: *wings, eyes, legs, antennae, head*. Ask learners to point to these body parts.

   Read the text with the class and discuss it briefly.

   Learners can then complete activities 1, 2 and 3 in the Workbook.

6. Teach the class how to make accurate descriptions of bugs. As you do this, learners will also be revising the use of determiners, adjectives and singular and plural nouns. Choose a few bugs and ask these questions:
   Does this bug have any wings/legs? How many wings/legs does it have?
   How many eyes does this one have? Are the eyes big or small? Are they round?
   Does the bug have antennae? Are they long or short?

7. **Link to art*. Let the class paint, draw or make models of bugs. The drawings and models should show the number of legs, wings, antennae and the colours accurately, although some artistic licence should be allowed. Learners can display their bugs and talk about them afterwards. Let them say what they can. (There is an assessment activity in Unit C in which learners give a formal talk about a bug. This activity could help them prepare for that.)

8. Let learners listen to a short text about the life cycle of a butterfly. Let them open their Workbooks. Tell them they are going to listen to information about butterflies and then complete the diagram and drawing in activities 4 and 5. Play **Audio 36** at least twice. You can also read the text to the class.

9. Learners read the poem *The incy wincy spider* on page 37 of the Student's Book in pairs. Draw a very simple flow chart on the board and then complete it with the class using simple past tense verbs. For example:

   The spider climbed up. → It rained. → The rain washed the spider down. → The sun came out. → The spider climbed up.

   Learners can also describe what spiders look like. Do this orally. For example: *They are small animals but they are not insects. They do not have wings. They have eight legs. They have round bodies.*

10. Revise singular and plural forms with the class. Write the following words from the texts in a table and let learners suggest how to complete it. The answers are in the texts on pages 37 and 38 of the Student's Book, so they can look for them there. Once you have completed the table, talk about how you need to change the singular nouns to make them plural.

    Learners can make oral sentences with the plural words. (Examples: *The beetle has two antennae. There are six butterflies on the flower.*)

singular (1)	**plural (more than 1)**
leg	
wing	
animal	
insect	
eye	
antenna	
egg	
butterfly	
worm	
spider	

11. Learners reread the non-fiction text *Most insects have wings* on page 38 of the Student's Book before they complete activities 6 and 7 in the Workbook.

12. Revise some vowel digraphs using words from the texts on pages 37 and 38 of the Student's

Book. Ask learners to find words with *ee* (*beetle*, *bee*) and *ea* (*beak*, *head*). Then talk about how we pronounce the words. Some words with *ee* and *ea* sound the same, and others do not.

Let learners try and complete the following familiar words with *ee* or *ea*. Write the words with missing letters on the board. Then say: *How do you spell ____________?* Read each word aloud and let learners suggest how to complete the word. Let them spell each word aloud. For example:

f _ _ t (*feet*) *k n _ _* (*knee*)
b _ _ ch (*beach*) *b r _ _ kfast* (*breakfast*)
f r _ _ (*free*) *c h _ _ se* (*cheese*)
d r _ _ m (*dream*) *s w _ _ t* (*sweet*)

13. Show the class some photographs of different spiders or any other mini-beast/insect. Then give learners a short talk about the animal. This should serve as a model for what you are going to ask learners to do, so it should be short and very structured. Use demonstrative pronouns (*this, these, those, that, one*) and determiners (*a*an+the*) in your statements.

Start like this for example:

These are ____________________.

They are ________________________.

Look at this picture. This is the ________________ and these are the ________________.

That one is the ______________. Those are the ________________________.

________________ *have* ____________________.

They also have ________________.

Learners listen carefully. Ask questions afterwards and let learners ask their own questions as well.

14. Learners complete activities 8, 9 and 10 in the Workbook.

15. Learners can make up riddles about insects and play a game in which other groups work out the answers to the riddles. For example:

It's a small animal but it's not an insect.
It doesn't have wings but it has eight legs.

16. Repeat your talk on a small animal. (See activity 13.) Then let learners work in pairs and prepare their own short talks about a small animal/insect using the same style as you did. They can use pictures and information from page 38 in the Student's Book or they can use their own pictures.

17. Learners write in their journals. Let them write about something interesting that they have learned about small animals. This can be free writing. Invite some learners (the ones who feel confident) to share what they have written afterwards.

18. Have a discussion about why insects are important. Learners should know what bees do. They may also know that caterpillars eat plants and that spiders can bite. Ask questions such as: *Should we kill caterpillars and spiders? Should you be careful of spiders?*

Wrap-up plenary

Have learners talk about their favourite small animals. They should share the reason for their choice. Write the names of the animals on the board and let learners think about what is the same and different (size, colours, wings, stings, dangerous).

Quick check

Divide learners into groups. They take turns to act as different mini-beasts. Everyone in the group asks the actor a question, such as:

Have you got wings?

How many legs have you got?

Is this how long your antennae are?

Can you hop?

Do you sting?

Where do you live?

The actor answers the questions and then chooses someone in the group to guess the animal.

Unit B Birds

Resources and materials

- Student's Book pp. 39–43
- Workbook pp. 100–105
- Audio files: Audio 37; Audio 38; Audio 39; Audio 40
- Photocopiable Master (PCM) PCM 18
- Coloured pencils
- Pictures and films of different birds

Key vocabulary

oxpecker, plover, crocodile, zebra, antelope, tick, danger, blood, skin, teeth, toothbrush, meat, bits, warn, suck, itchy, afraid

Lead-in ideas

- Show the class a film or pictures about birds and discuss what the birds look like, what noise they make and some of the things that they do.
- Teach learners simple action rhymes and songs about birds, for example *Little Bird* (**Audio 37**) and *This Is the Way* (**Audio 38**).

Script for the lesson

Introducing vocabulary

Introduce new vocabulary within the context of the texts in the Student's Book.

Sounds

You could focus on end phonemes in words from the texts in this unit, for example, *-ng* (*king*), *-ss* (*cross*) *–ch* (*itch*) *-ck* (*tick*), *-er* (*oxpecker, weaver*).

Introducing structures

In this unit you can continue to revise singular and plural nouns and the simple present tense, which is used in non-fiction texts. Focus on negative sentences in the present simple tense (with *not*). You can also revise the genitive (possessive *'s*) and conjunctions (*and, but*).

Previous knowledge

Learners should be familiar with some of the vocabulary in this unit and with common verbs in the simple present and simple past tenses.

Activities

Select from these activities depending on the level of challenge needed for different learners, interest levels and what you have time to include. Supplement these with additional activities of your own and/or digital activities from the online resource.

▲ **1.** Ask learners if they remember the story of Ant and Dove (*A Friend Helps* on Student's Book page 7). Let them find the story in the Student's Book and use the pictures to retell the story.

Let them look at the picture of Dove (or of any other bird) and name the different parts of a bird's body (*feathers, wings, beak, eyes, tail*). Write the parts on the board so they can refer to the names when they complete the activity.

Learners can colour in and label the picture of a bird whilst completing activities 1, 2 and 3 in the Workbook.

▲ **2.** Refer back to the poem *The bird* on page 37 in the Student's Book. Read the poem again and let learners recite it.

Then write the following on the board. Read the poem and let learners fill in the words. You can do this orally or as a simple written dictation.

Here are the __________
that ___________ *along.*
_______ *is the beak*
that ____________ *a song.*
Here ________ *the* _________
that flap ___________ *spread.*

▲ **3.** Learners find page 39 in the Student's Book. Ask them to look at the page and tell you what they think this is about. Is it a story or information? Read the title: *The helper birds.* Ask: *What does a helper bird do?* Show them the oxpecker on the antelope. Ask: *What is the bird doing? How is it helping? Who is it helping?* Accept all reasonable answers. Then point to the plover in the crocodile's mouth and ask the same questions.

Then teach the names *tick* and *crocodile*. Read the text with learners. You do not need to teach every word in this text, but make sure learners understand the main ideas. They should study the pictures carefully.

Learners can then complete activities 4 and 5 in the Workbook.

▲ **4.** Revise the possessive *'s*. Write some sentences on the board. Ask learners to choose the correct words to complete each sentence. For example:

This is (Anna/Anna's) bag.
This is the (bird/bird's) tail.
These are the (crocodile/crocodile's) teeth.
Ant was (Dove/Dove's) friend.

Then read each completed sentence and ask: *Whose bag is it?* Let learners reply: *It's Anna's bag*. Do this with all the sentences.

▲ **5.** Learners find the story *The Bird King* in the Student's Book, on pages 40–42. Do some pre-listening and pre-reading activities in the usual way. Teach the words *eagle* and *sparrow*. Then read the whole story to the class. Read or play the extended version (**Audio 39**) while learners follow the pictures in their books.

▲ **6.** Give learners copies of **PCM 18**. They cut out the pictures and put the pictures and sentences from the story in the correct order.

▲ **7.** Learners complete activities 6 and 7 in the Workbook to revise some of the new vocabulary in this unit.

● **8.** Learners practise making sentences. Write groups of words on the board (or write the words on prompt cards) and let learners make sentences using all the words. Include the word *not*, as well as conjunctions such as *and* and *but* in the groups of words. Learners can make sentences orally first and then in writing.

birds The did a king not have
have wings and feathers Birds
plovers Oxpeckers helper birds are and
not have wings Crocodiles do
An is big but sparrow small eagle a is

● **9.** Let learners read the text *The helper birds* in the Student's Book on page 39 again in pairs. They can ask each other questions about the text.

● **10.** Learners read the story *The Bird King* in the Student's Book on pages 40–42 in pairs and retell the story to each other. Learners can also work in groups and act the story, using some of the conversation from the Student's Book. They can add their own conversation as well where there is no conversation, by changing the tense of the verb, using a pronoun and letting someone say the words. For example:

All the animals had a king. = All the animals have a king.
The birds did not have a king. = We do not have a king.

11. Write some words on the board with missing end letters. Read each word aloud and let learners suggest how to complete the words. For example:

ki _ _ (king) *ti _ _ (tick)*
cro _ _ (cross) *oxpeck _ _ (oxpecker)*
it _ _ (itch) *weav _ _ (weaver)*

Learners can then complete activities 8 and 9 in the Workbook.

12. Learners find the non-fiction text *Making a nest* in the Student's Book on page 43. Let learners say what they can about the photographs first. Then read the text with them. Explain what an *entrance* is.

Learners can then complete activities 10 and 11 in the Workbook.

13. Talk about why animals need to build homes. Learners should remember some of this from Topic 2. Then ask learners what animals use to make their homes (things that are available in the environment: the ground, leaves, trees, etc.).

14. Let learners work in pairs and give a short talk based on the information in the non-fiction texts *The helper birds* or *Making a nest* in the Student's Book on pages 39 and 43. They should be familiar with the text at this stage. Let them use simple structures to present their talk.

These are ______________. *They are* ______________. *They* ______________.

They can point to the pictures as they talk.

15. Learners reread the story *The Bird King* in the Student's Book on pages 40–42 before completing activities 12, 13 and 14 in the Workbook.

16. Learners listen to the information about eagles (**Audio 40**). Then they answer questions about the main ideas in the listening text.

Here are some questions that you could ask:

What is a bird of prey?
Are eagles big or small?
Why do eagles have big wings?
Why do eagles have strong beaks?
Where do eagles make their nests?

Wrap-up plenary

Talk about some of the birds featured in this unit and let learners compare them. Write the names of the birds on the board and let learners think about what is the same and different (size, colours, beaks, tails, feathers).

You can also ask learners if they know the names of common birds found in the area where they live. Talk about the local names of the birds, what they eat, where they make their nests and the noises that they make.

Quick check

1. Hold a class brainstorming session in which learners call out vocabulary related to this topic. For example: *bird, beak, wing, oxpecker, eagle, fly*, and so on. Write the words on the board and have learners practise saying the words. Then ask each learner to say one sentence about the topic. Encourage them to include *and* or *but* in their sentence if possible, although this is not essential. Examples: *Birds don't have lips, but they do have beaks. Birds don't have fingernails, but they do have claws. I like sparrows, but I don't like eagles.*
2. Have learners create a page in a picture dictionary that includes some of the words on the board. Each learner only illustrates one word on their page. If there are enough words on the board every learner in the class can illustrate a different word. If there are not enough words, then have learners work in groups. Each learner in the group illustrates a different word. Collect the dictionary pages and either create a class or group dictionary that learners can page through.

Unit C Flying machines

Resources and materials

- Student's Book p. 44
- Workbook pp. 106–109
- Audio files: Audio 41; Audio 42; Audio 43
- Photocopiable Masters (PCMs) PCM 5; PCM 11; PCM 19; PCM 20
- Make a poster with pictures of different flying machines: a plane, a helicopter, a spaceship and a hot air balloon
- Prompt cards: helicopter, plane, spaceship, hot air balloon
- Paper to make paper aeroplanes
- Coloured crayons or pencils (per learner)
- 1–6 spinner (use PCM 11)

Key vocabulary

plane, helicopter, wings, fly, take off, land, rescue, blade, engine, tail, rotor, cockpit, passenger

Lead-in ideas

Teach learners a few songs or poems about aeroplanes and helicopters. For example: *Ten Little Aeroplanes* (**Audio 41**) and *Helicopter* (**Audio 42**).

Script for the lesson

Introducing vocabulary

Use pictures to introduce the vocabulary in this unit.

Sounds

Revise phonemes and sounds in context. In this unit, for example, there are opportunities to revise long vowel sounds in words such as *tail, mountain, fly, rescue, fight, seat.* You can also continue to teach and revise words with *vowel + consonant + -e*. For example: *take, blade, use, place, fire.*

Introducing structures

Introduce the structure *Have you (ever) been…?* in simple conversations about visiting different places and travelling by air. Revise the word *with* to mean accompaniment as it is used in the story *He Wanted to Fly* (**Audio 43**).

Previous knowledge

Some learners may have some experience of travelling by air. Help them to share their experiences in English.

Possible areas of difficulty

Some of the vocabulary in this unit may seem difficult (*helicopter, cockpit*) but there are not many new words. Don't expect learners to be able to spell and use all words, but help them to understand them and recognise some of the words by sight.

Activities

Select from these activities depending on the level of challenge needed for different learners, interest levels and what you have time to include. Supplement these with additional activities of your own and/or digital activities from the online resource.

1. Use the poster you have made and prompt cards to teach the names of different flying machines. Break words down into syllables if necessary. Let learners read the words and match the prompt cards to the pictures on the poster. Spell the names aloud and see if learners can recognise the word.

   Talk about the different machines. Ask questions such as: *What do they look like? Are they round, long, big or small? Do they all have wings? How do they get up into the sky? Are they fast or slow? Have you been in a/an ____________?*

2. Teach learners a short conversation, which they can practise in pairs.

   A: *Have you ever been in a/an ____________?*

   B: *Yes, I have./No, I haven't. What about you?*

   A: *When did you go?*

   B: *I went ____________. What about you?*

   A: *Yes, I have./No, I haven't.*

   B: *I would like to go in a/an ____________.*

   A: *Oh yes! Me too!*

3. Let learners find the labelled drawing of a helicopter on page 44 of the Student's Book. Let them read the title and look at the drawing. Help them read the labels. Then ask questions using prepositions of position and let them point to the appropriate parts to answer the questions. For example, ask: *Where is the engine? Is it in front of the cockpit? Is it under the rotor blades?*

   Learners can then complete activities 1 and 2 in the Workbook. Depending on learners' ability, encourage them to label parts of the aeroplane they draw.

4. Tell the class the story *He Wanted to Fly* (which is the story of Daedalus and Icarus). Tell them that it is an old story about a man who made wings to fly. Some learners may know the story in their first language. If they do, ask them to tell you about the story.

   Play the audio (**Audio 43**) and ask a few questions. Then let learners listen again. You can read the story or play the audio again.

   Ask some questions to check that the class have understood the main ideas in the story.

5. **Link to mathematics.* Revise number words from 1–50 by asking learners to solve some simple mathematical calculations orally. For example:

   If there are 20 feathers on one wing how many feathers are there on two wings?

   If Icarus has 33 feathers and then loses 11, how many feathers are left?

   If Daedalus needs 40 feathers to make a wing and he has 33, how many more does he need?

6. Let learners play a game similar to 'battleships' in pairs. Give learners copies of **PCM 5**. Remind them how to play (refer to the instructions on page 21 of this Teacher's Guide). Call the game 'Flying ships'. Have learners fill in the following flying ships on their sheet:

   1 block for a helicopter (x4)

   2 blocks for a small passenger plane (x2)

   3 blocks for a spaceship (x2)

   4 blocks for a big passenger plane (x1)

7. Revise prepositions of location, position and direction (*at, behind, between, in, in front of, near, next to, on, to*). Do this with familiar objects in the classroom.

   Then let learners complete activities 3 and 4 in the Workbook.

8. Let learners practise making up sentences with conjunctions. Draw this simple table on the board and let learners make sentences orally, using words from each column.

Helicopters can fly up		strong.
Birds have wings		they are useful.
Eagles are big	and	down.
You can go on a plane	but or	was the king of the birds.
Helicopters are small		on a boat.
The sparrow was small		feathers for flying.

9. Learners reread the text on page 44 of the Student's Book before completing activities 5, 6 and 7 in the Workbook.

10. On the board, make up a timetable like the one below. Explain that it shows at what time and on which days some planes will leave an airport. It also shows where the planes are going. Let the class ask and answer questions about the timetable. For example: *Which days does the plane go to Rome? At what time/When does the plane leave on Monday for London?*

(Note: learners are only expected to work with time on the hour and half hour in mathematics at this stage. They do not yet work with a.m. or p.m. and they are unlikely to know the 24-hour clock times.)

	Monday	**Tuesday**	**Wednesday**
Rome	7:30	-	7:30
London	11:30	9:00	-
Cape Town	12:30	4:00	-
Tokyo	5:30	7:00	8:30

Learners can then complete activities 8 and 9 in the Workbook.

11. Give learners a copy of **PCM 19**. Let them follow the instructions to make a simple paper aeroplane.

12. Work with groups of learners and make a story about a trip on a plane or a helicopter. Let learners make suggestions while you do the writing. Don't write down everything learners say; let them discuss and agree on things first. Write the story in very simple words. Start like this, for example:

Jo wanted to visit his cousin. His cousin lived in ________________. Then one day ________________.

13. Learners write in their journals about a trip in a plane or helicopter. If they haven't been on one of these, help them to imagine what it might be like. Encourage learners to write freely and to describe how they felt (*happy, afraid, excited*).

14. Let learners do some research using a simple picture dictionary or first encyclopaedia. They could also do an online search. Let them find a picture of a flying machine that they find interesting. They will need to draw or print out a picture of the machine and find out one or two interesting facts. Then they can prepare a short talk for the rest of the class. You can give them this basic frame to complete to help them prepare. Learners can do this alone if they feel confident, or they can do it in pairs.

This is a ________________.
It has ________________.
It can ________________
and ________________.

15. Make up a shape poem with the class in the shape of a hot air balloon or a spaceship. Draw a basic shape on the board and ask learners to suggest words or short sentences to fit on the shape. You can extend this activity by letting learners draw and write a shape poem about a flying machine.

16. Learners can listen to the story *He Wanted to Fly* (**Audio 43**) again. Talk about the sequence of events. Have learners draw a picture or a sequence of pictures to illustrate the story.

Wrap-up plenary

Let the class sing one of the songs or rhymes you have taught them. Change the words and use the names of different flying machines.

Quick check

Learners can play the games on **PCM 20**. Divide learners into pairs. Give each pair of learners one sheet and a 1–6 spinner (use **PCM 11**). Each learner in the pair must use a different colour crayon and they must use the same colour crayon throughout the game. Discuss how to play:

The players take turns to spin the spinner, find one of the corresponding numbers on the helicopter and then colour it in. While colouring in the part the learner tells their partner what they are doing. For example: *I am colouring in part of the blade.* The winner is the learner who has coloured in the most parts on the helicopter. They can then play the game again using the aeroplane picture.

Assessment

You can complete an oral assessment of the work done in this topic by asking learners to tell you about one of the creatures or machines with wings in the unit, using pictures in the Student's Book as prompts.

Learners can also complete Progress check activities 1, 2, 3 and 4 in the Workbook as a simple assessment.

You could allocate marks for these activities and record these as part of continuous assessment.

Topic 7 Wishes, feelings and needs

Overview

In this unit learners are encouraged to talk about their wishes, feelings and their need to feel safe. Vocabulary is developed using familiar topics and by encouraging learners to express themselves using whatever knowledge they already have. There are opportunities to integrate language lessons with other subjects in the curriculum, such as social sciences and drama.

Units in this topic

Unit A: I wish…

Unit B: Feelings

Unit C: I feel safe when…

Teaching focus

- **2Rg1** Recognise, identify and sound, with support, a limited range of language at text level
- **2Rg2** Begin to read, with support, very short simple fiction and non-fiction texts with confidence and enjoyment
- **2Rm2** Understand the main points of very short, simple texts on some familiar general and curricular topics by using contextual clues
- **2Rd1** Understand, with support, some specific information and detail in very short, simple texts on a limited range of general and curricular topics
- **2Rm1** Understand the meaning of very short, simple texts on familiar general and curricular topics by rereading them
- **2Rd2** Understand the meaning of simple short sentences on familiar general and curricular topics
- **2Wa1** Plan, write and check, with support, short sentences on familiar topics
- **2Ug14** Spell a growing number of familiar high-frequency words accurately during guided writing activities
- **2Wo2** Include a full stop and question mark during guided writing of short, familiar sentences
- **2Ug3** Use adjectives, including possessive adjectives, on familiar topics to give personal information and describe things
- **2Ut2** Use *who, what, where, how many* to ask questions on familiar topics
- **2Ut3** Use impersonal *you* in the question: *How do you spell that?*
- **2Ut4** Use demonstrative pronouns *this, these, that, those* and object pronoun *one* in short statements and responses
- **2Uf2** Use common simple present forms, including short answer forms and contractions, to give personal information
- **2Uf3** Use common past simple forms [regular and irregular] to describe actions and narrate simple events including short answer forms and contractions
- **2Ug9** Use prepositions of location, position and direction: *at, behind, between, in, in front of, near, next to, on, to* on personal and familiar topics
- **2Ug10** Use prepositions of time: *on, in, at,* to talk about days and times on personal and familiar topics
- **2Ug11** Use *with* to indicate accompaniment and instrument and *for* to indicate recipient on personal and familiar topics
- **2Ug13** Use *Would you like to …* to invite and use appropriate responses *yes please, no thanks*
- **2Ug12** Use declarative *what [a/an]* + adjectives + noun to show feelings
- **2Ut8** Use conjunctions *and, or, but* to link words and phrases
- **2Uf4** Use *when* clauses to describe simple present and past actions on personal and familiar topics
- **2Ut7** Use *so do I* to give short answers
- **2Ld5** Understand an increasing range of short supported questions on general and curricular topics
- **2Lm1** Understand the main points of short, supported talk on an increasing range of general and curricular topics
- **2Ld1** Understand some specific information and detail of short, supported talk on an increasing range of general and curricular topics
- **2Ld2** Use contextual clues to predict content and meaning in short supported talk on an increasing range of general and curricular topics
- **2Lg1** Understand short supported narratives on an increasing range of general and curricular topics
- **2Lg2** Identify initial, middle and final phonemes and blends

- **2S1** Make basic statements which provide personal information on a limited range of general topics
- **2S3** Describe basic present and past actions on a limited range of general and curricular topics
- **2S4** Use basic vocabulary for a limited range of general and curricular topics
- **2S5** Give short, basic descriptions of people and objects
- **2S6** Contribute a growing range of suitable words, phrases, and sentences during short pair, group and whole class exchanges
- **2S7** Take turns when speaking with others in a growing range of short, basic exchanges
- **2S8** Relate very short, basic stories and events on a limited range of general and curricular topics

Language patterns

Grammar summary for teachers:

***When* clauses:** Learners may be familiar with the word *when* as used in questions, but *when* can also be used to describe a point in time. In the following examples, the clause that begins with *when* describes the point in time:

When *I get home, I'll do my homework.* (*when* + present simple + *will*)

The traffic offer helps me ***when*** *I cross the street.* (*when* + present simple)

When *I got home it was dark.* (*when* + past simple)

Unit A I wish...

Resources and materials

- Student's Book pp. 45–47
- Workbook pp. 112–116
- Audio files: Audio 44; Audio 45; Audio 46
- Photocopiable Master (PCM) PCM 21
- Props to act the story, *The Magic Egg* (spoon, bucket, stool)
- Sentence strips with sentences from the stories *The Magic Egg* and *The Fisherman and the Golden Fish*.

Key vocabulary

wish, feel, still, stay, egg, camel, goat, water, egg, happy, angry, sad, scared, shy, hungry, thirsty, tired, wet, muddy

Lead-in ideas

Teach the class a poem or song about wishes or feelings. Examples: *Star Bright* (**Audio 44**) and *How I Feel* (**Audio 45**).

Script for the lesson

Introducing vocabulary

Use the texts to introduce new adjectives and verbs in this unit. You should also teach words for ideas that the class may try to express when they talk about feelings and wishes.

Sounds

Use words from the texts to revise initial phonemes and sounds *t/th, w* and the end sound *–y*.

Introducing structures

Learners should recognise some contractions in the simple present tense. You can now introduce a few common contractions in the simple past tense such as *I'd, we'd, they'd*.

Revise the structure *What a/an + adjective + noun* after reading the story *The Fisherman and the Golden Fish* (**Audio 46**).

Previous knowledge

Learners may already know some adjectives that describe feelings such as *happy* and *sad*.

Possible areas of difficulty

Some learners may feel shy to speak and act out *The Magic Egg* in front of the class. Make sure that the atmosphere is relaxed and non-threatening for learners. Explain that every learner will be trying their best so there should be no criticism. Don't worry too much about structures. Let learners say whatever they can. They can also act to show what they mean.

Activities

Select from these activities depending on the level of challenge needed for different learners, interest levels and what you have time to include. Supplement these with additional activities of your own and/or digital activities from the online resource.

▲ **1.** Write the words *I wish…* on the board and talk to the class or to groups of learners about their personal wishes. Give a few suggestions of your own to get started. For example: *I wish I had a sister. I wish people did not fight. I wish I could speak Japanese.* Let learners give their ideas.

Don't worry too much about structures at first, just prompt learners for words to express their ideas. Write some of the ideas on the board. Then sum up with oral sentences after your discussion. For example:

Jo wishes she had a swimming pool.

Lee wishes he had a new football.

2. Revise and talk about adjectives that express feelings. Give learners a copy of **PCM 21**, which is a picture dictionary page about feelings. Let them work in pairs. They take turns to point to pictures and make simple sentences, using contractions. For example: *He's angry./He's feeling angry. She's sad./She's feeling sad.* Do a few examples with the class first.

   Then extend the activity. Point to a picture and ask: *Why is he angry?* Let the class make suggestions. (Example: *The monkey broke the car. The monkey is bad.*) Do this with all the pictures. Learners can do the same in pairs afterwards if you feel they need the extra practice.

3. Let learners find the story *The Magic Egg* on pages 45–47 of the Student's Book. Read the title and ask learners what they think the story is about. Talk a little about the meaning of the word *magic*. In stories like this it means that it is not real. So the egg in this story is not like the normal egg that we eat.

   Read the story with the class or with groups. As you read, help learners to look carefully at the pictures in the story to understand what is happening. For example, read the text in the first picture (*I'm hungry! I wish I had an egg*). Then let learners look at the picture that follows, which has no text. Ask: *What did the boy get? What colour is the egg? Why?* Work through the rest of the story in the same way.

   Then let learners complete activity 1 in the Workbook.

4. Revise the adjectives that have been introduced in this unit and let learners use them in a short conversation. Demonstrate and teach the conversation. You can focus on the adjectives *hungry* and *thirsty*, but learners could use other adjectives as well. Use facial expressions and body language to help convey the meaning of the adjectives. For example, if someone is angry or tired, they might like some tea. You could illustrate this with a conversation such as:

   A: *I'm ________. (hungry*thirsty+sad*tired+angry)*

   B: *Would you like some ______________? (milk, tea, sleep, food, water, etc.) Would you like to _______? (sleep/eat/drink)*

   A: *Yes, please./No, thanks. I would like some _____________.*

   B: *What a nice ________. (cup of tea/glass of water, etc.)*

5. Revise contractions with subject pronouns and adjectives. Learners can play a quick game. They sit in a circle and exchange simple sentences. For example:

   A: *I'm hungry.*

   B: *She's/He's hungry but I am thirsty.*

   C: *He's/She's thirsty but I am angry.*

   And so on.

6. Use words from the texts to revise initial phonemes and sounds *t/th, w* and the end sound *–y*. For example, write the words below on the board. Ask learners to suggest or find other words with the same sounds (the sound could be in any part of the word). They can look at the **PCM 21** dictionary page and in the Student's Book on pages 45–47.

   angry (thirsty, hungry, happy)

   table (tired, wet, goat, water)

   Thursday (thirsty)

   Wednesday (wet, wish)

   They can also look for more words with these sounds. You can then write some of the words on the board with some letters missing and let learners complete the words and spell each word aloud.

7. Learners complete activities 2 and 3 in the Workbook to revise spelling and contractions.

8. Learners find and reread the story *The Magic Egg* on pages 45–47 of the Student's Book. Then they complete activities 4 and 5 in the Workbook

9. **Link to drama*. Talk about the story *The Magic Egg*. Talk about the characters in the story and make a list on the board: *the boy, the hen, the goat, the camel, the woman with the basin of water.*

   Then talk about where the story takes place (*near a home/on a farm/on a family compound*).

   Then tell learners that they are going to work in groups of five and act the story. They will need to make up things for some of the characters to say. Discuss some ideas with the class. For example, the hen could say: *You want an egg? Here you are!* The goat could say: *You want some milk? You must milk me! Here you are!* and so on. Encourage them to use props.

   Let the groups perform their stories for the rest of the class.

10. Write a simple wish poem with the class. Let learners provide ideas as you write on the board. The poem does not need to rhyme. You will need to use ideas from learners and write them in simple sentences. For example:

    I wish…

    I had a baby brother.

    I wish there was no rain.

    I wish____________________.

    That is what I wish.

11. Learners write their own wish poems in their journals. The poems can be short. Don't correct the poems but invite some learners to read their

poems aloud to the rest of the class if they feel confident in doing so.

12. Learners listen to the story about a poor fisherman and his wife and the wishes that they made in *The Fisherman and the Golden Fish* (**Audio 46**). Let learners listen to the story several times. Then ask some simple questions to see if learners have understood the main ideas. The story is long but it is repetitive and easy to follow. Ask learners if they enjoyed this story. Let them say what they can about it.

13. What does the fish mean when it says *What a greedy man you are!* What does *greedy* mean? How does the fish feel? Who was greedy in the story of *The Fisherman and the Golden Fish*? Is it good to be greedy?

14. Learners reread the story *The Magic Egg* on pages 45–47 of the Student's Book. Then let them write sentences to match the story map in activity 6 in the Workbook.

15. Learners listen to the story *The Fisherman and the Golden Fish* (**Audio 46**) again in groups. Then let the groups retell the story. Start off the retelling yourself and then ask for a volunteer to continue the story. Each learner in the group makes a contribution to the retelling. Encourage learners to use the structure *What a/an adjective +noun* as they retell the story. Some learners will be able to say more than others. Choose learners who are not so confident to retell the sections that are repeated in the story.

Learners complete the flow chart in activity 7 on page 116 of the Workbook.

Wrap-up plenary

Re-visit some feelings that you have discussed with the class in this unit. Start to talk about when we have these feelings. This will be explored further in Unit C. Do the same with wishes. This will be explored in Unit B.

Quick check

1. Use the sentence strips from the stories in this unit. Learners use them to retell the stories.
2. In groups, have learners take turns to mime a wish from *The Magic Egg* or *The Fisherman and the Golden Fish*. Their group members must guess what they are wishing for. You can extend this by having learners act out wishes of their own.

Unit B Feelings

Resources and materials

- Student's Book pp. 48–50
- Workbook pp. 117–121
- Audio files: Audio 46; Audio 47; Audio 48
- Photocopiable Masters (PCMs) PCM 2; PCM 22
- A big analogue clock to revise times on the hour and half hour
- A beanbag, ball or soft toy that can be thrown in the classroom

Key vocabulary

bottom, carry, clean, cried, dive, dolphin, drown, fishermen, heal, hunt, hurled, kill, king, knight, promise, save, scream, sea, spear, storm, strange, waves, whisper, wound

Lead-in ideas

- Tell the class any story you know about someone who was kind to animals. Then ask the class what it means to be cruel to animals. Have a short discussion about this.
- Teach the class a tongue-twister with some of the vocabulary in this unit, for example, *Danny the Dolphin* (**Audio 47**). Explain that this is a nonsense rhyme and ask the class to identify the letter that is repeated.

Script for the lesson

Introducing vocabulary

There is quite a lot of new vocabulary in the story *The Dolphin King*. You do not need to teach every new word. Learners need to understand the main ideas of the story and get used to hearing stories with some words that they do not understand yet. See the key vocabulary list for words that you could teach.

Sounds

You could focus on end phonemes in simple past tense verbs and initial consonant digraphs, such as *sp, cl, pr* and *fr* using words that are used in the story *The Dolphin King*.

You could also teach the class that the letters *ph* are sometimes used to make an 'f' sound (as in the word *dolphin*). If you feel the class is ready, you can also introduce the silent 'k' in the the word *knight*. Learners may already be familiar with other words that start like this (*knee, know*).

Introducing structures

Revise and extend learners' knowledge of the simple past tense by letting them add *–ed* to verbs to make this form and helping them to recognise irregular forms of verbs.

Previous knowledge

Learners should be able to recognise some regular and irregular simple past tense verbs.

Possible areas of difficulty

Learners may not always recognise irregular forms of verbs in the simple past tense because they are spelled differently to the simple present tense. Help them to make the connections by matching verbs. You can also ask questions which use the infinitive forms of verbs. For example: *She wrote a letter. What did she write?*

Activities

Select from these activities depending on the level of challenge needed for different learners, interest levels and what you have time to include. Supplement these with additional activities of your own and/or digital activities from the online resource.

1. Learners listen again to the story that was introduced in Unit A, *The Fisherman and the Golden Fish* (**Audio 46**). Give each learner a copy of **PCM 22**. Learners cut out the pictures and sequence them. They use the pictures to retell the story in pairs or small groups.
2. **Link to mathematics*. Revise times with the class. Show them different times on the clock and let them say the times like this: *It's six o'clock. It's half past seven.*

   If you have several clocks available let learners work in pairs to ask and tell the time. One learner shows the time on a clock and asks: *What's the time?* The other learner replies: *It's ____________ o'clock.*
3. Revise the way we talk about days and times. Make sure learners use the correct prepositions in phrases like these: *in the morning, in the afternoon, at night, at lunch time, on Monday*. You can practise these orally by asking questions and letting learners give full answers. For example:

   What do you do in the morning? (I get dressed and have breakfast in the morning.)

   What do you do in the afternoon?

   What do you eat at lunch time?

   What do you do on Sundays?

   Where are you going on Monday?

   You could also play a guessing game. Give learners a few clues about something you do. Include time phrases in your clues. Let them guess what it is. For example, say:

   I am thinking about something. I do this at lunchtime. I do it every day. What is it?

   Learners can try and play this game in groups too. Work out with them how to take turns and how to score.
4. Learners can complete activities 1, 2 and 3 in the Workbook to consolidate the time phrases they have practised.
5. Learners find the story *The Dolphin King* in the Student's Book on pages 48–50. Do some pre-reading activities with the class before reading this story aloud. For example:
   - Read the title. Ask learners to find a *dolphin* and a *king* in the pictures. Ask: *How do we know he is a king?* (He is wearing a crown.)
   - Ask the class to find a *fisherman, a spear* and a *knight* in the pictures.
   - Ask learners what they know about the sea. Ask: *Does it change? Is it safe?* Let them look at the pictures and look at how the sea changes in the pictures. (It is calm and clear at first and then dark and stormy.)
   - Explain what *drown* means.
   - Ask learners what they think story is about.

   Read the story aloud while learners follow the pictures in their books.

   Ask a few questions to make sure that learners have understood the main ideas. They do not have to be able to read and understand every word of the text to do this.
6. Explain what a *character* is. Then let learners work in pairs and make lists of all the characters (Jean, the other fishermen, the dolphin king, the knight, other dolphins) in the story. When they have finished, they can compare their lists.
7. Revise and extend learners' knowledge of the simple past tense by letting them recognise and spell verbs with regular past tense forms. Write these sentences on the board and underline the verbs. Then let learners look in the story and find out how the verbs are spelled in the story. Let the class spell each word aloud. As they spell, replace the verb in the sentence.

   Jean (hurl) his spear at the dolphin.

   The animal (scream) and (dive) beneath the waves.

   The knight (shout), "You nearly (kill) the dolphin king."

   The knight (carry) Jean down to the bottom of the sea.

   The knight (whisper) to Jean.

   Learners can then do activity 4 in the Workbook.
8. Revise some initial consonant digraphs such as *sp, cl, dr, pr* and *fr* using words from the story *The Dolphin King*. Write these words on the board and ask learners to fill in the initial letters.

   _ _ *iend (friend)*

   _ _ *ear (spear)*

   _ _ *own (drown)*

   _ _ *eaned (cleaned)*

   _ _ *omise (promise)*

   Then add other words with the same initial digraphs and let learners try and work out what the words are. For example:

   _ _ *ize (prize)*

   _ _ *og (frog)*

   _ _ *ap (clap)*

   _ _ *oon (spoon)*

   _ _ *aw (draw)*

9. Write some irregular past tense verbs from the story *The Dolphin King* on the board in the present tense. Ask learners find the matching past tense verbs in the story. For example, you could use: *were* (are), *said* (say), *saw* (see), *cried* (cry).

10. Learners reread the story *The Dolphin King* in the Student's Book on pages 48–50 before completing activities 5 and 6 in the Workbook.

11. **Link to drama*. Learners can work in big groups or as a class to act the story of the *The Dolphin King*. Then ask learners to name all the characters in the story. (They can look at the lists that they made in a previous activity.) Then choose who will play each character. Help the class or groups to rehearse.

12. Let learners listen to the story *Kind Emma* (**Audio 48**). Let them listen at least twice. Then ask a few questions to check that they have understood the main ideas of the story. Talk about what it means to be kind to other people (and other creatures/ animals).

13. Talk about the stories *The Dolphin King* and *The Fishermen and the Golden Fish* and help learners to compare the stories. Here are some questions you could ask:

What are the titles of the stories?
Who are the characters in the stories?
Are all the characters real?
Which characters are magic?
Who is kind in each story?
Who is not good and kind in each story?
How does each story end? Is the ending happy or sad?
What can we learn from each story?

Then let learners complete the comparison table in activity 7 in the Workbook.

14. Learners write about one of the characters that they liked in the stories in this unit. Let them write freely and draw pictures too. Encourage them to share what they have written afterwards, or make time to listen to them read what they have written individually.

15. Learners first work in pairs to retell the story *The Dolphin King*. They can use the pictures in the Student's Book as prompts. Then learners work by themselves to complete the sentences in activity 8 in the Workbook. The sentences tell the story in a very simple way, using words from the story. Learners check their answers with their partners afterwards.

16. Talk about being kind and cruel and what the stories in this unit tell us about being kind and cruel. Ask: *Do people always think before they do something?* You can have this discussion in the learners' first language and then give learners a few sentences in English to remember, for example: *Think before you do something*.

Wrap-up plenary

Talk about how we should treat animals and why this is important.

Quick check

1. Write vocabulary words from this unit on the board. Give learners Bingo sheets (use **PCM 2**) and let them choose words to complete their sheets. Then play 'Bingo' in the usual way.
2. Play 'toss the tense' with the class or with small groups. A beanbag (or ball or balloon or soft toy) represents the past tense. The game begins with all learners standing. Call out a verb used in this unit in the present tense and toss the beanbag to a learner. The recipient of the verb (beanbag) calls out the past tense form of the verb you called out and then throws the verb (beanbag) back to you. Carry on like this until all learners have had a turn.

   Examples of verbs in the unit:

want – wanted	*show – showed*
choose – chose	*ask – asked*
find – found	*know – knew*
write – wrote	*feel – felt*
come – came	*marry – married*
arrive – arrived	*stay – stayed*

Unit C I feel safe when...

Resources and materials

- Student's Book p. 51
- Workbook pp. 122–126
- Audio files: Audio 49; Audio 50
- Photocopiable Masters (PCMs) PCM 21; PCM 23
- Pictures and/or videos about people in the community who keep us safe: nurses, doctors, police, firefighters, ambulance staff, rescue pilots, life guards (on a beach), security guards
- Prompt cards with the names of community workers

Key vocabulary

safe, feel, when, look after, scared, nurse, doctor, sick, firefighter, police (officer), life guard, security guard, danger, cross, street, parents

Lead-in ideas

- Let the class sing any safety songs that they know about crossing a road safely or about using sharp utensils safely.
- Teach the class one or two simple poems about other ways of staying safe. For example, *Be Safe* (**Audio 49**).

Script for the lesson

Introducing vocabulary

Introduce the new vocabulary in the context of the non-fiction text *People who keep us safe* in the Student's Book.

Sounds

You could focus on initial consonant digraphs and blends such as *wh, sc, tr, str, cr* using words that are used in the non-fiction text *People who keep us safe* in the Student's Book.

Introducing structures

In this unit introduce *when* clauses to describe simple present tense actions. Learners can use these clauses along with the adjectives they have learned to describe feelings. (Example: *I feel happy when…*)

Previous knowledge

Learners should be able to recognise and use some personal pronouns and the simple present tense.

Activities

Select from these activities depending on the level of challenge needed for different learners, interest levels and what you have time to include. Supplement these with additional activities of your own and/or digital activities from the online resource.

▲ **1.** Have a general discussion with the class about their need to feel safe. You can focus on road safety, safety in the streets or safety at school. Ask the class for some suggestions about how to stay safe. You can do this in the first language. Then write a few key instructions in English for the class to remember. For example: *Stop, look and listen before you cross a road. Wear a seatbelt in the car. Wear a helmet when you ride your bike.*

▲ **2.** Let the class look at the picture dictionary page (**PCM 21**) again and say the adjectives aloud. Then talk about when people have these feelings.

Introduce *when* clauses by making sentences about the pictures. Give the class some examples, and then let them try and make more sentences, for example:

I feel angry when… (someone is rude/someone cheats/people hurt other people)

I feel happy when… (it rains/I get a present/I read a good story)

I don't like it when… (someone is rude/someone is unkind)

I feel sad when… (my friends don't play with me/ my sister cries)

I feel scared when… (it is stormy/the bus drives fast)

I say sorry when… (I make a mistake)

I say thank you when… (someone gives me something/someone helps me)

I feel safe when… (I wear my seatbelt in the car)

▲ **3.** Use the pictures you have collected about people in the community who help us and keep us safe (or let the class find pictures in their picture dictionaries if the dictionaries have such pictures). Revise or teach the following names. Use the names given to people such as these in your country or community: *nurse/doctor, firefighter, police officer, security guard, life guards, helicopter rescue pilots, ambulance staff.* If you have a video available about the work done by any of these workers, show it to the class and discuss it.

▲ **4.** Learners find the non-fiction text *People who keep us safe* in the Student's Book on page 51. Help learners to read the title. Then ask learners to name the people in the photographs before reading the text with them.

▲ **5.** Learners match the names and pictures in activity 1 in the Workbook.

▲ **6.** Write some words with initial consonant digraphs and blends, such as *wh, sc, tr, str, cr,* on the board. Let learners look for the words in the Student's Book on page 51, fill in the missing consonants and spell the words aloud.

_ _ *en (when)*

_ _ *ared (scared)*

_ _ *affic (traffic)*

_ _ _ *eet (street)*

_ _ *oss (cross)*

▲ **7.** Give learners copies of **PCM 23**. Learners listen to sentences that you read aloud and then tick the picture that matches the sentence.

Describe what one of the people in each pair of pictures does to keep us safe. For example:

1. *He helps when there is a fire.* OR *He keeps us safe on the beach.*
2. *He keeps us safe.* OR *She keeps us safe.*
3. *She helps us when we have an accident.* OR *She helps us when we are sick.*
4. *He helps us cross a road safely.* OR *He keeps us safe in the shops.*
5. *She looks after us when we are scared.* OR *He helps us when we are sick.*

This sheet could also be used for assessment.

● **8.** Learners reread the text *People who keep us safe* in the Student's Book on page 51 in pairs. Then they complete activities 2 and 3 in the Workbook.

● **9.** Teach the class a simple conversation in which they talk about feeling safe. Give them a basic structure but allow them to change words. Encourage them to use short answers when they reply. For example:

A: *I feel safe when I am __________ [at home].*

B: *So do I.*

A: *Do you feel safe ____________ [at school]?*

B: *Yes, I do.*

A: *And do you feel safe when* ____________ *[you cross the street]?*

B: *Yes. The traffic warden is there.*

10. Let learners look at the pictures in activity 4 in the Workbook. Tell them that they are going to listen to a story about the pictures. Read the labels in the pictures before you play the story. Explain the words *train, platform, train guard, driver, horse, boy, bridge, storm.* Some of the words should already be familiar. Ask learners what time of day they think it is in the story. Ask: *What is the weather like– sunny or stormy?*

After learners have listened to the story *The Red Light* (**Audio 50**), at least twice, ask a few simple questions to see if they have understood the main ideas in the story. For example, ask:

Where was the train?

Why did it stop?

Who had a red light?

Why did he tell the train to stop?

What would have happened if the train did not stop?

11. Write these sentences on the board. They tell the story *The Red Light* in a simple way. Help learners to read the sentences. Then let them read the sentences in the correct order to retell the story.

A boy came to the station on his horse.

He said the storm broke the bridge.

The boy saved the people on the train.

The boy told the train to stop.

It was a stormy night.

The train stopped at the station.

The train driver saw a red light.

12. Learners complete activities 5 and 6 in the Workbook. They read the short report about a story and then write their own report about a story they have enjoyed.

13. Learners write in their journals about how they are feeling that day. Encourage them to try and say why they feel that way. As before, do not correct this writing, just encourage learners to share what they have written or to read it to you.

14. Tell learners that they are going to work in pairs and prepare a short talk about someone in the community who keeps them safe. They can do this by interviewing a person, or by doing some research in the library or online. They will need your help with this.

Give them a few questions to answer to help them to know what information to look for. For example:

What job does the person do? (name of job)

Where does he or she work?

Does he or she wear special clothes?

How does he or she help people?

Show learners some simple picture dictionaries or first encyclopaedias where they can get information. Remind them that pictures give us a lot of information. They don't need to read long texts. If you know some good websites for children of this age, show learners how to get information from this source. There are many songs and pictures about community helpers online.

Learners can complete activities 7 and 8 in the Workbook with the information they have collected. They can then use this information to give a talk to the rest of the class.

15. Talk about why we need people in the community who can help us. For example, ask:

Why do we need firefighters?

- *They know how to put out fires.*
- *They have equipment to put out fires.*
- *They can help lots of people in different places.*

Wrap-up plenary

Summarise what you have discussed about what makes us feel safe and how other people can help us feel safe. Go around the class and ask individual learners to complete this sentence orally: *I feel safe when…*

Quick check

1. Learners can work in groups and role-play somebody who is helping someone else. The other learners can guess who the helper is.
2. Learners can recite a safety song.

Assessment

You can complete an oral assessment of the work done in this topic by asking learners to tell you how one of the people in the pictures on Student's Book page 51 helps.

Learners can also complete Progress check activities 1, 2, 3, 4 and 5 in the Workbook as a simple assessment.

You could allocate marks for these activities and record these as part of continuous assessment.

Topic 8 Cities

Overview

In this topic the focus is on sharing information about buildings and transport in the city, building on familiar vocabulary and structures to build confidence and then introducing new vocabulary to develop language skills.

There are opportunities to integrate activities with other curricula such as mathematics, art, drama and social sciences.

Units in this topic

Unit A: What's that building?

Unit B: Fun in the city

Unit C: Getting about

Teaching focus

- **2Rg1** Recognise, identify and sound, with support, a limited range of language at text level
- **2Rg2** Begin to read, with support, very short simple fiction and non-fiction texts with confidence and enjoyment
- **2Rm2** Understand the main points of very short, simple texts on some familiar general and curricular topics by using contextual clues
- **2Rd1** Understand, with support, some specific information and detail in very short, simple texts on a limited range of general and curricular topics
- **2Rm1** Understand the meaning of very short, simple texts on familiar general and curricular topics by rereading them
- **2Rd2** Understand the meaning of simple short sentences on familiar general and curricular topics
- **2Ug15** Use, with more infrequent support, a simple picture dictionary
- **2Wa1** Plan, write and check, with support, short sentences on familiar topics
- **2Ug14** Spell a growing number of familiar high-frequency words accurately during guided writing activities
- **2Wo2** Include a full stop and question mark during guided writing of short, familiar sentences
- **2Ug1** Use singular nouns, plural nouns – including some common irregular plural forms – and uncountable nouns, genitive 's/s' to name and label things
- **2Ug2** Use numbers 1–50 to count
- **2Ug3** Use adjectives, including possessive adjectives, on familiar topics to give personal information and describe things
- **2Ut1** Use determiners *a, the, some, any, this, these, that* to refer to familiar objects
- **2Ut2** Use *who, what, where, how many* to ask questions on familiar topics
- **2Ut3** Use impersonal *you* in the question: *How do you spell that?*
- **2Uf2** Use common simple present forms, including short answer forms and contractions, to give personal information
- **2Uf3** Use common past simple forms [regular and irregular] to describe actions and narrate simple events including short answer forms and contractions
- **2Ut6** Use *there is/are* to make short statements and descriptions
- **2Uf6** Use *Have you [ever] been?* to talk about experiences
- **2Ug5** Use adverbs of time and place *now, today, over, there* to indicate when and where
- **2Ug6** Use common *–ly* adverbs to describe actions
  2Ug7 Use the adverb *too* to add information
- **2Uf7** Use *can* to make requests and ask permission and use appropriate responses *here you are, OK*
- **2Uf8** Use *must* to express obligation
- **2Uf9** Use *have + object + infinitive* to talk about obligations
- **2Uf10** Use *will* to talk about future intention
- **2Ug8** Use *What/How about* + noun/*-ing* to make suggestions
- **2Ug9** Use prepositions of location, position and direction: *at, behind, between, in, in front of, near, next to, on, to* on personal and familiar topics
- **2Ug10** Use prepositions of time: *on, in, at,* to talk about days and times on personal and familiar topics
- **2Ug11** Use *with* to indicate accompaniment and instrument and *for* to indicate recipient on personal and familiar topics
- **2Ld5** Understand an increasing range of short supported questions on general and curricular topics

- **2Lm1** Understand the main points of short, supported talk on an increasing range of general and curricular topics
- **2Ld1** Understand some specific information and detail of short, supported talk on an increasing range of general and curricular topics
- **2Ld2** Use contextual clues to predict content and meaning in short supported talk on an increasing range of general and curricular topics
- **2Lg1** Understand short supported narratives on an increasing range of general and curricular topics
- **2Lg2** Identify initial, middle and final phonemes and blends
- **2S1** Make basic statements which provide personal information on a limited range of general topics
- **2S3** Describe basic present and past actions on a limited range of general and curricular topics
- **2S4** Use basic vocabulary for a limited range of general and curricular topics
- **2S5** Give short, basic descriptions of people and objects
- **2S6** Contribute a growing range of suitable words, phrases, and sentences during short pair, group and whole class exchanges
- **2S7** Take turns when speaking with others in a growing range of short, basic exchanges
- **2S8** Relate very short, basic stories and events on a limited range of general and curricular topics

Language patterns

Grammar summary for teachers:

Verb 'must': This is a modal or auxiliary verb. It expresses a firm obligation or necessity. It only exists in the simple present (*must*) and present perfect forms (*must have*). The verb does have a negative form (*must not/mustn't, must not have/mustn't have*).

Unit A What's that building?

Resources and materials

- Student's Book p. 52
- Workbook pp. 129–133
- Audio files: Audio 51
- Photocopiable Masters (PCMs) PCM 2; PCM 24; PCM 25
- Pictures of buildings in cities
- Prompt cards about buildings in cities and towns
- Picture dictionaries (one per group or per learner)
- Internet (to access Google Earth or something similar)

Key vocabulary

shop, supermarket, shopping, mall, hospital, library, garage, station, bus stop, building, bank, office, restaurant, post office, internet café, stadium, museum, harbour (and any other building that is important in your community)

Lead-in ideas

- If you have access to the internet, show the class what your city (or a city near to where you live) looks like from above. Use a programme such as Google Earth, which allows you look at individual buildings in a town or city. Ask learners to try and identify buildings and make simple sentences. (*That's the stadium. The shopping mall is over there.*)
- Take the class for a walk around town and identify the buildings that you see. You could take the class to a museum, for example, and talk about the buildings that you see on the way there. This could link with activities that the class are doing in social sciences.

Script for the lesson

Introducing vocabulary

Revise familiar vocabulary and teach new vocabulary by using pictures or by visiting or viewing real places in your own community. Focus on buildings that are important in your own community. For example, there may be an important memorial building or sports stadium in your area.

Sounds

Learners should use their knowledge of phonemes to start recognising and pronouncing new words. Help learners to break longer words or compound words into sections in order to read and understand them. Don't expect learners to be able to spell these long words at this stage.

Introducing structures

Revise the following structures in this unit in conversations and discussions about buildings:

Have you ever been to __________?

How do you get to ______________?

Where is _______________? It's over there.

Genitive (possessive *'s*).

Previous knowledge

Learners should know the names of some buildings from Stage 1. They may also know names in their first language. Some names may be similar in different languages, but pronounced differently (examples: *restaurant/ristorante, bank/banque/banco/banca*).

Possible areas of difficulty

Simple maps are used in this unit to encourage learners to talk about buildings and to use prepositions. Some learners may still find it difficult to interpret and even draw simple maps. Focus on the language and not the drawing skills.

Activities

Select from these activities depending on the level of challenge needed for different learners, interest levels and what you have time to include. Supplement these with additional activities of your own and/or digital activities from the online resource.

1. Use the pictures you have collected to talk about buildings in a town or city. Write words up on the board as you talk, or make prompt cards. Then let learners read the words on the board and match them to the pictures. Alternatively, place the prompt cards face down on a table. Let learners choose a card, read the name aloud and match the card with a picture.

2. If learners have picture dictionaries, tell them to look for a page about towns or cities. (Write *town* and *city* on the board.) Let them work in pairs and read the names of all the buildings. Then let them make a list of the names of buildings they have found. (They could do this in alphabetical order, which will reinforce the idea of how a dictionary works.)

3. Learners open their Workbooks and look at activities 1 and 2. Ask them to name the buildings that they know. Then let them work alone to read the names of the buildings and copy the correct name under each building.

4. Revise prepositions of location, position and direction (*at, behind, between, in, in front of, near, next to, on, to*). You can do this with classroom objects.

5. Give learners copies of **PCM 24** which is a simple map of a town. Learners work in pairs and practise finding places on the map and giving each other directions. For example:

Where's the harbour?

It's over there, near the ____________.

How do you get to the funfair?

You go up this road. It's next to the ______________.

6. Learners find page 52 of the Student's Book, *What's that building?*

Talk about the buildings in the photographs with the whole class. Ask them to name the buildings if they can and say what people do in the buildings. Make sure learners know the words *bank, office, restaurant* and *post office.*

Learners work in pairs, asking and answering questions about the photographs:

What's that building?

It's a _______________. *It's where you* ______________________. *It's for* ____________.

7. Give each learner a copy of **PCM 25**. Learners listen to sentences and tick the picture that matches the sentence you say. Describe one of the buildings in each pair of pictures. For example:

1. *The cars are parked in front of the supermarket.* OR *The cars are parked behind the supermarket.*
2. *The library is next to the shop.* OR *The library is next to the school.*
3. *There is a big ship in the harbour.* OR *There is a big ship sailing into the harbour.*
4. *The bus stopped at the bus stop.* OR *The bus stopped near the school.*
5. *The man is walking to the bank to get some money.* OR *The man is getting some money inside the bank.*
6. *The menu is between the two restaurant windows.* OR *The menu is on the restaurant window.*

8. Learners work in groups. Tell them that they are going to make up names for a restaurant. Each group must think of five names. They need to write the names on a sheet of paper. The names must have an *'s* in them. The names can include the names of people and foods. For example:

Jo's restaurant

Lee's chicken

The class will then vote for the name that they like the best. Learners can then draw a picture of a restaurant and complete activities 3 and 4 in the Workbook. They need to follow the instructions.

9. Teach learners a song about a famous bridge in London (**Audio 51**). Explain that the song is about fixing a bridge. Wood, clay, bricks, mortar, iron and steel are all materials that are used for building. Silver and gold are not usually used for building because they are too expensive. They are used for making jewellery.

10. Learners look at page 52 of the Student's Book again and then complete activities 5, 6 and 7 in the Workbook.

11. Have a discussion with the whole class. Ask them which buildings every town needs. Then choose a few of the buildings and ask questions such as: *Do we need a bank? Why? Do we need a post office? Why not?*

12. Let learners revise the names of buildings by completing the crossword puzzle in activity 8 in the Workbook. They may have to refer to activities

5, 6 and 7 in the Workbook and a completed version of **PCM 24** to complete the crossword accurately.

13. Learners write in their journals. They write about a place (building) they like to visit. Let them write freely using any words or structures that they know. Make sure learners have an opportunity to read what they have written.

14. Learners work in groups and play a game in which they mention places that they visited. Each learner adds to what the previous learner says until they can't remember the sequence of events any longer. Groups of six to eight learners work well. For example:

I went to town yesterday. I went to the museum.

I went to town yesterday. I went to the museum and the library.

I went to town yesterday. I went to the museum, the library and the harbour.

I went to town yesterday. I went to the museum, the library, the harbour and a restaurant.

And so on.

15. Tell learners a simple story about a trip to town. Give each learner a copy of **PCM 24** again or let them use the copies they have**.** Learners listen and number the pictures in the order in which the person in the story visits the places in the town. Read the story twice and then check how learners have numbered their pictures. You can insert the names of places in any order that makes sense.

You could tell the following story, for example:

Story: Raj and David go to the harbour

Listen to the story. Raj and David are in New Town. They want to visit many different places. First, they go to ______________. Then they go ______________. After that they go to ______________. Then they have lunch at the restaurant. After lunch they visit the ______________ and the ______________.

16. Learners complete activities 9, 10 and 11 in the Workbook. They draw a simple map of part of a town. They should draw at least five buildings on the map. Then they imagine that they walked around the town. They draw a route through the town and complete a few sentences about where they walked in the town.

Wrap-up plenary

Talk about buildings of cultural heritage in a town in your country. Help learners to name and describe buildings in the country that are culturally important. Ask them if they have been to visit them. Let them try and describe what they look like in very simple ways.

Quick check

Let learners make up Bingo sheets with the names of places. Write the names of all the buildings you have discussed in this unit on the board for learners to choose from. Give learners copies of **PCM 2** and play 'Bingo' in the usual way.

Unit B Fun in the city

Resources and materials

- Student's Book pp. 53–55
- Workbook pp. 134–138
- Audio files: Audio 52; Audio 53; Audio 54
- Photocopiable Master (PCM) PCM 26
- Pictures of funfairs or posters advertising funfairs

Key vocabulary

fun, funfair, tall, thin, small, fat, around, up, down, out, in, entrance, exit, mirror, swing, ride, slide, big wheel (Ferris wheel), bumper car, roller coaster, hall of mirrors, merry-go-round, swing, game

Lead-in ideas

Teach the class a song about a funfair or about the people who sell things at funfairs. You can adapt well-known songs to the vocabulary you would like to teach. For example: *The Bumper Cars* (**Audio 52**) and *Here We Go Round on the Ferris Wheel* (**Audio 53**).

Script for the lesson

Introducing vocabulary

Use pictures and the story in the Student's Book to teach the names of some of the attractions that are common at funfairs, for example: *bumper cars, big wheel (Ferris wheel), roller coaster, hall of mirrors, merry-go-round, swings, games, rides.*

Sounds

The story in the Student's Book has rhyming sentences. Use the story to revise rimes such as '-out', '-all', '-at', '-air' and let learners build words with them.

Introducing structures

There are no new structures in this unit, but learners will continue to recognise and use the simple present and simple past tenses. They will also use adjectives in different types of sentences.

Previous knowledge

Learners should recognise some common verbs in the present and past simple tense, as well as some adjectives.

Possible areas of difficulty

Some learners may struggle to position adjectives correctly in a sentence. Cut up sentence strips and have learners practise arranging the words into the correct order before they do activities 2 and 3 in the Workbook. Example sentences for strips:

She saw a big wheel.

There was a fat girl in the mirror.

I won a fluffy toy.

He got a small bear.

They ate sour sweets.

Activities

Select from these activities depending on the level of challenge needed for different learners, interest levels and what you have time to include. Supplement these with additional activities of your own and/or digital activities from the online resource.

▲ **1.** Ask learners if they have ever been to a funfair. Show learners some pictures of funfairs. You can use your own pictures or the pictures in activity 4 in the Workbook. Let learners suggest the names that they know for the various rides, machines and activities. Then teach some key words from the key vocabulary list. Ask learners what they enjoy at the funfair, if they do go.

▲ **2.** Learners find the story *Rebecca at the Funfair* on pages 53–55 of the Student's Book. Read the title and give learners time to look at the pictures. Read the words in the pictures (*Hall of mirrors*, etc.). Discuss what these places are. Then read the whole story while learners follow the pictures in their books. Let them read the story again in pairs or alone. Many of the words should be familiar.

Learners then complete **PCM 26** to reinforce the key vocabulary in the story before they do activity 1 in the Workbook. Have learners keep the pictures and labels on **PCM 26** so they can play a game with them later.

▲ **3.** Revise adjectives with the class, by referring to the story *Rebecca at the Funfair.* Ask: *How did Rebecca look in the hall of mirrors?* Find four words in the story that describe how she looked (*thin, fat, tall, small*). Then ask them to find a word that describes how Rebecca felt on the roller coaster in picture 8 (*green*). Explain that this means that she was feeling sick. Then ask if learners can think of a word to describe how Rebecca felt in pictures 4 and 12 (*unhappy, scared, happy*).

Learners can then complete activities 2 and 3 in the Workbook.

▲ **4.** Learners work in small groups and pretend they are at a funfair. They role-play what they would say. You could read or play the example, *At the Funfair* (**Audio 54**) first.

▲ **5.** Revise numbers and shapes. Let learners look at the picture of the funfair in activity 4 in the Workbook.

- Let them count the number of people on the roller coaster and at the funfair.
- Let them find these shapes in the picture (rectangle, circle, triangle). Let them count the number of each shape they can find.
- Let them count black and white triangles.
- Learners can also work in pairs and ask each other questions. For example: *How many triangles are there on top of the hall of mirrors?*

▲ **6.** Write some simple questions and sentences on the board, *without* question marks and full stops and capital letters. For example:

rebecca went to the funfair

where did rebecca go

what did she enjoy

she felt sick on the roller coaster

Ask learners what is wrong with the sentences. Ask: *What did I forget?* Prompt learners to point out that the sentences and names should have capital letters. Make the changes on the board.

Then read the sentences and questions aloud, paying careful attention to the intonation differences. Ask the class where you should put a full stop (.) and where you should put a question mark (?).

Remove the capital letters and let the class copy the sentences into their exercise books and insert the correct punctuation.

▲ **7.** Have learners play a memory game with the pictures and the words on **PCM 26**. Let them play the game in pairs. They can combine their packs of word and picture cards to make the game more challenging.

How to play

Learners shuffle the cards and lay them face down on their desk.

The youngest player goes first.

Players take turns turning over a picture card and a label. They read the label aloud and see if it matches the picture.

If the picture matches the label, the player keeps the two cards.

The player's turn continues until they do not make a match.

If the two cards do not match, the player turns them back over and it is the next player's turn.

Players need to try to remember where the cards are.

The winner is the player with the most cards once all the cards have been turned over.

8. Learners find the story *Rebecca at the Funfair* on pages 53–55 of the Student's Book. They read the story again by themselves. Then they complete activity 4 in the Workbook.

9. The story *Rebecca at the Funfair* has rhyming sentences. Use the story to revise rimes such as *'-out', '-all', '-at', '-air'* and let learners build words with them. For example, ask the class to find words in the story that rhyme with these words:
that (fat, cat) *shout (out)*
tall (small, all) *bear (fair)*

Then make word spiders with these rhymes so that learners can build words with them. The class can spell the words and say them aloud. Learners can then write the words as they complete activities 5 and 6 in the Workbook.

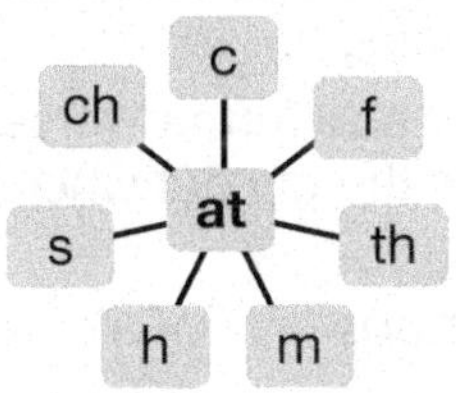

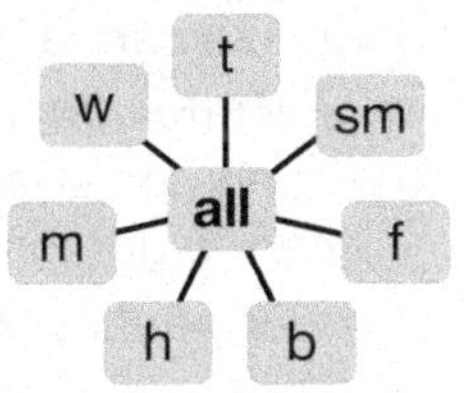

10. Give learners some oral mathematics problems to solve, to revise numbers. Use some of the vocabulary from this unit. For example:
- *How long did Rebecca spend on the roller coaster? She bought a ticket. That took 10 minutes. Then she went on the ride. That took 5 minutes.*
- *Rebecca and her parents went to the funfair at 1 o'clock. They left at half past four. How long were they at the funfair?*

11. Have a short discussion with the class about safety at a funfair. Let them suggest a list of rules. For example:
- *Don't run near the machines.*
- *Don't throw things.*
- *Put your seatbelt on.*

12. Learners read the story *Rebecca at the Funfair* on pages 53–55 of the Student's Book and then complete the comprehension questions in activities 7, 8 and 9 in the Workbook. Discuss the meaning of the word *strange* before learners do the activity.

13. Learners write in their journals. They can imagine that they are Rebecca and they have been to the funfair, or they can write about their own experiences. They should say what they did and how they felt. Encourage them to share what they have written afterwards.

14. **Link to drama*. Learners can work in groups and create a short play about a family that goes to the funfair. They can use ideas from this unit. Give them some sentence frames to use:

Can I go on the ____________?

Let's go to the ____________ first.

I don't want to ____________.

I want to ____________ and I want to ____________.

So do I.

Wrap-up plenary

Let learners talk about what they enjoy and don't enjoy about funfairs.

Quick check

1. Let learners sing one of the songs from the beginning of the unit and change the words.
2. Learners work in groups and make up riddles about different rides and games at a funfair. For example: *This looks like a snake. You go up and down on it. You go fast. It makes me feel green.* (A roller coaster)

Unit C Getting about

Resources and materials

- Student's Book p. 56
- Workbook pp. 139–142
- Audio files: Audio 55; Audio 56; Audio 57
- Photocopiable Master (PCM) PCM 27
- Pictures of different types of transport (buses, trains, trucks, boats, metro, horses, cars, etc.)
- Two sets of prompt cards with names of types of transport to play a game
- A simple bus, metro or train timetable
- Paper to make posters (one sheet per pair)

Key vocabulary

bus, train, truck, boat, metro, horse, car, cart, plane, scooter, bike (and any other common forms of transport)

underground, tunnel, bridge

quickly, slowly

Lead-in ideas

Teach learners a song about moving around. For example: *Row, Row, Row Your Boat* (**Audio 55**).

Script for the lesson

Introducing vocabulary

Revise and teach the names of the main types of transport used in the community where you live and in other places.

Sounds

Learners should use their knowledge of phonemes to start recognising and pronouncing new words. Help learners to break longer words or compound words into sections, in order to read and understand them. Don't expect learners to be able to spell these long words at this stage.

Introducing structures

You can revise simple sentences in the present and past tense with adjectives and adverbs in this unit.

Previous knowledge

Learners should recognise, and be able to use, some simple adjectives already.

Possible areas of difficulty

Some learners may struggle to understand the train timetable on **PCM 27** as they have not learned these real methods of working with time formally yet. Let these learners work together with a learner who does understand it.

Activities

Select from these activities depending on the level of challenge needed for different learners, interest levels and what you have time to include. Supplement these with additional activities of your own and/or digital activities from the online resource.

▲ **1.** Use a poster or make a display of pictures of different types of transport. Label the pictures. Let the class play 'I spy' referring to the pictures or poster.

▲ **2.** If learners have picture dictionaries, tell them to look for a page about transport. (Write: *transport, trains, planes, boats, etc.* on the board.) Let them work in pairs and read the names of all the types of transport they can find. Then let them make a list the names of transport they have found. (They could do this in alphabetical order, which will reinforce the idea of how a dictionary works.)

▲ **3.** Learners complete activity 1 in the Workbook. They can refer to their picture dictionary or the pictures on display to spell the transport names correctly.

▲ **4.** Teach learners to use simple adjectives and adverbs to describe and compare the actions of different types of transport.

Write these sentences on the board and let learners complete them.

A ______________ is quick.

A ______________ is slow.

Then write these frames on the board:

A train moves ______________.

A plane moves ______________.

Show the class how we can add *–ly* to the words *quick* and *slow* to complete the sentences. These words describe the ways the train and the plane move. They are adverbs.

Learners complete activities 2 and 3 in the Workbook. Discuss the vocabulary before learners begin.

▲ **5.** Play the song *The Boy Went Over the Mountain* (**Audio 56**). Then ask learners to suggest how the boy got over the mountain (*by road, on foot, in a helicopter, in a truck*, etc.) and over the river (*in a boat, in a canoe, by swimming*, etc.).

Then let the class help you add further verses to the song and suggest how the girl got where she wanted to go, for example:

The girl went over the treetops (*by hot air balloon, by plane*).

The girl went down through the tunnel (*by train, by car, by truck*).

▲ **6.** **Link to art*. Let the class paint a picture of a train or boat and write a sentence about it. Alternatively let them build a small model of a train in clay or wire or with recycled materials.

● **7.** Learners find the non-fiction text *Under your feet* on page 56 of the Student's Book. Discuss the photographs first and write words such as *train, tunnel, ticket, passengers* and *subway* on the board. If you live in a city where there is a subway system, discuss this with the class. Ask questions such as *Where does it go? How much does it cost?*

Then read the text with groups of learners.

● **8.** Revise singular and plural nouns. Let learners find the plural forms of words in the text *Under your feet.* Make a table like this on the board.

singular	**plural**
foot	
city	
bus	
train	
tunnel	

Then make oral sentences with both forms of the nouns to practise using the correct form of the verb with each in the present tense. For example, say:

This is my foot.

These are my feet.

London is a big city.

Paris and Tokyo are big cities.

Learners can complete activities 4 and 5 in the Workbook.

9. Learners listen to a short talk about the subway network in London (**Audio 57**). Ask a few questions afterwards to check that they have understood the main ideas. You could ask, for example:

   Who uses the underground trains in London?

   Why do they need to use these trains?

   What is the other name for the London Underground?

   Can you get on a Tube on Tuesdays?

   Can you get on a Tube at night?

10. Use one of the timetables you have collected. Choose a simple one. Enlarge it or copy it on the board. Then help learners to read the timetable. Ask questions such as: *When can you get a [bus/train] to [name of place]? How long does it take? If you want to get to [name of place] before [time], which [bus/train] must you take?*

    Learners can then work through **PCM 27**. Make sure that they understand the information and questions before they start. (Again, note that these are realistic times for a timetable and you may need to pair learners up with other learners who know how to read and interpret timetables.)

11. Teach the class to use *must* to express obligation. Talk about the things we must do when we move around a town or city using different types of transport.

    Write some examples on the board, for example:

    You must buy a ticket.

    You must put on a seatbelt.

    You must wear a helmet.

    Then let learners work in pairs and tell each other what to do while travelling. Teach a short conversation, for example:

    A: *I want to go on the ____________ [train/bus/bike].*

    B: *OK. You must ____________ [buy a ticket/ask your mother].*

    A: *Can I get on any ____________?*

    B: *No. You must ____________ [look at the timetable/ask that man].*

12. Learners read the non-fiction text *Under your feet* on page 56 of the Student's Book again before they complete activities 6, 7 and 8 in the Workbook.

13. Talk about the quickest way of moving about the place where you live. Then ask: *What is a healthy way to move around? What is a safe way to move around?* Let learners share their ideas and thoughts in their first language. Then translate and write a few simple sentences in English to sum up your discussion.

14. Tell learners that they are going to give a short talk on different types of trains. They can work in pairs.
    - First they need to find some pictures of different trains, for example, an old train, a subway train, a high-speed train, a steam train.
    - Then they need to find out something interesting about the trains (for example: when it was made, how fast it can go, how many people can go in the train).
    - Then each pair can prepare their talk. They can make a poster to show the trains and then talk about the poster.
    - Each pair gives their talk to the class. They can use simple sentences, such as: *This is an old train. This is a fast train. That is a steam train. They burn coal in the train.*
    - Encourage the class to respond to the talk and ask questions about the pictures. For example: *Why do they burn coal in that train? Does this train also use coal?*

15. Learners write a journal entry about a trip on a train, boat or bicycle. Let them write freely and share their stories afterwards if they want to.

Wrap-up plenary

Let learners sing the song *Row, Row, Row Your Boat* again. Then help them to change the words to sing about other forms of transport.

Quick check

Use the two sets of prompt cards with names of types of transport to play a game. Learners can play in small groups. They place the cards face downwards and then pick up two cards at a time, attempting to match the words on the cards. If a learner finds a matching pair, he or she has another turn. The learner with the most matching pairs wins the game.

Assessment

You can complete an oral assessment of the work done in this topic by asking learners to talk about the things they must do when using a certain form of transport. Examples:

What must you do when you go in a car?

I must put my seatbelt on.

I must sit in the back.

I mustn't disturb the driver.

Learners can also complete Progress check activities 1, 2 and 3 in the Workbook as a simple assessment.

You could allocate marks for these activities and record these as part of continuous assessment.

Topic 9 Music

Overview

In this topic, the focus is on sharing information about music and musical instruments, building on familiar vocabulary and structures to build confidence and then introducing new vocabulary to develop language skills.

There are opportunities to integrate activities with other curricula such as art, science, mathematics and drama.

Units in this topic

Unit A: Sounds

Unit B: Can you play…?

Unit C: Let's make music

Teaching focus

- **2Rg1** Recognise, identify and sound, with support, a limited range of language as text
- **2Rg2** Begin to read, with support, very short simple fiction and non-fiction texts with confidence and enjoyment
- **2Rm2** Understand the main points of very short, simple texts on some familiar general and curricular topics by using contextual clues
- **2Rd1** Understand, with support, some specific information and detail in very short, simple texts on a limited range of general and curricular topics
- **2Rm1** Understand the meaning of very short, simple texts on familiar general and curricular topics by rereading them
- **2Rd2** Understand the meaning of simple short sentences on familiar general and curricular topics
- **2Ug15** Use, with more infrequent support, a simple picture dictionary
- **2Wa1** Plan, write and check, with support, short sentences on familiar topics
- **2Wo1** Link with support words or phrases using basic coordinating connectors
- **2Ug14** Spell a growing number of familiar high-frequency words accurately during guided writing activities
- **2Wo2** Include a full stop and question mark during guided writing of short, familiar sentences
- **2Ug1** Use singular nouns, plural nouns – including some common irregular plural forms – and uncountable nouns, genitive 's/s' to name and label things
- **2Ug3** Use adjectives, including possessive adjectives, on familiar topics to give personal information and describe things
- **2Ut1** Use determiners *a, the, some, any, this, these, that* to refer to familiar objects
- **2Ut5** Use personal subject and object pronouns, including possessive pronouns *mine, yours* to give basic personal information and describe things
- **2Uf2** Use common simple present forms, including short answer forms and contractions, to give personal information
- **2Uf3** Use common past simple forms [regular and irregular] to describe actions and narrate simple events including short answer forms and contractions
- **2U10** Use common present continuous forms, including short answers and contractions, to talk about what is happening now on personal and familiar topics
- **2Ug4** Use *–ing* forms *swimming, spelling* as nouns to describe familiar and classroom activities
- **2Ut6** Use *there is/are* to make short statements and descriptions
- **2Uf6** Use *Have you [ever] been?* to talk about experiences
- **2Uf7** Use *can* to make requests and ask permission and use appropriate responses *here you are, OK*
- **2Uf8** Use *must* to express obligation
- **2Uf9** Use *have + object + infinitive* to talk about obligations
- **2Uf10** Use *will* to talk about future intention
- **2Ug8** Use *What/How about* + noun/*-ing* to make suggestions
- **2Ut8** Use conjunctions *and, or, but* to link words and phrases
- **2Uf4** Use *when* clauses to describe simple present and past actions on personal and familiar topics
- **2Ut7** Use *so do I* to give short answers
- **2Ld5** Understand an increasing range of short supported questions on general and curricular topics
- **2Lm1** Understand the main points of short, supported talk on an increasing range of general and curricular topics

- **2Ld1** Understand some specific information and detail of short, supported talk on an increasing range of general and curricular topics
- **2Lg1** Understand short supported narratives on an increasing range of general and curricular topics
- **2Lg2** Identify initial, middle and final phonemes and blends
- **2S1** Make basic statements which provide personal information on a limited range of general topics
- **2S3** Describe basic present and past actions on a limited range of general and curricular topics
- **2S4** Use basic vocabulary for a limited range of general and curricular topics
- **2S5** Give short, basic descriptions of people and objects
- **2S6** Contribute a growing range of suitable words, phrases, and sentences during short pair, group and whole class exchanges
- **2S7** Take turns when speaking with others in a growing range of short, basic exchanges
- **2S8** Relate very short, basic stories and events on a limited range of general and curricular topics

Language patterns

Grammar summary for teachers:

There are no new structures to be taught in this topic. Instead, structures that have already been introduced will be revised and practised.

Unit A Sounds

Resources and materials

- Student's Book pp. 57–60
- Workbook pp. 145–149
- Audio files: Audio 58
- Photocopiable Master (PCM) PCM 28
- Instruments and objects that make different sounds (for example, bells, recorders, drums, tin cans, bottles)
- Prompt cards with the names of objects and musical instruments

Key vocabulary

sound, ear, around, bell, drum, drumstick, string, guitar, recorder, blow, pluck, hear, hurt, whisper, roar, squeak, miaow, howl, buzz, shout, voice, soft, loud

Lead-in ideas

- Let learners close their eyes for a minute and listen to all the sounds they can hear. Let them open their eyes and talk about what they heard in their first language. Then help them identify sounds in English. Write some words on the board as you talk (for example: *bells, cars, talking*).
- Use some of the instruments and objects you have collected and make sounds with them. Let learners name the objects and instruments if they can and imitate the sounds.

Script for the lesson

Introducing vocabulary

Introduce new vocabulary within the context of the texts in the Student's Book.

Sounds

There are many onomatopoeic words in this unit (words that echo the sounds they describe) which are useful for practising English sounds in a fun way.

Introducing structures

Structures such as the simple present and past tense and the present continuous tense can be revised in this unit, as they are used in the reading texts and other activities. Introduce the structure *have + object + infinitive* to express obligation. Use this structure in questions and simple conversations. You can also revise conjunctions with *and,* the impersonal *you* and determiners (*some*).

Previous knowledge

Learners should be familiar with some of the vocabulary and the structures used in the activities in this unit.

Possible areas of difficulty

Some learners may struggle to join two sentences with *and*. Write sentences on strips and cut them up into words. Jumble the words and remove *and*. Let learners first arrange the words into two sentences and read the sentences. Then add *and* to the words and ask the learner to rearrange the words to make one sentence. Discuss which words are left out of the new sentence (the repetitive words). Examples:

The drums are loud The bells are loud and (The drums and bells are loud.)

The recorder is noisy The alarm is noisy and (The recorder and alarm are noisy.)

You get big drums You get small drums and (You get big and small drums.)

Activities

Select from these activities depending on the level of challenge needed for different learners, interest levels and what you have time to include. Supplement these with additional activities of your own and/or digital activities from the online resource.

1. Ask learners about the sounds that animals such as cows and hens make. Let them make the sounds. Then sing a familiar song with sound effects, for example, *Old MacDonald Had a Farm.*

2. Learners find the non-fiction text *Sounds* on pages 57–59 of the Student's Book. Start by letting them use their knowledge of phonemes to read all the sound words in the pictures (*buzz, bang, boom*, and so on). Then let them talk about the pictures, naming as many of the instruments as they can. Then read the text and let the class listen and follow as you read.

   Then ask a few questions such as: *What sound does a bell make? What goes bzzz?*

3. Learners read *Sounds* again and then complete activities 1 and 2 in the Workbook.

4. Revise adjectives with the class. For example, let learners look at picture 4 on page 57 of the Student's Book. Ask them to find two words (adjectives) that describe the bells (*little, big*). Then look at picture 6 and ask them to find two words that describe the drums (*big, small*). Finally, look at picture 9 and ask them to find two words that describe sounds (*loud, soft*). Write the adjectives on the board. Explain that *little* and *small* have the same meaning.

   Learners can then work in pairs and make sentences with each of the adjectives.

5. Learners find the poem *Sounds like me* on page 60 in the Student's Book. Read the poem aloud to the class with as much expression as possible.

   Poem: Sounds like me

   Roar like a lion,
   Squeak like a mouse.
   Miaow like a cat
   Locked out of the house.
   Howl like a wolf,
   Buzz like a bee.
   Then shout, with your own voice,
   Hello! This is me!

   Check that learners understand the poem. Read it again and let them try and read along with you.

6. Look at the vowel digraphs and rhyming words in the poem *Sounds like me*, in words such as *mouse, house, shout, howl, own.*

   Ask the class if there are words that rhyme in the poem. Let them identify: *mouse/house, bee/me.*

   Then write the words *mouse, house, shout, howl, own* on the board. Underline the vowel digraphs. Ask: *Which words sound the same? Which sounds are spelled in the same way?*

   Then remove the vowels from each word and let learners complete the words.

7. Let learners work in groups. This may be noisy! Give each group a musical instrument and/or a set of four or five different objects (tin cans, plastic balls, pencils, etc.)

   The groups use different objects to make sounds. Let them experiment and then report back to the class. They must be able to answer these two questions about each object:

   - *What sound does this make?* Prompt the groups to make the sounds and to describe them using adjectives like *loud* and *soft*.
   - *What do you have to do to make the sound?* Prompt learners to use verbs like *tap, blow, hit* and *pluck* to describe how they made the sounds. For example: *You have to blow into the flute to make a sound*.

8. Give each learner a copy of **PCM 28**. This is a picture dictionary page about musical instruments. Learners use the information on this page to complete the activities 3 and 4 in the Workbook.

9. Let learners listen to the song *Let's Play Music* (**Audio 58**) and learn it.

10. Learners find the non-fiction text *Sounds* on pages 57–59 of the Student's Book. Let them read the text in pairs and ask each other questions about it.

11. Write these sentences on the board:

    There are little bells. There are big bells.

    Some drums are big. Some drums are small.

    Some sounds are soft. Some sounds are loud.

    Ask learners to suggest what word we can use to join each pair of sentences (*and*). Read the sentences joined together with the word *and.*

    Then show the class how you add *and,* changing the punctuation and reducing the repeated information, for example: *There are little bells and big bells. Some drums are big and some are small.*

    Learners then complete activities 5 and 6 in the Workbook.

12. Learners find the poem *Sounds like me* on page 60 in the Student's Book. Let them learn the poem and recite it in groups of three. For example: One learner says line 1, the next learner line 2 and the third learner lines 3 and 4.

13. Learners find the poem *My Big Band* on page 60 in the Student's Book. Read the poem aloud with as much expression as possible so that learners enjoy listening to the poem.

    Poem: My Big Band

    "Ting" went the triangle.
    "Foo" went the flute.
    "Whee" went the whistle.
    The horn went "Toot".
    "Crash" went the cymbal.

"Boom" went the drum.
"Ta-ra" went the trumpet.
"Quiet!" yelled Mum.

Then read or play it again and let learners join in as they can.

Note that learners can re-visit this poem in the next unit.

14. Tell learners that they are going to plan, write and edit a piece of writing about music. Show them how this works by doing an example with the whole class.

PLAN

Let them choose a musical instrument that interests them. They can look in the Student's Book or on the dictionary page, or they can choose another instrument. Then they make a word spider with words they can use to describe the instrument. For example:

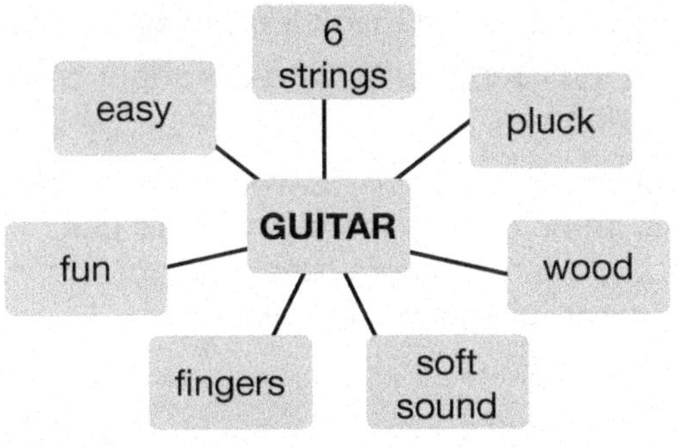

WRITE

Then make sentences using the words in the word spider. Do this orally with the class. (Example: *A guitar has six strings.*)

EDIT

Write a sentence using words from the spider diagram. Misspell one word and leave out the punctuation. Ask the class to tell you what is wrong with the sentence and let them correct it. Explain that this is what editing means.

Learners complete activities 7 and 8 in the Workbook.

15. Learners reread the non-fiction text *Sounds* on pages 57–59 of the Student's Book by themselves and then complete activities 9, 10 and 11 in the Workbook.

16. Learners work in groups and write their own poems about sounds. Give them a template like this:

_______________ *went the* _______________
_______________ *went the* _______________
_______________ *went the* _______________
_______________ *went the* _______________

They don't need to worry about making this rhyme. Encourage them to read their poems aloud afterwards.

17. Talk to the class about loud noise and soft noise.

Ask: *Which music do you like – loud or soft music? Which sounds do you like: loud or soft noises? Why? Do you like to hear noise all the time? Why is it good to have no sounds sometimes?*

Wrap-up plenary

Let the class recite a poem or sing one of the songs they have learned, with sound effects.

Quick check

1. Hold up a prompt card with the name of an instrument or object and ask learners: *What sound does this make? What do you do to make the sound?*
2. Write a few familiar sentences from the unit on the board but jumble the word order. Ask learners to say the sentences in the correct word order.

Unit B Can you play...?

Resources and materials

- Student's Book pp. 60–61
- Workbook pp. 150–153
- Audio file: Audio 59
- Photocopiable Masters (PCMs) PCM 28; PCM 29
- Instruments and objects that make different sounds (for example, bells, recorders, drums, tin cans, bottles)
- Prompt cards with the names of objects and musical instruments
- Blank A4 sheets of paper

Key vocabulary

instrument, metal, steelpan, festival, violin, bow, string, orchestra, xylophone, wood, hammer, didgeridoo, blow, pipe, difficult, musician

Lead-in ideas

- Invite someone in the school to come and play a musical instrument for the class. Let them talk about the instrument, how they play it and why they play it. Encourage the class to ask questions. If you have learners in the class who are accomplished, you could get them to play for the class instead.
- Invite learners to mime playing a musical instrument. The class must guess what they are playing.

Script for the lesson

Introducing vocabulary

Introduce new vocabulary within the context of the texts in the Student's Book.

Sounds

Revise initial, middle and end phonemes according to the needs of your class, but within the context of this theme.

Introducing structures

Learners are introduced to longer sentences with prepositional phrases in this unit, with the aim of increasing their general understanding.

Previous knowledge

Most of the vocabulary used in this unit has already been introduced.

Possible areas of difficulty

Although learners are introduced to prepositional phrases, they may struggle to use them. They are not expected to use them when writing their own sentences at this stage.

Activities

Select from these activities depending on the level of challenge needed for different learners, interest levels and what you have time to include. Supplement these with additional activities of your own and/or digital activities from the online resource.

▲ **1.** Talk to the class and find out which musical instruments they like most and which they can play. Teach the word *musician*. You can also invite a few learners to perform for the class if they are comfortable doing so.

▲ **2.** Learners find the poem *My Big Band* on page 60 in the Student's Book (this poem is from the previous unit). Teach them to recite it.

▲ **3.** Let learners find the non-fiction text *All sorts of music* on page 61 in the Student's Book. Give them time to look at the photographs and say what they can about them. Ask questions such as: *Who is playing? What are they playing? What sounds do the instruments make?*

Ask learners to choose two pictures that they like best. Read and discuss the text under these two pictures.

▲ **4.** Learners complete activities 1, 2 and 3 in the Workbook.

▲ **5.** Let learners play 'I spy'. They use pages 57–61 of the Student's Book as a reference.

▲ **6.** Write a few simple sentences on the board. Leave one word out. Ask learners to read the sentences and suggest a word to complete the sentence. You can choose to leave out nouns or verbs. For example:

A violin ______________ *a musical instrument.*
It ______________ *strings. You play with a* ______________.

Learners can then complete activity 4 in their Workbooks.

▲ **7.** Give learners copies of **PCM 29**. They read and follow the instructions to make a simple drum. It is important to stretch the plastic tightly over the opening or else they won't hear any sound.

● **8.** Learners read the text *All sorts of music* on page 61 in the Student's Book in pairs. They can ask and answer questions about the texts.

● **9.** Learners describe how to play different musical instruments. Write this list of verbs on the board. Let them make sentences with each verb.

beat (You need to beat or hit a drum.)

play (You play a violin.)

hit (You need to hit the strips in a xylophone.)

blow (You need to blow into a trumpet or a didgeridoo.)

● **10.** Teach learners a short conversation to practise using some of the vocabulary in this unit. Introduce the structure *have + object + infinitive* to express obligation. For example:

A: *How do you play a* ______________ *[violin]?*

B: *You have to* ______________ *[move a bow across the strings].*

A: *Do you have to press hard?*

B: *No, you don't.*

A: *Is it difficult?*

B: *You have to practise every day.*

A: *Oh, like dancing. I have exercises to do every day!*

● **11.** Learners listen to a short text about people who play different musical instruments (**Audio 59**). They complete activities 5, 6 and 7 in the Workbook.

■ **12.** Learners plan, write and edit a text about someone from their own country who plays a musical instrument. Help learners to do some research in the library. Alternatively, provide information about two or three musicians from your country - pictures and very short articles. You can put this information on cards.

Learners complete activities 8 and 9 in the Workbook. They choose one musician. They make a word spider with words and facts about the person. Then they draft 3–4 sentences. They check their spelling and punctuation and improve their work. Learners can do the activity in pairs or alone.

■ **13.** Have learners make cards with pictures and names of musical instruments. They fold a piece of paper in half lengthwise. Then they fold that piece of paper in half and in half again. They unfold the piece of paper and cut along the fold lines to make eight cards. They draw the musical instrument on one card and write the matching name on another card. They end up with four picture cards and four name cards. They can then use the cards to play the memory game.

14. Learners work in pairs and find out about a traditional musical instrument. They draw a picture (or bring a real instrument to class) and explain how the instrument is played. (They do not have to play the instrument themselves, the focus is on language.)

Wrap-up plenary

Let the class talk about traditional music that they enjoy. Tell them about some traditional instruments and talk about how they are played.

Quick check

1. Have learners take turns to describe a musical instrument. The other learners guess what is being described.
2. Learners can play the memory game again with the cards they made in activity 12.

Unit C Let's make music

Resources and materials

- Student's Book pp. 62–63
- Workbook pp. 154–157
- Audio files: Audio 60; Audio 61
- Photocopiable Master (PCM) PCM 30

Key vocabulary

love, music, own, drums, recorder, join, concert, watch, practise, need

Lead-in ideas

Teach learners a rhythmic song about dancing, singing and playing music. They may enjoy the traditional song, *As I Was Walking Down the Street* (**Audio 60**).

Script for the lesson

Introducing vocabulary

Introduce new vocabulary within the context of the texts in the Student's Book.

Sounds

Revise initial, middle and end phonemes according to the needs of your class, but within the context of this theme.

Introducing structures

All the structures introduced in this unit have already been introduced, except the use of *when* clauses in the simple past tense. Introduce this during discussions and practise during the wrap-up at the end of the unit.

Previous knowledge

Learners should be familiar with a mix of questions and answers in the present simple tense and familiar with verbs in the simple past tense in simple stories.

Possible areas of difficulty

Learners may struggle to complete activities 2, 3, 4 and 5 in the Workbook if you haven't revised personal subject and object pronouns as well as the genitive (possessive 's) before they do it.

Activities

Select from these activities depending on the level of challenge needed for different learners, interest levels and what you have time to include. Supplement these with additional activities of your own and/or digital activities from the online resource.

1. Play a familiar game (such as 'Bingo' or a matching game) to revise number words from 1–50.
2. Teach learners these two short conversations to revise the use of the word *can* to express ability and to ask permission and to revise pronouns. For example:

   A: *Are those your drums?*
   B: *No, they're my dad's drums.*
   A: *Can you play the drums?*
   B: *Yes, I can.*
   A: *So can I! Let's play.*
   B: *I must ask my dad.*

   B: *Dad, please can we play your drums?*
   Dad: *No, not now.*
   B: *But Dad, my friend wants to play.*
   Dad: *Can she play?*
   B: *Yes, she can.*
   Dad: *OK. You can play my drums. But I have work to do. Play softly, please!*
   B: *OK. Thanks, Dad. We won't be loud!*
3. Write some familiar irregular verbs on the board. Ask learners to read the words and then make sentences with them. For example:

   went (*We went to the concert.*)
   had (*They had a good time!*)
   were (*There were nine people in the orchestra.*)
   made (*She made a drum from an old plastic bottle.*)
   came (*They came to my party.*)

   Learners do activity 1 in the Workbook.

4. Learners find the story *Our Band* on pages 62–63 in the Student's Book.

   Let learners practise the present continuous tense as you do some pre-reading activities. Learners look at each picture in turn and answer the questions: *What are they doing? What is he/she doing? Is he/she singing? Is he/she clapping?*

   Then read the story with learners.

   Ask about the characters in the story. Ask learners to find the names. They should know that names begin with capital letters.

5. Learners complete activities 2, 3, 4 and 5 in the Workbook.

6. Learners find the story *Our Band* on pages 62–63 in the Student's Book. They reread the story in pairs and then tell the story to their partner.

7. Let learners look through the Student's Book and choose the story that they like the best. They can read it aloud to the class and give a short review of the story. They could write their reviews first. Write this frame on the board:

   Name of story:

   ____

   The story is about ______________________

   ______________________.

   I liked the story. It ______________________

   ______________________.

8. Let learners pretend that they have been in a band and had a concert. What did they enjoy? Give them some examples, using *when* clauses in the simple past tense:

   I liked it when we practised.

   I liked it when the people clapped.

   I liked it when I got a hug from my grandpa.

   Let learners make their own oral suggestions.

9. Tell learners that they are going to listen to a story and answer some questions in activities 6 and 7 in the Workbook. Play **Audio 61** and then read the story aloud as well.

10. Learners reread the story *Our Band* on pages 62–63 in the Student's Book and then complete a simple summary of the story in activities 8, 9 and 10 in the Workbook.

11. Talk about doing things in groups. Ask questions such as: *Is it fun to do things in groups, like play in a band? Or do you prefer to do things by yourself? Why?*

Wrap-up plenary

Talk about some of the activities you have done in class this year. Let learners use the structures *I enjoyed ________ing. I liked it when we ____________.*

Quick check

Have learners complete the puzzle on **PCM 30**.

Assessment

You can complete an oral assessment of the work done in this topic by asking learners to retell the story *Our Band* using pictures from the Student's Book as prompts.

Learners can also complete Progress check activities 1, 2, 3, 4 and 5 in the Workbook as a simple assessment.

You could allocate marks for these activities and record these as part of continuous assessment.

Review Activity Guidelines

There is a Review Activity on pages 127–132 of this Teacher's Guide which you can use at the end Stage 2 to monitor progress in an informal way. (Please note that there is no allocated mark scheme and it is not intended that performance in this review activity equates in any way with Cambridge grades or levels.)

Print out some copies of the relevant part of the review activity for learners. Permission is granted by the Publisher for the photocopying of these pages. You can also play the audio files (**Audio 62** and **Audio 63**).

- **Part 1** (the listening section) requires you to read out instructions as supplied below.
- **Part 2** (the reading and writing section) can be done individually or collaboratively if you feel learners are not ready to work individually.
- **Part 3** (the speaking section) needs to be done in small groups with learners, with you guiding them through it orally.

Use the guidelines below to prepare for each section. We would recommend that the review activity should be kept informal and enjoyable so learners don't feel anxious. It is not intended that this review activity should be used for summative assessment, but only as a tool to guage general progress. Depending on the class you may decide to go through the review activity and to discuss the answers together, so it becomes a collaborative activity.

Before tackling the activities: Discuss the title of the book, *Bob's Secret Hideaway* so learners are familiar with the scene and the vocabulary. Tell learners that Bob's secret hideaway is a little house in a tree called a treehouse.

Part 1: Listening

This activity allows you to assess learners' listening skills.

Question 1: This is a pre-listening and reading comprehension activity which learners can either do on their own, or with your help.

Ask learners to listen carefully and then circle the correct answers for question 1.

Read out *a): The main character is a girl/boy.*

Repeat it once. Give the class a minute or so to circle the correct answer (boy). Repeat this process for sentences b) and c).

Questions 2 and 3: Read the story, or play **Audio 62** to the class.

Learners need to tick the boxes for things they hear about in the story (question 2) and circle the correct answers in question 3. If they still don't understand what to do you could help them and demonstrate.

Question 4: Read or play **Audio 63**.

Give learners pencils. Tell them to look at the picture and listen carefully. They need to draw lines to link the small pictures with the larger illustration as they hear each item. Support them as needed so that they get this right.

Answer key: Listening

1. a) boy b) Bob c) happy
2. These items should be ticked: treehouse, moon, toys, door, friends
3. a) The moonlight glowing
   b) They made a noise.
   c) Sad
4. Learners should have drawn lines joining the aeroplane, train, green car, fire engine and football to the large illustration.

Part 2: Reading and writing

This activity will allow you to assess learners' reading and writing skills including their use of English.

If learners are not ready to complete this part individually they can work together in pairs, or this section can be done collaboratively as a class, led and directed by you.

Before learners complete question 4, you may like to play **Audio 62** again.

Answer key: Reading and writing

1. a) ✓ b) ✗ c) ✓ d) ✓ e) ✗ f) ✓
2. a) helicopter b) truck c) treehouse
   d) window
3. I am a bird. I have two eyes on my head and two legs. I can fly because I have two wings. I have feathers, but I don't have fur. Yesterday I sat on an elephant's head.
4. a) 4 b) 2 c) 3 d) 1
5. a) No, he isn't. b) Yes, he does.
   c) Yes, he can. d) No, she isn't.
6. a) Yes, please b) When my friends leave.
   c) No, I haven't. d) So do I.

Part 3: Speaking

This activity can be used to assess learners' speaking skills. Have learners look at the pictures while you ask them questions.

Have a question and answer session with learners. If possible, work in small groups with learners. Make sure you go around and include everyone in the discussions and keep the atmosphere fun, relaxed and collaborative so that they have natural curiosity and interest in the activity, and so they don't feel stressed or worried. Start by pointing to objects in the picture. Ask learners to say what you are pointing to. Encourage them to help each other if some cannot remember words. Also, name some items yourself and ask learners to point to them.

Ask questions which include numbers, activities/games and prepositions (position of objects) as well as to elicit preferences from learners.

Alternatively, have learners use the picture clues and retell the story.

Audio scripts

Topic 1

Audio 1

Song: *Hello!*

Hello [name]. Hello [name].
Are you well? How are you?
I'm good, thank you.
Very good, thank you.
How about you? How about you?

Audio 2

Song: *Saying Hello*

This is the way we say hello,
say hello, say hello,
This is way we say hello,
When we get to school in the morning.
This is the way we say goodbye,
say goodbye, say goodbye,
This is the way we say goodbye,
When we leave the school building.

Audio 3

Poem: *My Friends*

My friends are kind
The best you can find.
When I feel sad
They make me smile.
When I feel bad
They make me laugh.
Friends make me happy
They always play with me.
That is why
I have friends, you see!

Audio 4

Poem: *Friends at School*

Friends at school
Are rather cool
They play with you
And help you too!

Audio 5

Story: *A Friend Helps*

One day, Ant is thirsty. He goes down to the river to drink water. He falls into the water.

Dove is sitting up in a tree near the river. She sees Ant. She feels sorry for him. She throws a leaf into the river. Ant climbs up on the leaf and floats to the riverbank. "Thank you, Dove!" he shouts. "You're a good friend."

The next day, Ant sees a boy setting a trap to catch birds. Dove can't see what the boy is doing. Ant is worried Dove will get caught in the trap so he bites the boy's foot. The boy shouts and the trap falls over with a crash. Dove hears it and flies off.

"Thank you, Ant!" says Dove. "You're a good friend."

Audio 6

Story: *The Stupid Goats and the Clever Goats*

Some goats lived near a river. There was a small bridge across the river.
One day, two goats were on a small bridge. They both wanted to go across the bridge.
"Let me go," said the first goat.
"No. *You* let me go," said the second goat.
"I am bigger," said the first goat.
"So you can let me go first," said the second goat.
The two goats had a fight.
They both fell into the water!
Stupid goats!
The next day, two more goats were on the same bridge.
They both wanted to go across the bridge.
"You can go first," said the first goat.
"Thank you," said the other goat.
They both crossed the river safely.
Clever goats!

Audio 7

Story: *The Street Party*

The children who live in Third Street want to have a party.
"Let's have a street party," said Halina.
"That's a good idea," said Akeem.
"We can make cakes," said Jafar.
"We can dance," said Amena.
"We can have fun!" said Sanjeev. "Let's ask my parents."
So the children went to ask Sanjeev's parents.
"OK," says Sanjeev's mother.
"That's fine," said Sanjeev's father, "But you must ask all the neighbours."
So the children went to ask all the neighbours.
They all said, "OK."
The children made cakes. They also made lemonade.
Everyone had fun!

Topic 2

Audio 8

Song: *The House That Jack Built*

This is the house that Jack built.

This is the corn
That lay in the house that Jack built.

This is the rat,
That ate the corn
That lay in the house that Jack built.

This is the cat,
That killed the rat,
That ate the corn
That lay in the house that Jack built.

This is the cock,
That pecked the cat,
That killed the rat,
That ate the corn
That lay in the house that Jack built.

This is the cow,
That chased the cock,
That pecked the cat,
That killed the rat,
That ate the corn
That lay in the house that Jack built.

This is the girl,
Who milked the cow,
That chased the cock,
That pecked the cat,
That killed the rat,
That ate the corn
That lay in the house that Jack built.

This is the man,
Who kissed the girl,
Who milked the cow,
That chased the cock,
That pecked the cat,
That killed the rat,
That ate the corn
That lay in the house that Jack built.

Audio 9

Story: *Fixing Our House*

Last month there was a big storm. There was a strong wind and lots of rain. The roof of our house came off. Everything inside the house got wet. What a mess!

But we are lucky. We have good neighbours. They are helping us to fix the house. They are fixing the roof. My family are painting the walls of the house. We are painting the walls inside the house. The walls are white.

Audio 10

Text: *A walk around the house*

Ben is walking through the house. He starts at the front door. He goes into the living room. He walks to the window in the living room. Then he walks into the kitchen. After that he walks to the back door and goes outside. Then he goes back into the house. He goes to the small bedroom. Then he goes into the bathroom. Then he turns around and walks back to the living room. He walks out of the front door.

Audio 11

Story: *The Three Goats*

Once upon a time there were three goats - a little goat, a big goat and a middle-sized goat. They lived near a river. They ate lots of grass.
"The grass is brown here," said the big goat. "The grass is green on that side of the river."
"Let's go there," said the middle-sized goat.
So the goats went to the bridge to cross the river.
A big giant lived under the bridge.
The little goat walked onto the bridge.
Trip trap trip trap!
"Who is on my bridge?" shouted the giant.
"It's me. I'm the little goat."
"I'm hungry. I want to eat you!" shouted the giant.
"No, I'm little. You can eat my brother. He is big," said the little goat.
"OK. You can go," said the giant.
Then the middle-sized goat walked on to the bridge.
TRIP TRAP TRIP TRAP!
"Who is on my bridge?" shouted the giant.
"It's me. I'm the middle-sized goat."
"I'm hungry. I want to eat you!" shouted the giant.
"No, I'm little. You can eat my brother. He is big," said the little goat.
"OK. You can go," said the giant.
Then the big goat walked on to the bridge.
TRIP TRAP TRIP TRAP!
"Who is on my bridge?" shouted the giant.
"It's me. I'm the big goat."
"I'm hungry. I want to eat you!" shouted the giant.
"Huh!" said the big goat. "Oh no you won't!"
The big goat ran across the bridge. He hit the giant with his head.
The giant fell into the river.
"Let's eat some green grass," said the big goat.

Audio 12

Song: *The Little Blue Bird*

The little blue bird flaps its wings,
Flaps its wings, flaps its wings
The little blue bird flaps its wings,
As it flies back to its nest in the trees.

The little brown monkey jumps and swings,
Jumps and swings, jumps and swings
The little brown monkey jumps and swings,
From branch to branch up in the trees.

The little brown rabbit hops around,
Hops around, hops around
The big brown rabbit hops around,
In and out of the holes in the ground.

Audio 13

Story: ***It Was a Cold, Dark Night***

It was a cold, dark night and the wind was blowing.
Ned, the hedgehog, was looking for a home.
He looked down a little hole.
The rabbits said, "This is *our* home! Look next door."
He looked down a big hole.
The fox said, "This is *my* home! Look next door!"
He looked up at a tree.
The owls said, "Whoo-oo! This is *our* home. Look next door!"
The hedgehog looked up at the old barn. The bats said, "This is *our* home. But look down, Ned!"
Ned looked down and there was a big pile of leaves.
Ned said, "My home!" and he went to sleep all winter.

Topic 3

Audio 14

Story: ***The Hare and the Tortoise***

One day, Hare and Tortoise were talking.
"I'm big and I can run fast," said Hare. "You walk slowly."
"Yes," said Tortoise. "I walk slowly, but I am clever."
"Let's have a race now," said Hare.
"OK," said Tortoise. "See that tree over there? Let's go there."
"Let's go!" said Hare. The race started.
Tortoise walked slowly. Hare ran fast.
"Tortoise is too slow," said Hare. He stopped running.
He ate some carrots. Then he played.
"I can sleep now," said Hare.
So Hare slept, but Tortoise walked. Tortoise walked and walked.
Then Hare opened his eyes. "Oh no!" he said. "Tortoise is at the tree!"
So Hare ran fast. He ran and ran, but Tortoise won the race.
"Ha ha!" said Tortoise. "I walk slowly, but I am clever!"

Audio 15

Rhyme: ***Two Little Bears***

Two brown bears went out one day
Over the hills and far away.
They saw a tiger and he said "Let's play!"
But the two brown bears ran away.

Two brown bears went out one day
Over the hills and far away.
They saw an elephant and he said "Let's play!"
But the two brown bears ran away.

Two brown bears went out one day
Over the hills and far away.
They saw a black bear and he said "Let's play!"
So the two little bears said "OK!"

Audio 16

Story: ***The Lion and the Mouse***

Lion liked to sleep in the sun. One day, Mouse climbed on the lion's back. Mouse jumped and danced on Lion's back. "This is fun!" he said.
Then Lion opened his eyes. He saw Mouse.
"What are you doing there?" he roared.
He caught Mouse in his big paws.
"Oh please," said Mouse. "Let me go. I am too small to eat."
"Mmmm," said Lion. "Yes, you are. OK. Go away then. Let me sleep!"
Lion let Mouse go and Mouse ran away.
The next day Mouse came back. He saw Lion, but Lion was not asleep. Lion was in a net and he was scared.
"Help me!" roared Lion.
"Yes! I will help you," said Mouse.
Mouse chewed the net. He chewed and he chewed. He bit the net.
"Now you are free!" said Mouse.
"Thank you," said Lion. "You are so small but you saved me!"

Audio 17

Story: ***The Ants and the Grasshopper***

It was summer. It was warm and sunny. There was lots of grass. A grasshopper hopped and sang in the grass. Then some ants walked by.

"What are you doing?" asked the grasshopper.

"We're working," said the ants. "We're collecting food for winter."

"Why?" said grasshopper. "There's lots of food! Come and play with me."

The ants did not stop.

Then winter came. It was cold. The grasshopper's tummy was empty. He was hungry but he had no food. Then he saw the ants. They had lots of food.

"Please give me some food," said the grasshopper. "I'm hungry but I have no food."

"No," said the ants. "We worked in summer. You played and sang."

So the grasshopper was hungry all winter!

Audio 18

Poem: ***Spiders***

I like spiders.
Do you know why?
  Because they are so small
  And I am so big
  Because they can spin
  And I can't even knit
  Because they have eight legs
  And I have only two.
Spiders.
I like them.
This is why.

Audio 19

Story: *The Bear and the Bees*

One day, a big bear was in the forest. He saw a beehive on a tree.
"Yum! I smell honey," he said. The bear liked honey. He put his paw on the beehive.
One little bee came up to the bear and stung him on his nose.
"Bzzz," said the bee. "Go away. This is our honey!"
"Ow!" shouted the bear. It was cross. "That hurts! I can hurt you too, little bee." The bear hit the beehive with his big paws.
And what do you think happened?
All the little bees came out of the beehive and they stung the big bear.
"Ow! OW! **OW!**" shouted the bear and he ran away.

Audio 20

Story: *Goldilocks and the Three Bears*

Once upon a time there were three bears, Papa Bear, Mama Bear and Baby Bear. They lived in a house in the forest.

One day, a little girl called Goldilocks went for a walk in the forest. She saw the bears' house. She walked into the house.

She went into the kitchen. There were three bowls of food on the table. Goldilocks tasted the first bowl.
"This is hot," she said.
Then she tasted the second bowl of food.
"This is cold," she said.
Then she tasted the third bowl of food.
"This is good," she said. She ate all the food in the bowl.

Then Goldilocks walked in to the living room. There were three chairs in the living room.
Goldilocks sat down in the first chair.
"This is hard," she said.
So she sat down in the second chair.
"This is soft," she said.
So she sat down in the third chair.
"This is nice," she said. And then "Oh no!" The chair broke and Goldilocks fell on the floor.

Goldilocks was tired now. She went to the bedroom. There were three beds in the bedroom.
She lay down on the first bed.
"This is hard," she said.
She lay down on the second bed.
"This is soft," she said.
She lay down on the third bed and she fell asleep.

Then the three bears came home.
"Who ate my food?" cried the Baby Bear?
"Who broke your chair?" cried Mama Bear.
"Someone is in our house," said Papa Bear.

Baby Bear went into the bedroom.
"Someone is on my bed," he shouted.

Goldilocks woke up and ran out of the house.

Topic 4

Audio 21

Rhyme: *Five Fat Peas*

Five fat peas in a pea pod pressed,
One grew, two grew and so did the rest.
They grew, and they grew,
and they grew and they grew,
Until one day,
The pea pod POPPED!

Audio 22

Tongue-twisters

Peter Piper picked a packet of pink peppers.

The caterpillar chomps and chews crunchy carrots and cabbages.

What a wonderful well of white water.

Audio 23

Chant: *Let's Make Fruit Salad*

Here's a banana.
– Peel it and cut it up.
Here's an orange.
– Peel it and cut it up.
Here's a mango.
– Peel it and cut it up.
Here's an apple.
– Wash it and cut it up.
Here's a plum.
– Wash it and cut it up.
Here's a spoon.
– Take it and mix everything up!

Audio 24

Radio talk: *How to make a milkshake*

Hello everybody! Today I'm going to tell you how to make a good milkshake. Listen carefully! It's easy!

What do you need? You need a cup of milk and some fruit or chocolate powder. You can also add some of your favourite ice cream.

You will need a blender or food mixer. If you don't have one, you can use a fork. (My aunty uses a fork and her milkshakes are VERY good!)

This is what you do.

First wash or peel the fruit. Then cut it into small pieces.

Then mash the small pieces with a fork or mix them in a machine.

Add the milk and ice cream or chocolate powder and mix well.

Pour this into a glass.

What a good milkshake! And it's easy! Enjoy!

Audio 25

Story: *Rice and Gold*

Once there was a boy called Han Xin. His family were very poor. They did not have much food. Han Xin was very skinny.

Every day, Han Xin went down to the river to fish. But he didn't catch any fish.

A woman saw Han Xin. The woman was doing her washing in the river. "That boy is very skinny," she said to her friend.

So the next day, the woman brought Han Xin a bowl of rice.

"Oh thank you!" said the boy. He ate all the rice and gave the bowl back to the woman.

The next day she brought him a bowl of rice too.

Again Han Xin said, "Thank you" and he ate all the rice.

The woman brought him a bowl of rice every day.

Soon Han Xin was not so skinny. He grew into a healthy man.

Later, Han Xin became an important leader of the Chinese people. He lived in a palace and had lots of money. But he was also very kind.

One day, he went to look for the old woman.

He found her at the river. She was doing her washing.

He gave her a basket with many gold coins. "These are for you," he said. "You gave me rice. I'm giving you gold."

"No," said the old woman. "You are a kind leader. I don't want gold."

So Han Xin invited the old woman to come and live with his family at the palace.

Audio 26

Story: *Stone Soup*

Once, long ago, there was a drought in a village. There was no rain. The animals and plants died because there was no water. The people in the village were very hungry. They did not want to share their food.

One day, a stranger came into the village. He asked for some water. The people in the village gave him some water. Then he asked for some food.

"We have no food," said one woman.

"You must go," said a man.

"It is my birthday today. Would you like me to make a special soup?" asked the stranger.

"Yes, please," they all said.

"Well, bring me a pot and some water, please," said the stranger.

The stranger made a small fire and put the pot on the fire. Then he took a stone out of his pocket. He put the stone in the water. Soon the water boiled. The stranger tasted the water.

"Mmm," he said. "It's good. But an onion will make it nicer."

An old man said, "I have one onion. You can use that."

"Thank you," said the stranger. He cut the onion and put it in the soup.

Then the stranger tasted the soup again.

"Mmm," he said. "It's good. But a carrot will make it nicer."

A woman said, "I have one carrot. You can use that."

"Thank you," said the stranger. He cut the carrot and put it in the soup.

Then the stranger tasted the soup again.

"Mmm," he said. "It's good. But some salt and pepper will make it nicer."

A woman said, "I have some salt and pepper. You can use that."

"Thank you," said the stranger. He put the salt and pepper in the soup.

Then the stranger tasted the soup again.

"Mmm," he said. "It's good. But some meat will make it nicer."

A man said, "I have some bones. You can use them."

"Thank you," said the stranger. He put the bones in the soup. The soup smelled very good!

Then people in the village found some tomatoes and potatoes to put into the soup. An hour later, the soup was ready to eat.

"What a tasty soup!" they said.

"Now we can all have some soup," said the stranger. "You shared your food with me, so I will share my meal with you!"

Audio 27

Poem: *Stone Soup*

Put a stone into your pot.
Add some water, make it hot.

Add some spices and some oil.
Stir the pot and let it boil.

Add some onions, carrots too.
Stir the pot to mix them through.

Add something salty or a bone,
To your pot of soup and stone.

When your soup is good and done.
Share the meal with everyone.

(By Karen Morrison)

Topic 5

Audio 28

Chant: *I Can Do It!*

I can do it
You can do it
She can do it
He can do it
We can do it
Everyone can do it!

Audio 29

Story: *The Best Runner*

Usain Bolt is from Jamaica and he is very good at running. He's the fastest runner in the world.

He enjoyed playing cricket and football with his brother and his friends.

He started to play cricket at school. Then the coach said: "What about running? You're good at running!"

"I don't think so," said Usain.

Usain started to practice. He didn't believe he was a good runner but he trained hard.

He won many medals and now everyone knows that he is the best!

Audio 30

Conversation: *I like it when...*

Voice A (boy): Do you enjoy dancing?

Voice B (boy): Yes, I do.

Voice C (girl): I like it when we play dance music.

A: Yes, so do I.

B: I like it when we sing.

C: Yes, so do I.

A: Do you enjoy playing drums?

C: Yes, I do.

B: I LOVE it when we play drums.

A: So do I.

C: It's fun to sing and dance and play!

Audio 31

Rhyme: *Thirty Days Has September*

Thirty days has September,
April, June and November.
All the rest have thirty-one
Except for February alone
which has twenty-eight most times
And in a leap year, twenty-nine.

Audio 32

Radio announcement: *A competition*

Hi everyone. It's April again, which means that it is competition time.

This April we invite you to make something out of paper. You can make anything you like. It can be big or small! You must make it with your own hands.

We will announce the winners on 28 April.

Audio 33

Radio announcement: *The kite flying competition*

Hi everyone. It's competition time again. There will be a kite flying competition during the holidays.

The competition is on Sunday 21 December.

It starts at 3 o'clock in the afternoon.

You need to go down to Blue Beach. Get there early.

All you need is a kite.

It's free! And there will be prizes!

Topic 6

Audio 34

Rhyme: *The Little Insect*

The little insect flaps its wings
Flaps its wings, flaps it wings
The little insect flaps its wings
And flies away when it sees me!

[You can change the insect to another noun (bird, moth, bee) and you can also change the last line of the poem.]

Audio 35

Rhyme: *Fly, Fly, Butterfly*

Fly, fly, butterfly,
come and see your friends!
Fly, fly, butterfly,
come and see your friends!
The little bee, the ladybird, the caterpillar, ant!
The little bee, the ladybird, the caterpillar, ant!

Audio 36

Text: *Butterflies*

Butterflies are insects. They have four wings, six legs and two antennae. The wings often have bright colours.

Butterflies change during their lives. A butterfly with wings is an adult butterfly. The adult butterfly lays eggs. Caterpillars hatch out of these eggs. The caterpillars then change into pupae. The adult butterflies come out of these pupae.

Audio 37

Song: ***Little Bird***

I saw a little bird go hop, hop, hop.
I told the little bird to stop, stop, stop.
I went to the window to say "How do you do?"
He wagged his little tail and far away he flew!

Audio 38

Song: ***This Is the Way***

This is the way we flap our wings, flap our wings, flap our wings
This is the way we flap our wings on a warm spring day.
This how we scratch for worms, scratch for worms, scratch for worms
This is how we scratch for worms on a summer day.
This is the way we peck for food, peck for food, peck for food
This is the way we peck for food on an autumn day.
This is the way we fly away, fly away, fly away
This is the way we fly away on a winter day.

Audio 39

Story: ***The Bird King***

Long ago, all the animals had kings. The big animals had a lion king. The small animals had a spider queen. But the birds did not have a king or a queen. So one day, the birds had a meeting. They wanted a king.

"Who can be our king?" asked one bird.

"How do we choose?" asked another bird.

"I think the bird who can fly high should be king," said one bird.

"Then I will be king," said the eagle. "I can fly very high."

"No," said the little sparrow. "Let's have a race. The bird that flies the highest will be our king."

Lots of birds wanted to be king. They all lined up and owl said, "Too-whit-too-woo" when it was time to start.

The birds flew up in the sky. The little sparrow flew up under the wing of the eagle, but no one saw that.

After a while, some birds came back down to the ground. They were tired. But the eagle went on flying high up in the sky.

"I will be the king," shouted the eagle and he came back down to the ground. The sparrow came out from under the eagle's wing and flew high up in the sky.

"But look. There's the sparrow," shouted one bird. "He is still flying high. He will be our king."

The eagle was very cross. He flew back up in the sky and tried to pull the sparrow down. He pulled some feathers out of his tail. But the sparrow became king. But sparrows still have short tails!

Audio 40

Text: ***Eagles***

There are many different eagles. Condors, buzzards and hawks are all eagles. Eagles are birds of prey. This means that they catch small animals and eat them.

Eagles are big and strong. They have big wings. They can fly high and they fly fast. They have big beaks and big claws to catch small animals. They can see very well too.

Eagles make their nests in tall trees and up in the mountains.

Audio 41

Song: ***Ten Little Aeroplanes***

Ten little aeroplanes flying in the sky
One landed on the ground and now there are …

Nine little aeroplanes flying in the sky.
Nine little aeroplanes flying in the sky
One landed on the ground and now there are …

Eight little aeroplanes flying in the sky.
Eight little aeroplanes flying in the sky
One landed on the ground and now there are …

Seven little aeroplanes flying in the sky.
Seven little aeroplanes flying in the sky
One landed on the ground and now there are …

Six little aeroplanes flying in the sky.
Six little aeroplanes flying in the sky
One landed on the ground and now there are …

Five little aeroplanes flying in the sky.
Five little aeroplanes flying in the sky
One landed on the ground and now there are …

Four little aeroplanes flying in the sky.
Four little aeroplanes flying in the sky
One landed on the ground and now there are …

Three little aeroplanes flying in the sky.
Three little aeroplanes flying in the sky
One landed on the ground and now there are …

Two little aeroplanes flying in the sky.
Two little aeroplanes flying in the sky
One landed on the ground and now there is…

One little aeroplane flying in the sky.

Audio 42

Song: ***Helicopter***

Helicopter, helicopter
Buzzing up on high
Where are you going?
Flying up in the sky.

Helicopter, helicopter
Out over the sea
Where are you going?
Can you take me?

Audio 43

Story: *He Wanted to Fly*

Long ago there was a scary creature called a Minotaur. This Minotaur terrified the people. King Minos thought of a plan. "Can you build me a maze that nothing can escape from?" asked the King.

"Yes, I can," said Daedalus.

Daedalus built the maze. Then he left a pile of meat in the centre of the maze. The Minotaur smelt the meat. He went into the maze to look for it. He could not find his way out again.

King Minos was a cruel king. He threw Daedalus and his son Icarus into the maze with the terrifying Minotaur. Daedalus had built the maze so he knew the way out. Daedalus built wings with feathers and wax to fly away with his son. "With these wings you will fly like a bird," Daedalus told his Icarus, "but be careful. Don't fly too close to the sun."

Daedalus and Icarus tied the wings onto their arms. They ran and flapped their arms. Up and up they went. Icarus had lots of fun flying. He didn't see how close he was to the sun. The wax started melting. The feathers floated down towards the sea. Down, down, down went Icarus...

Topic 7

Audio 44

Rhyme: *Star Bright*

Star light, star bright,
The first star I see tonight.
I wish I may, I wish I might,
Have the wish I wish tonight.

Audio 45

Song: *How I Feel*

I am hungry. I am hungry.
Burgers, fries!
I am thirsty. I am thirsty.
Pour me some milk!
I am happy. I am happy.
Cuddle my cat!
I am tired. I am tired.
Let's go to bed.

Audio 46

Story: *The Fisherman and the Golden Fish*

One day, a poor fisherman caught a big golden fish. He was surprised but he pulled the fish out of the water.
"Please let me go," said the fish. "I can help you. You can make a wish."
"OK," said the fisherman and he put the fish back in the water.
The fisherman went home to his small house.
"I have no fish for us to eat," says the fisherman. He told his wife about the golden fish.
The wife was angry. "You stupid man!" she shouted.
"Go to the fish and make a wish. I want some food," she said.

So the fisherman went back to the sea and called the fish.
"Fish, oh beautiful big fish
I want to make a wish."
The fish came up out of the water.
"What is your wish?" asked the fish.
"We want some food," said the fisherman.
"Go home," said the fish.
The fisherman ran home. There was a big table with a lot of food outside the house.

"You see?" said his wife. "Go back to the fish and make a wish. I want some new clothes!" she said.

So the fisherman went back to the sea and called the fish.
"Fish, oh beautiful big fish
I want to make a wish."
The fish came up out of the water.
"What is your wish?" asked the fish.
"My wife wants new clothes," said the fisherman.
"Go home," said the fish.
The fisherman ran home. His wife had new clothes.
"Now I want a new house," said the fisherman's wife.

So the fisherman went back to the sea and called the fish.
"Fish, oh beautiful big fish
I want to make a wish."
The fish came up out of the water.
"What is your wish?" asked the fish.
"We want a new home," said the fisherman.
"Go home," said the fish.
The fisherman ran home. There was a beautiful big home.
"What a small house!" said his wife. "I want a palace. I want to be a queen."

So the fisherman went back to the sea and called the fish.
"Fish, oh beautiful big fish
I want to make a wish."
The fish came up out of the water.
"What is your wish?" asked the fish.
"We want a palace," said the fisherman. "My wife wants to be a queen."
"No!" says the fish. "What a greedy man you are! Go home."
The man went home. There was no food. There were no new clothes. There was no palace. But the small house was there.
The man was happy! His wife was angry!

Audio 47

Tongue-twister: *Danny the Dolphin*

Danny the Dolphin dreamed and danced down in the water.

Dreamed and danced did Danny down in the water.

Then why did Danny dive down under the water?

Because other dolphins screamed "Danger! Danger! Danger!"

Audio 48

Story: *Kind Emma*

Kind Emma lived all alone with no one to talk to.

One night, a little voice called,
"Oh, dear Emma, oh!
Where can I go
in the wind and in the snow?"

"Come into my house,"
said Kind Emma.

She opened the door and
a tiny *thing* scuttled in.
It was almost too small to be seen.

The the little voice said,
"Oh, dear Emma, oh!
Your fire has burned low
and I shiver so!"

"I'll make the fire glow for you,"
said Kind Emma, and
she poked the fire.

Then the little voice said,
"Oh, dear Emma, oh!
I ate long ago.
I need food so!"

"You can share what I have,"
said Kind Emma.

She put a dish of hot soup and a very small spoon on the table.

The tiny *thing* stayed hidden.
It was afraid to come out.

"Goodnight!" said Kind Emma.

She hoped the tiny *thing* would come out and eat if she left the room.

Next morning, when Emma awoke …

… the fire burned and
the water was hot.
Fresh bread was ready.
The floor was scrubbed and the house was tidy and clean.

"Good food and a fire, and
someone to talk to!
What more could I want?"
said Kind Emma.

The tiny *thing* stayed with Kind Emma for the rest of her days.

Audio 49

Poem: *Be Safe*

Wear a helmet on your head
When you ride, on your bike
Wear a helmet on your head
Then you can go, as fast as you like!

Don't take gifts from people
You don't know, that you meet.
Don't take gifts from people
Near your school or in the street.

Audio 50

Story: *The Red Light*

It was a black, stormy night.
The train stopped at an empty station. The platform was dark and silent.
No one got on or off, but the train didn't leave.
The guard stepped down from the train.
A passenger leant out of the train window.
"Why have we stopped?" he called to the guard.
"I don't know," the guard said.
The guard walked along the platform to the driver's cabin.
"What's the problem?" he asked the driver.
"There's a red light," replied the driver. "I don't know why."
"Look!" exclaimed the driver, pointing.
The red light was coming closer through the darkness.
Suddenly a white horse galloped onto the platform.
The rider was holding a red lantern.
"Halt!" he cried, "you mustn't go on."
The bridge had been blown away in the storm.
If the train had gone on, it would have fallen into the river far below.

Topic 8

Audio 51

Song: *London Bridge Is Falling Down*

London Bridge is falling down,
Falling down, falling down.
London Bridge is falling down,
My fair lady.

Build it up with wood and clay,
Wood and clay, wood and clay,
Build it up with wood and clay,
My fair lady.

Wood and clay will wash away,
Wash away, wash away,
Wood and clay will wash away,
My fair lady.

Build it up with bricks and mortar,
Bricks and mortar, bricks and mortar,
Build it up with bricks and mortar,
My fair lady.

Bricks and mortar will not stay,
Will not stay, will not stay,
Bricks and mortar will not stay,
My fair lady.

Build it up with iron and steel,
Iron and steel, iron and steel,
Build it up with iron and steel,
My fair lady.

Iron and steel will bend and bow,
Bend and bow, bend and bow,
Iron and steel will bend and bow,
My fair lady.

Build it up with silver and gold,
Silver and gold, silver and gold,
Build it up with silver and gold,
My fair lady.

Silver and gold will be stolen away,
Stolen away, stolen away,
Silver and gold will be stolen away,
My fair lady.

Audio 52

Song: *The Bumper Cars*

Do you know the bumper cars,
The bumper cars, the bumper cars,
Do you know the bumper cars,
They're what I like the best!

Oh yes, I know the bumper cars
The bumper cars, the bumper cars,
Yes, I know the bumper cars,
I also like them the best.

Audio 53

Song: *Here We Go Round on the Ferris Wheel*

Here we go round
On the Ferris wheel,
The Ferris wheel, the Ferris wheel.
Here we go round on the Ferris wheel,
At the funfair in the morning.

Audio 54

Conversation: *At the funfair*

A: Here we are!

B: Wow. I want to go on the roller coaster.

A: So do I. Come, let's go.

B: OK. After that can we play a game?

C: No, let's go on the bumper cars. That's fun!

A: Yes, it is.

D: And can we go to the hall of mirrors.

B: OK! The mirrors make you look funny!

Audio 55

Song: *Row, Row, Row Your Boat*

Row, row, row your boat,
Gently down the stream.
Merrily, merrily, merrily, merrily
Life is but a dream.

Ride, ride, ride your bike
Quickly down street.
Merrily, merrily, merrily, merrily
Pedal with your feet!

Audio 56

Song: *The Boy Went Over The Mountain*

The boy went over the mountain,
The boy went over the mountain,
The boy went over the mountain,
To see what he could see.

And all that he could see,
And all that he could see,
Was the other side of the mountain,
The other side of the mountain,
The other side of the mountain,
Was all that he could see.

The boy went over the river,
The boy went over the river,
The boy went over the river,
To see what he could see.
And all that he could see,

Was the other side of the river,
The other side of the river,
The other side of the river,
Was all that he could see.

Audio 57

Text: *The London Underground*

London is a big, busy city. Millions of people need to move around every day. Children need to go to school and adults need to go to work. There are also lots of tourists in London.

People in London call the underground trains "the Tube" because the tunnels look like tubes. Tubes are long, thin, round pipes. Taking "the Tube" is a quick and easy way to move around.

There are trains every day of the week from 5 o'clock in the morning until 12 o'clock at night. You must buy a ticket or an Oyster card to use the Tube. Then look at the map to see where you want to go.

Topic 9

Audio 58

Song: *Let's Play Music!*

Let's play music!
Let's play music!
The violin and the xylophone,
the triangle and the drum!
The violin and the xylophone,
the triangle and the drum!

Drum, drum, Keekee, play the drum!
Daisy plays the trumpet! Ben – the tambourine.
Daisy plays the trumpet! Ben – the tambourine.
Drum, drum, Keekee,
Play the drum!

Audio 59

Text: *The musicians*

Betty, Ken, Akim, Sara and Lori are from different countries. They are musicians. They all play different musical instruments. Betty is from America. She plays drums. Ken is from Australia. He plays the trumpet. Sara is from Korea and Akim is from Germany. They play the violin. And Lori is from Trinidad. She plays the steelpan.

Audio 60

Song: *As I Was Walking Down the Street*

As I was walking down the street,
Down the street, down the street,
A very good friend I chanced to meet;
Hi Ho, Hi Ho, Hi Ho.

Rig a jig jig and away we go,
Away we go, away we go;
Rig a jig jig and away we go,
Hi Ho, Hi Ho, Hi Ho.

We clapped our hands and stomped our feet,
Stomped our feet, stomped our feet,
We clapped our hands and stomped our feet,
Hi Ho, Hi Ho, Hi Ho.

We jumped up high and came back down,
Came back down, came back down,
We jumped up high and came back down,
Hi Ho, Hi Ho, Hi Ho.

Rig a jig jig and away we go,
Away we go, away we go;
Rig a jig jig and away we go,
Hi Ho, Hi Ho, Hi Ho.

We climbed on a train and tooted the horn,
Tooted the horn, tooted the horn,
We climbed on a train and tooted the horn,
Hi Ho, Hi Ho, Hi Ho.

Rig a jig jig and away we go,
Away we go, away we go;
Rig a jig jig and away we go,
Hi Ho, Hi Ho, Hi Ho.

Audio 61

Story: *The End of the Year Concert*

Suri, Mike and Meena loved music. They decided to make a band.

Suri had some drums.

Mike had a guitar.

Meena liked to sing.

They practised every Saturday.

At the end of the year, they gave a concert at Suri's house.

Everyone enjoyed the concert.

Review Activity

Audio 62

Bob's Secret Hideaway

Bob had a secret hideaway, that only he would know.
He crept up there alone at night, to watch the moonlight glow.

Then Bob invited all his friends, but all they brought was noise.
So Bob decided not to share, his treehouse or his toys.

Now Bob was left alone again, in his treehouse feeling sad.
He found his secret was no fun, without the friends he had.

He heard a knock upon the door, and opened it a crack.
He peeped outside and happily saw, that his friends had all come back!

Audio 63

Help Bob put his toys in the right place.

The aeroplane goes on the shelf under the window.

[pause]

The train goes against the wall under the three long shelves.

[pause]

The car goes next to the toy on the second shelf.

[pause]

The fire engine goes on the shelf above the train.

[pause]

The musical instrument goes on the floor near the aeroplane.

(Topic 1 Unit A)

Listen and draw pictures.

1	2
3	4
5	6
7	8

(Topic 1 Unit A, Unit C; Topic 2 Unit C; Topic 5 Unit A; Topic 7 Unit B; Topic 8 Unit A)

Bingo

- Complete the card.
- Listen and cross out the words as you hear them.

(Topic 1 Unit B)

Listen and tick (✓) the correct picture.

1. a)

b)

2. a)

b)

3. a)

b)

4. a)

b)

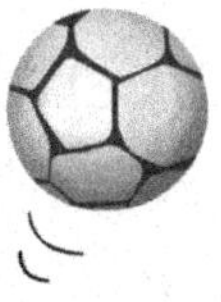

5. a)

b)

6. a)

b)

(Topic 2 Unit A)

Make a paper house

Read the instructions carefully. Make the paper house.

1. Fold a square piece of paper in half to make a crease line.

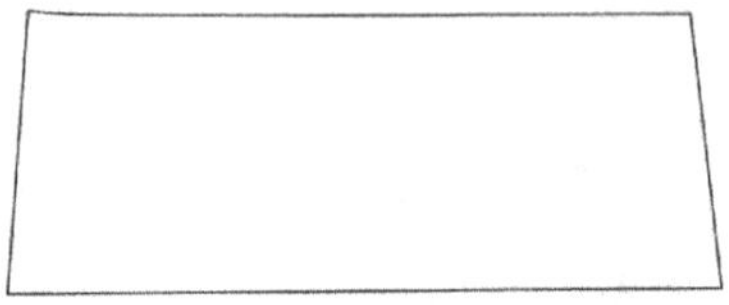

2. Open up the paper.

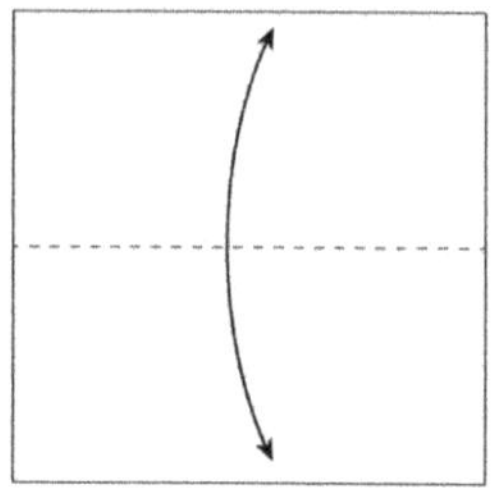

3. Fold the bottom edge to meet the crease line.

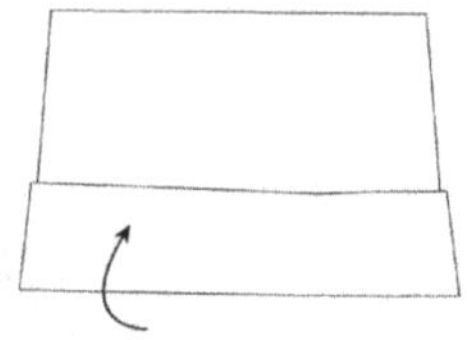

4. Fold the top edge to meet the crease line.

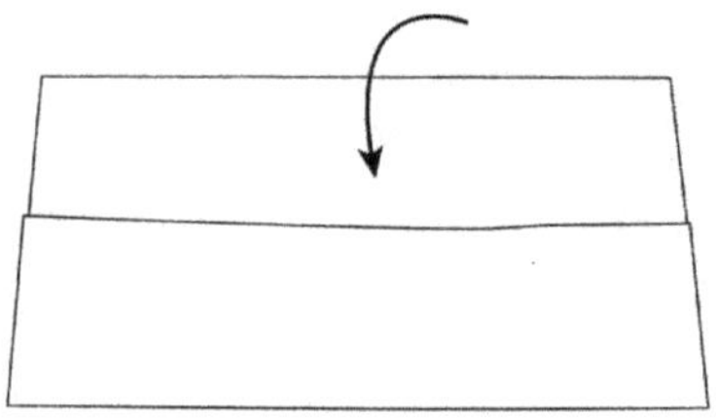

5. Fold the paper in half to make a crease.

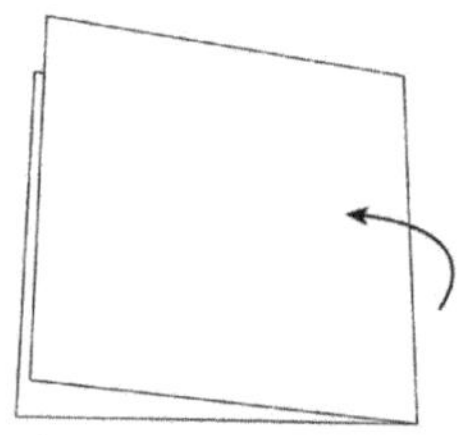

6. Unfold it.

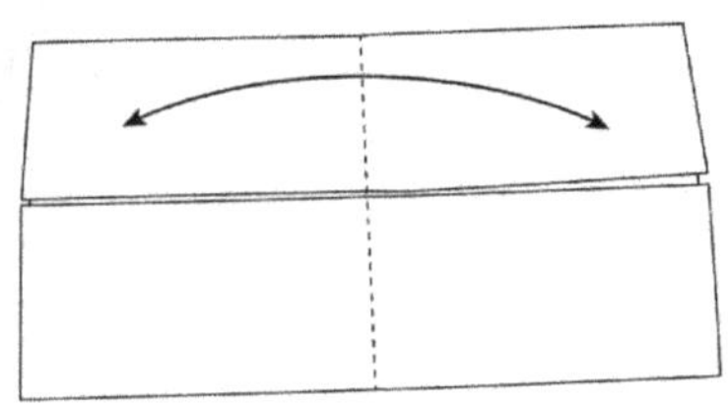

7. Turn the paper over. Fold both sides to meet the crease.

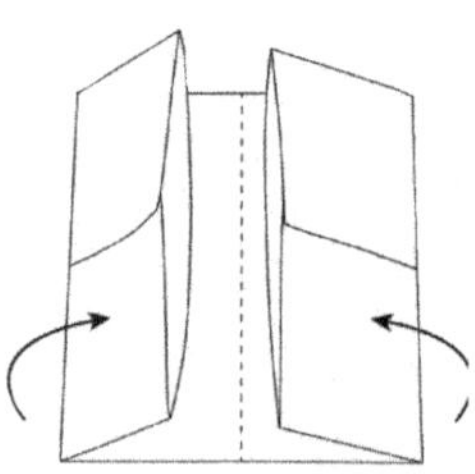

8. Pull open the top left corner.

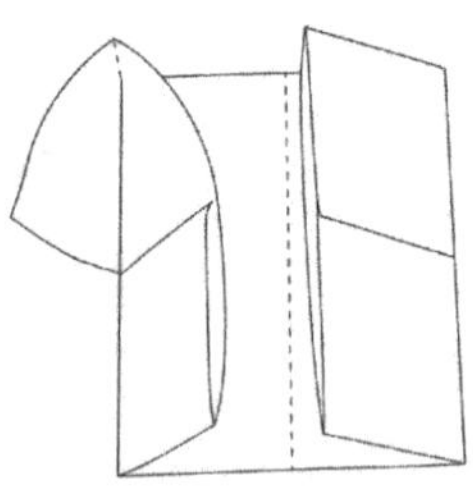

9. Press down to make a triangle.

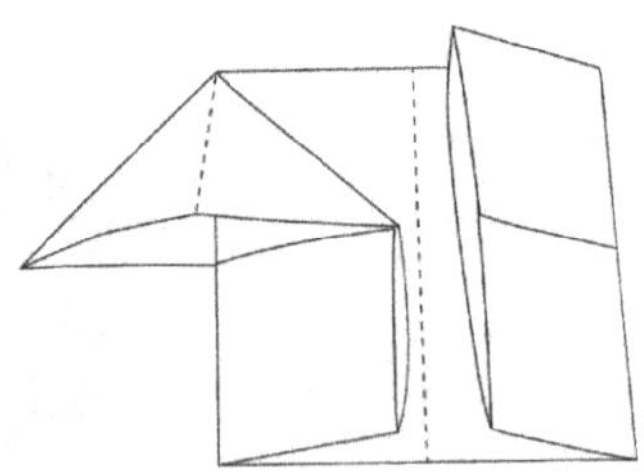

10. Do the same to the top right corner.

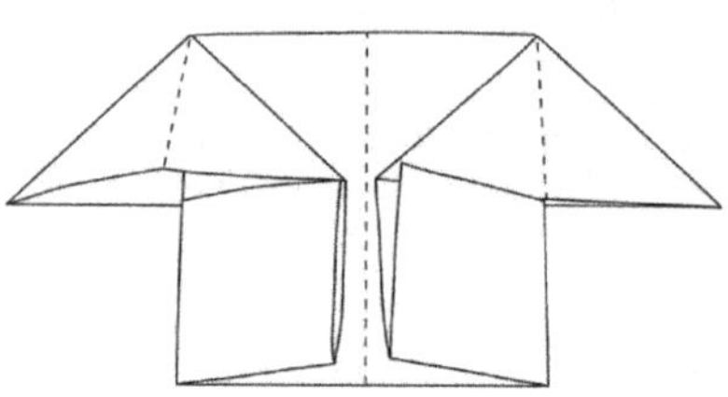

11. Flip the paper over.

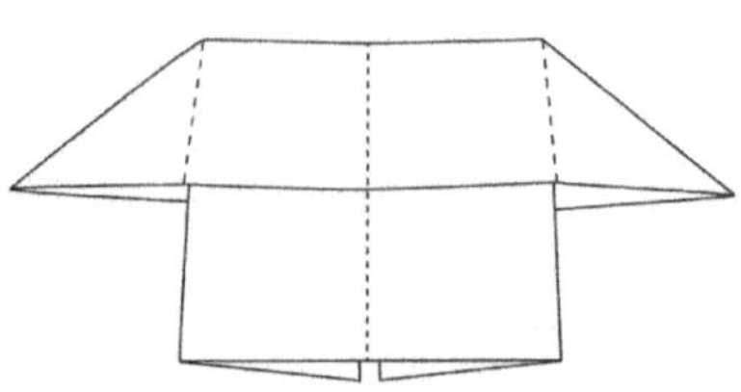

12. Colour and decorate your house.

(Topic 2 Unit A; Topic 6 Unit C)

Battleships game

	A	B	C	D	E	F
1						
2						
3						
4						
5						
6						
7						
8						
9						
10						

(Topic 2 Unit B)

The Three Goats

- Listen to the story *The Three Goats.*
- Cut out the pictures and put them in the correct order.
- Tell the story to your partner.

(Topic 3 Unit A)

The Hare and the Tortoise

- Cut out the pictures.
- Put them in order.
- Tell the story of *The Hare and the Tortoise.*

(Topic 3 Unit B)

Listen and tick (✓) the correct picture.

1. 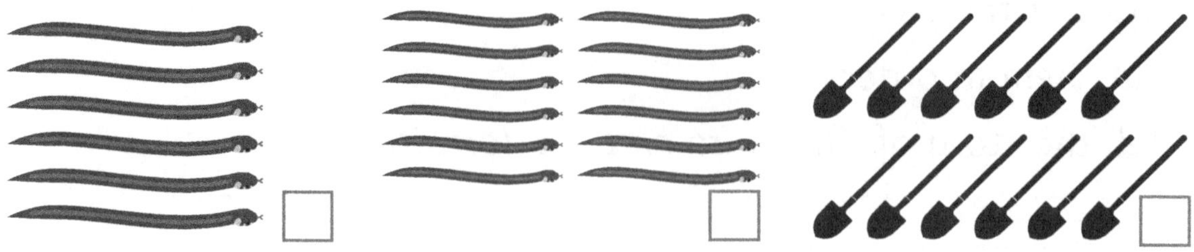

2. 

3. 

4. 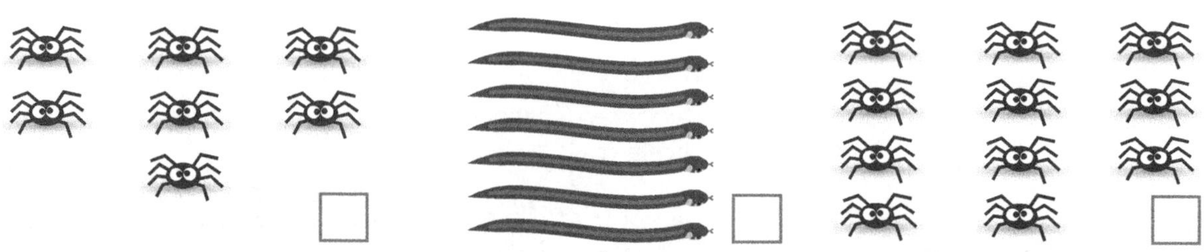

5. 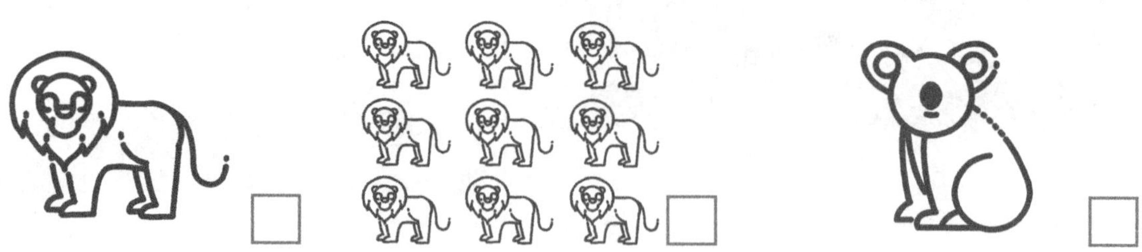

6. 

(Topic 3 Unit B)

Listen and draw lines to show which way the animals move.

	A	B	C	D
1.				
2.				
3.				

	A	B	C	D
1.				
2.				
3.				

	A	B	C	D
1.				
2.				
3.				

	A	B	C	D
1.				
2.				
3.				

(Topic 4 Unit A)

Read the pie chart.

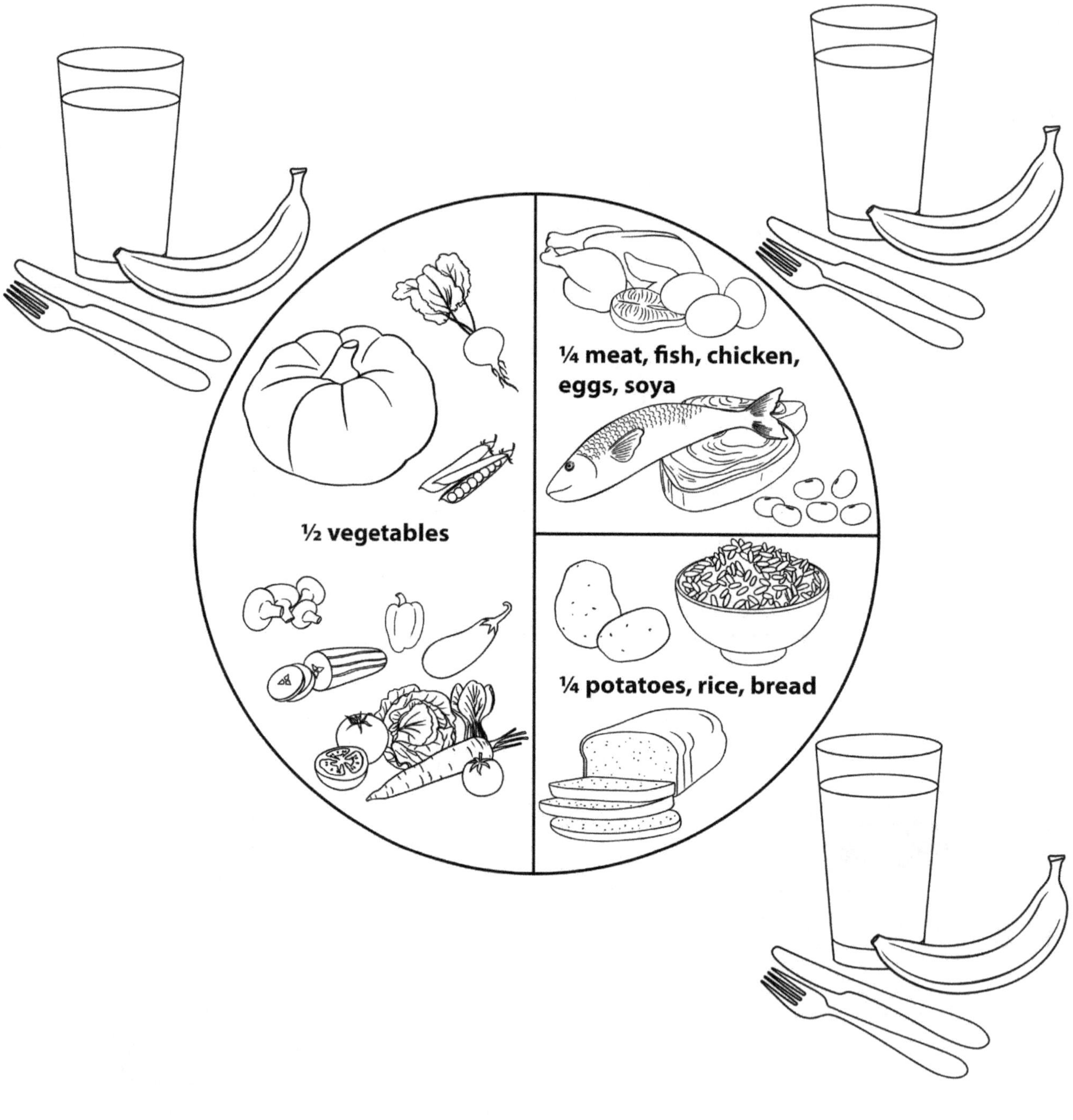

(Topic 4 Unit A; Topic 5 Unit A, Unit B; Topic 6 Unit C)

1–6 Spinner

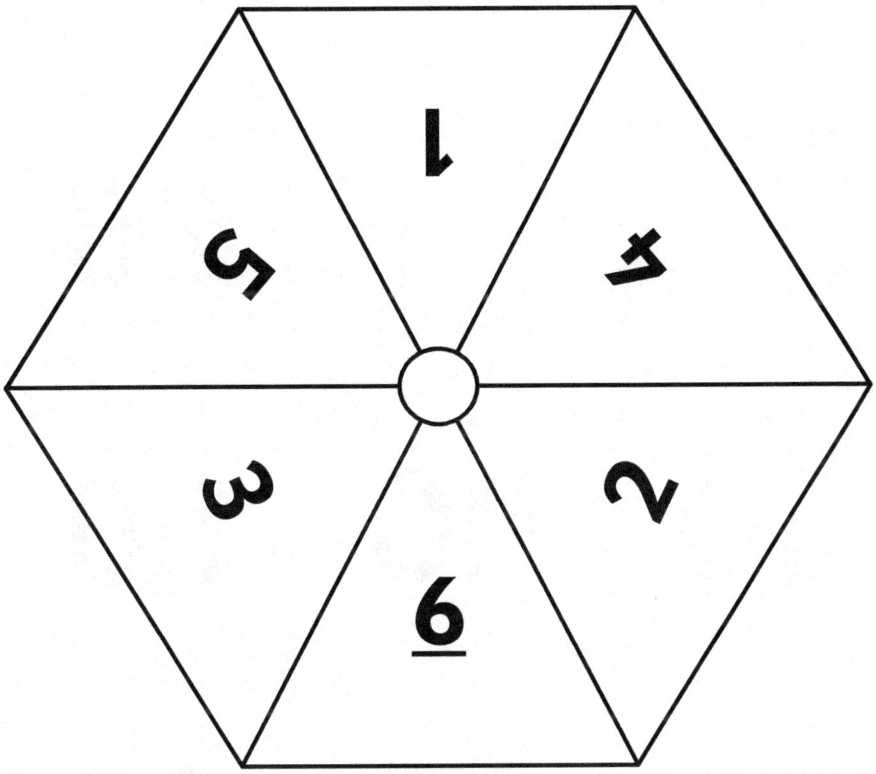

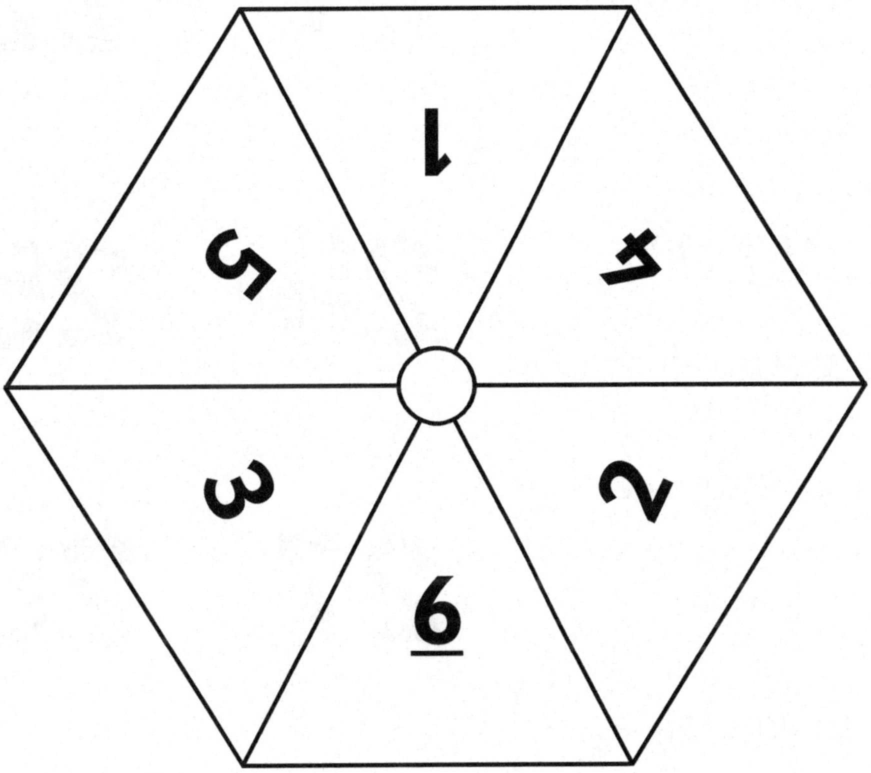

(Topic 5 Unit A)

Numbers

- Cut out the numbers and the number words.
- Match them.
- Then put them in the correct order.

twenty

thirty

forty

fifty

twenty-one

twenty-two

twenty-three

twenty-four

twenty-five

twenty-six

twenty-seven

twenty-eight

twenty-nine

		20
30	40	50
21	22	23
24	25	26
27	28	29

(Topic 5 Unit A)

Complete the bar graph.

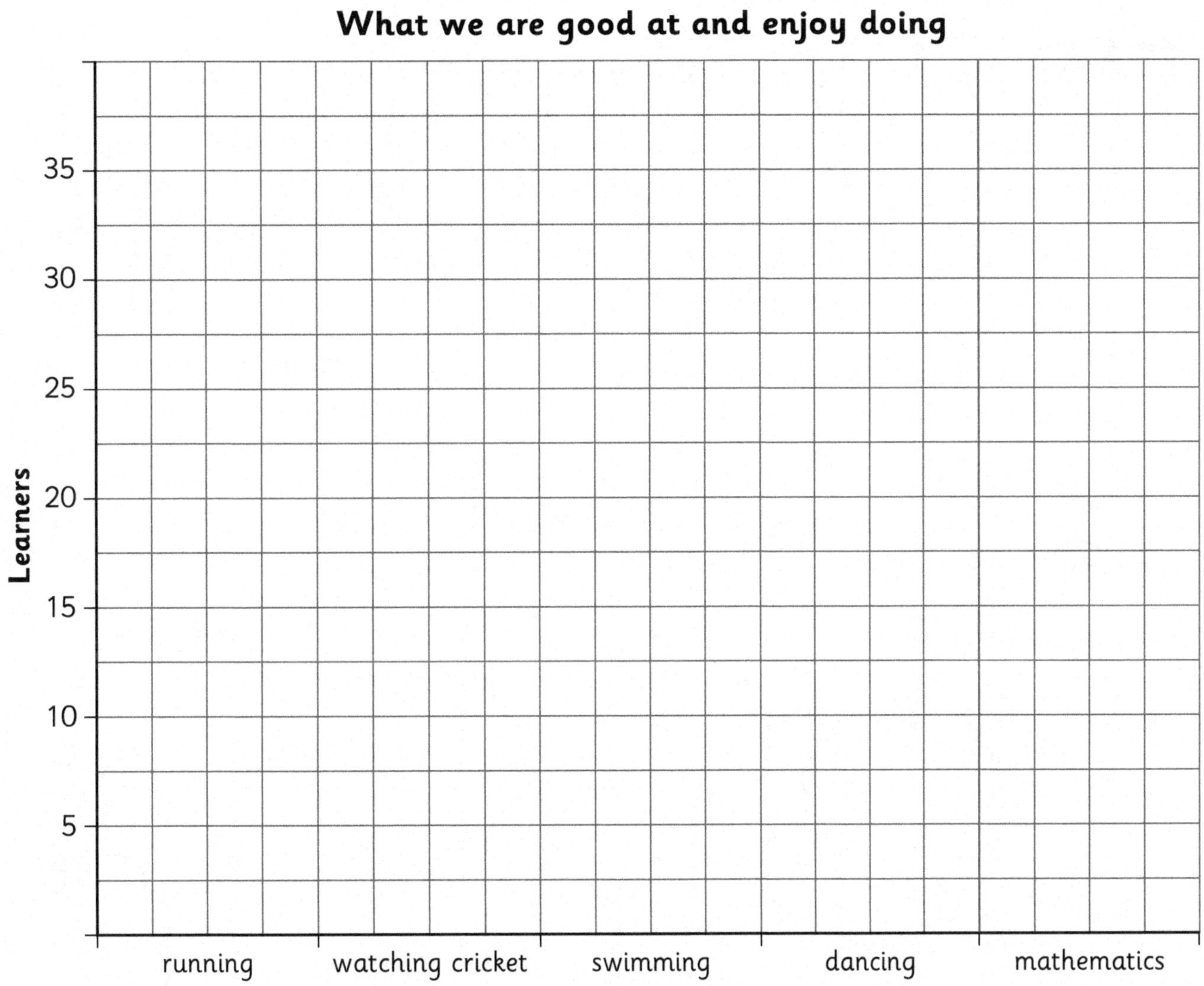

(Topic 5 Unit A)

- Make your own game.
- Write your own instructions in blocks 3, 7, 11, 14 and 19.

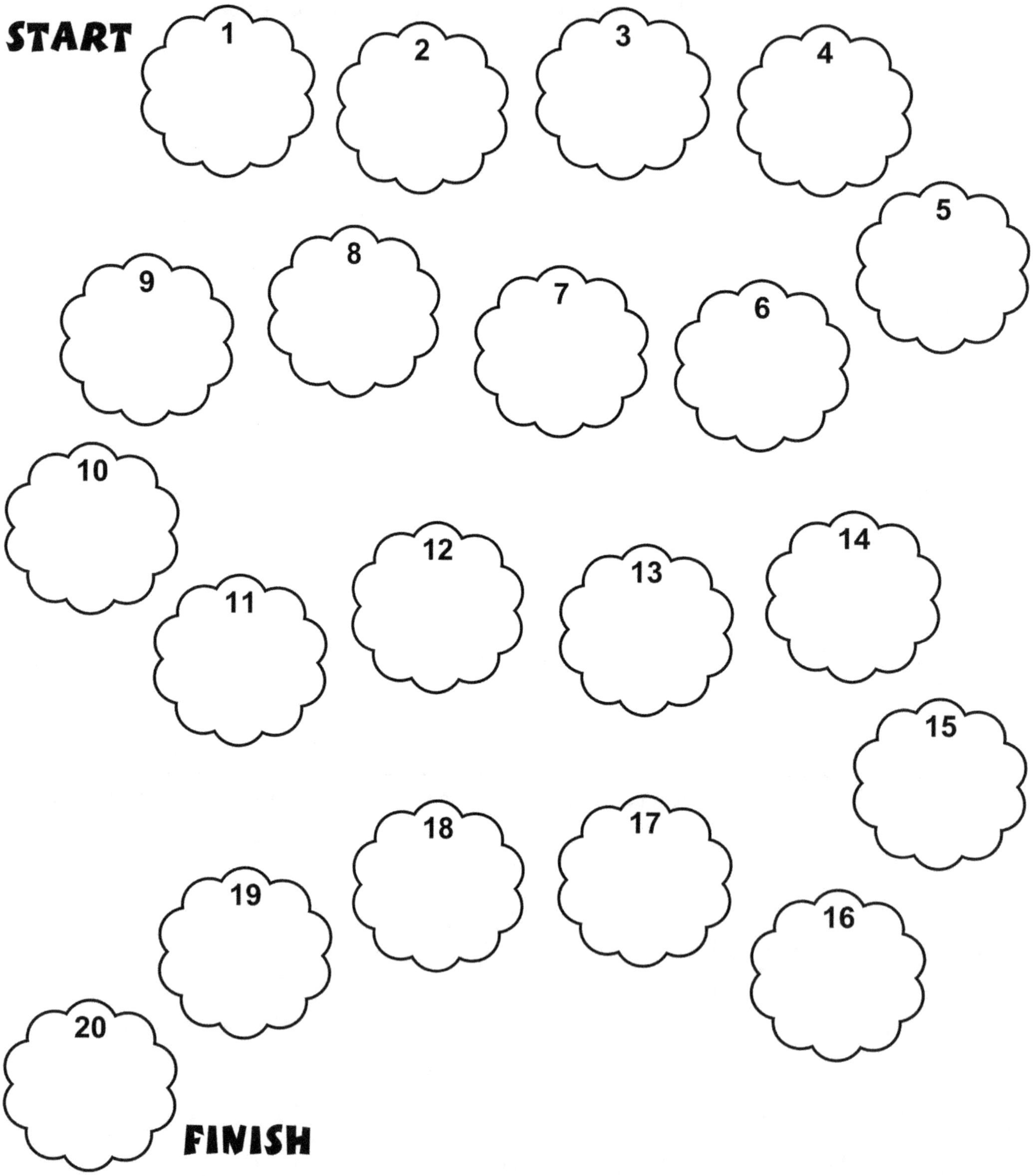

(Topic 5 Unit C)

Look at the calendar. Circle the answers.

JULY

Sunday	Monday	Tuesday	Wednesday	Thursday	Friday	Saturday
						1
2	3	4	5	6	7	8
9	10	11	12	13	14 School closes	15
16	17	18	19	20	21	22
23	24 Mountain hike	25	26 Kim's birthday	27	28	29
30	31					

1. Which month does the calendar show?

a) January b) June c) July

2. How many days are in this month?

a) 29 b) 30 c) 31

3. What day of the week is Kim's birthday?

a) Monday b) Thursday c) Wednesday

4. On which day will school close?

a) Friday b) Saturday c) Sunday

5. On which date will they go hiking?

a) 14 July b) 24 July c) 26 July

(Topic 5 Unit C)

How to make a ladybird

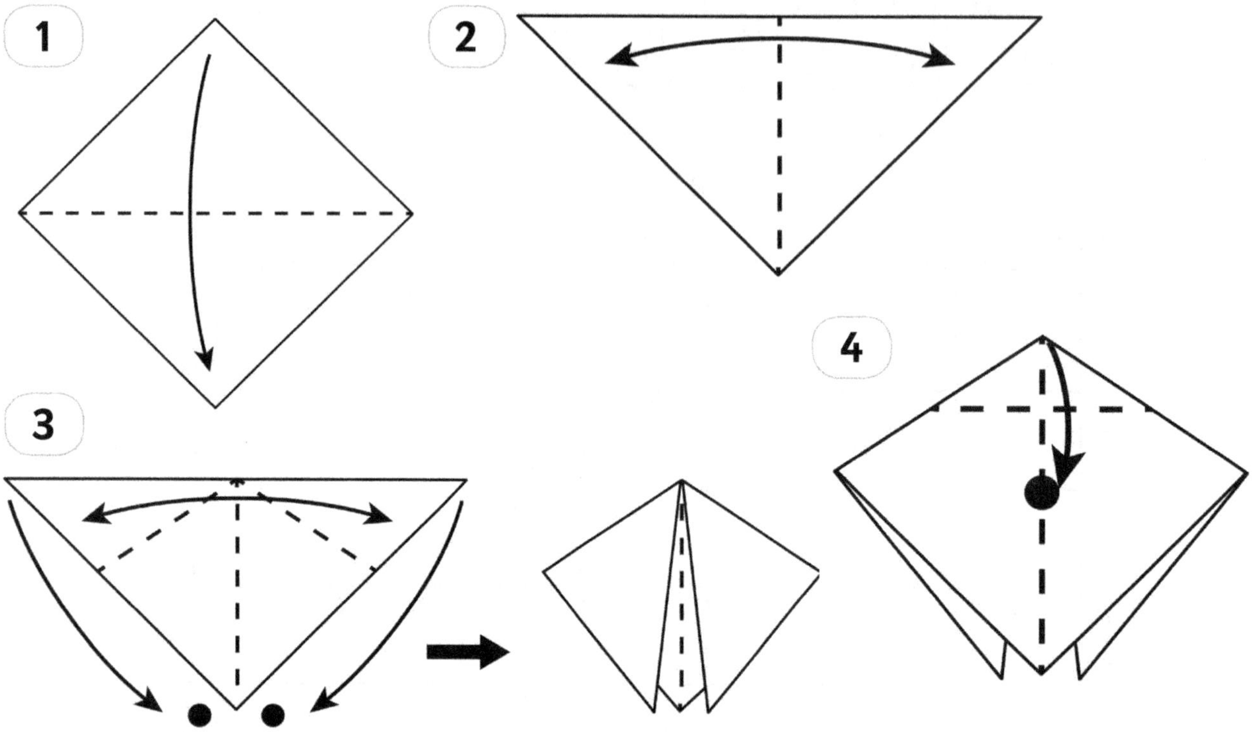

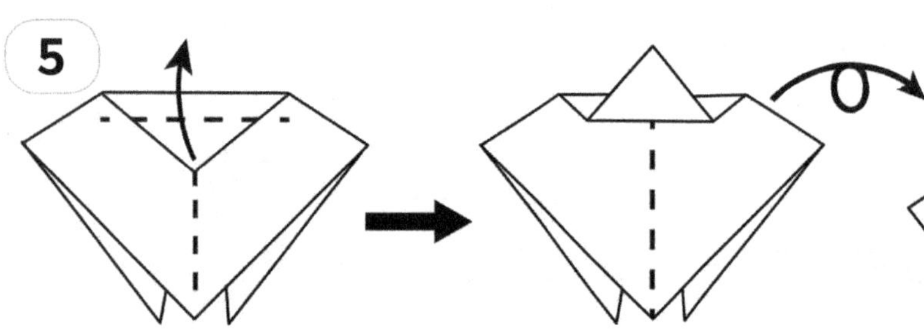

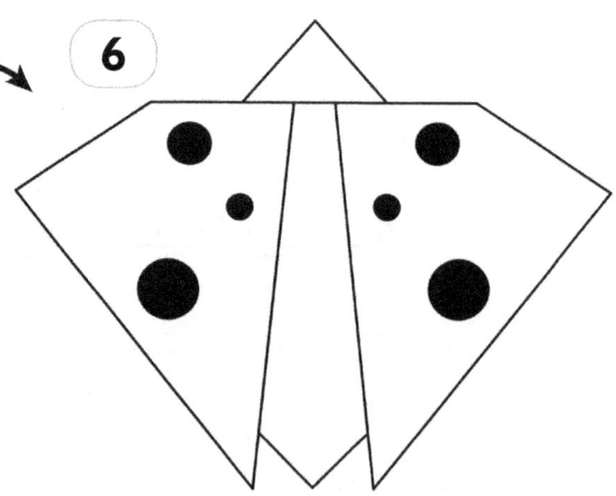

Instructions

1. Fold a square piece of paper in half.
2. Fold it again. Press hard to make crease lines. Open it.
3. Fold the two corners down. Leave a little gap in the centre.
4. Turn it over. Fold down the top corner to the centre.
5. Now fold the same corner up and press down.
6. Turn the shape over. Decorate your ladybird.

(Topic 6 Unit A)
My First English Words Dictionary

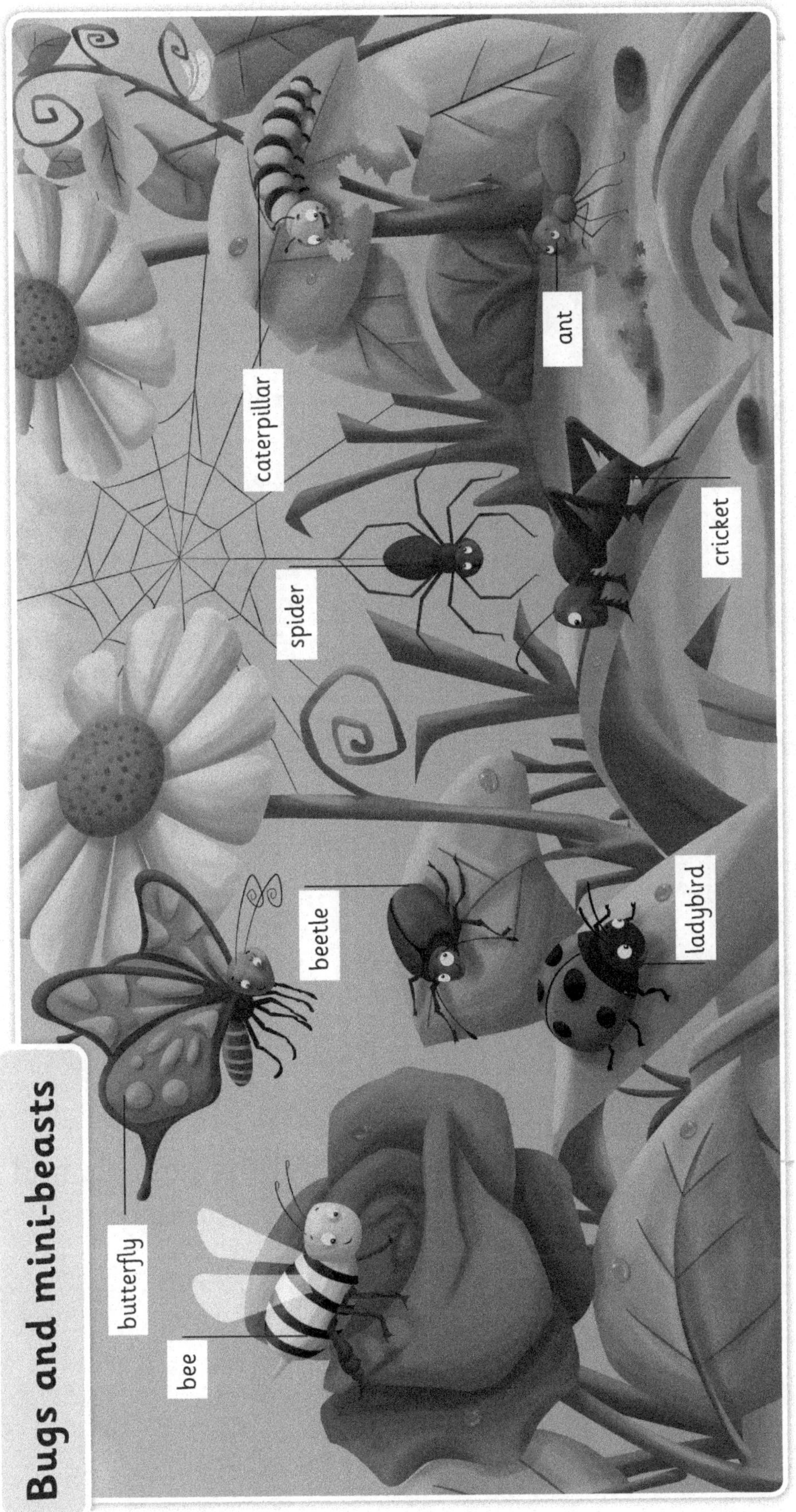

(Topic 6 Unit B)

Listen to the story, *The Bird King*.

1. Cut out the pictures and put them in the correct order.

2. Cut out the sentences and match each sentence to the correct picture.

The birds did not have a king.	They had a race.	Sparrow flew the highest.
They had a meeting.	Sparrow became king.	All the animals had a king.

(Topic 6 Unit C)

Make a paper aeroplane

Read the instructions.

1. Fold the paper in half long-ways. Open the paper again.

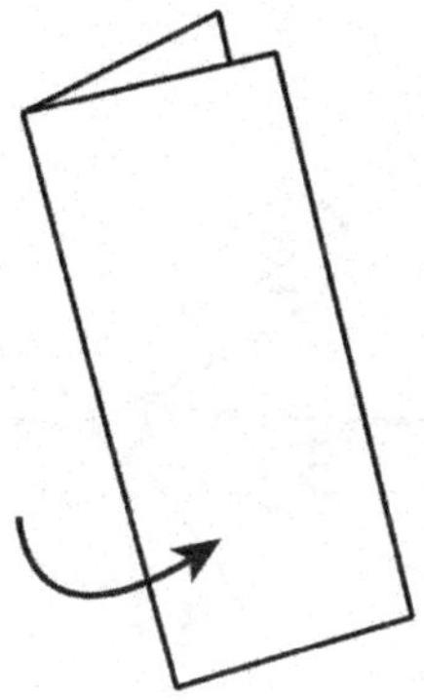

2. Fold the top corners down.

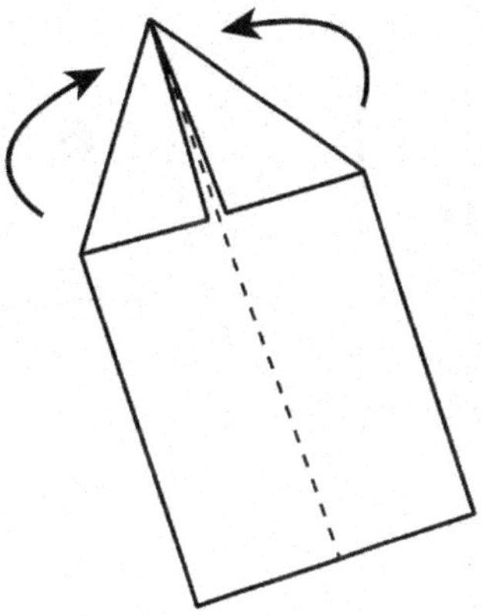

3. Fold the bent corners to the centre.

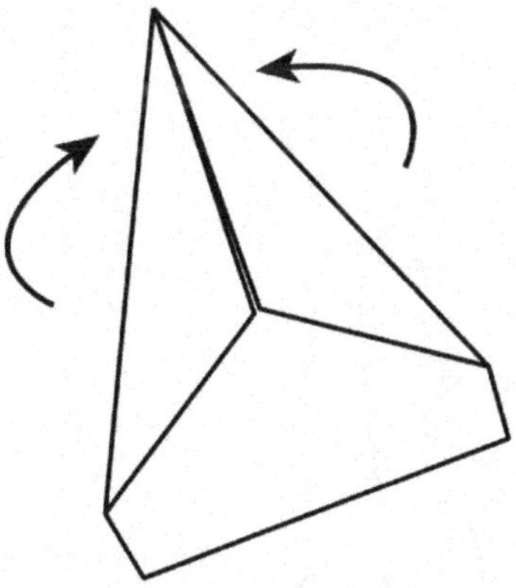

4. Fold the paper in half.

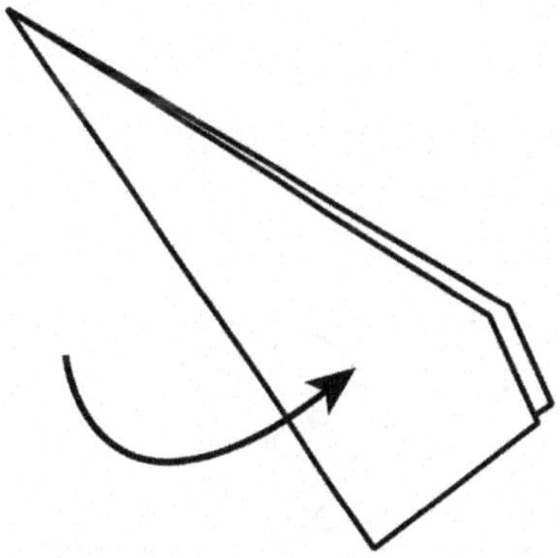

5. Fold the wings down.

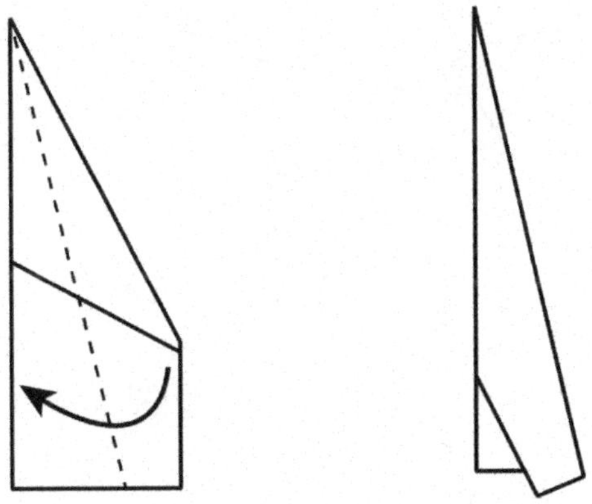

6. Fly your aeroplane.

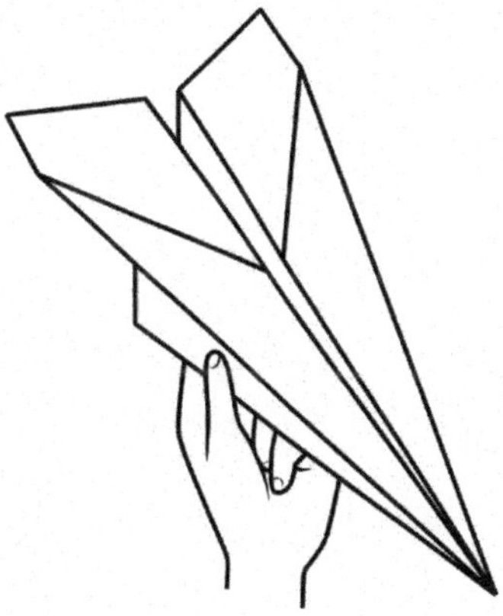

(Topic 6 Unit C)

Play the helicopter game.

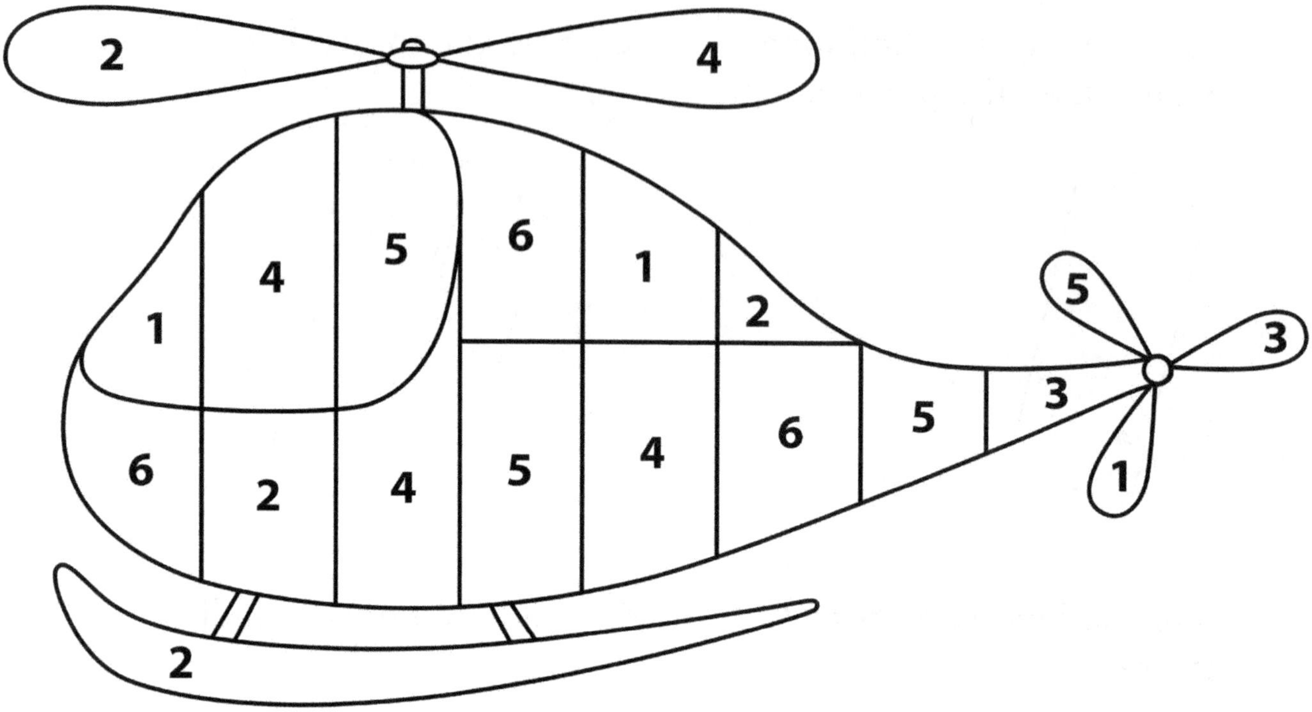

Play the aeroplane game.

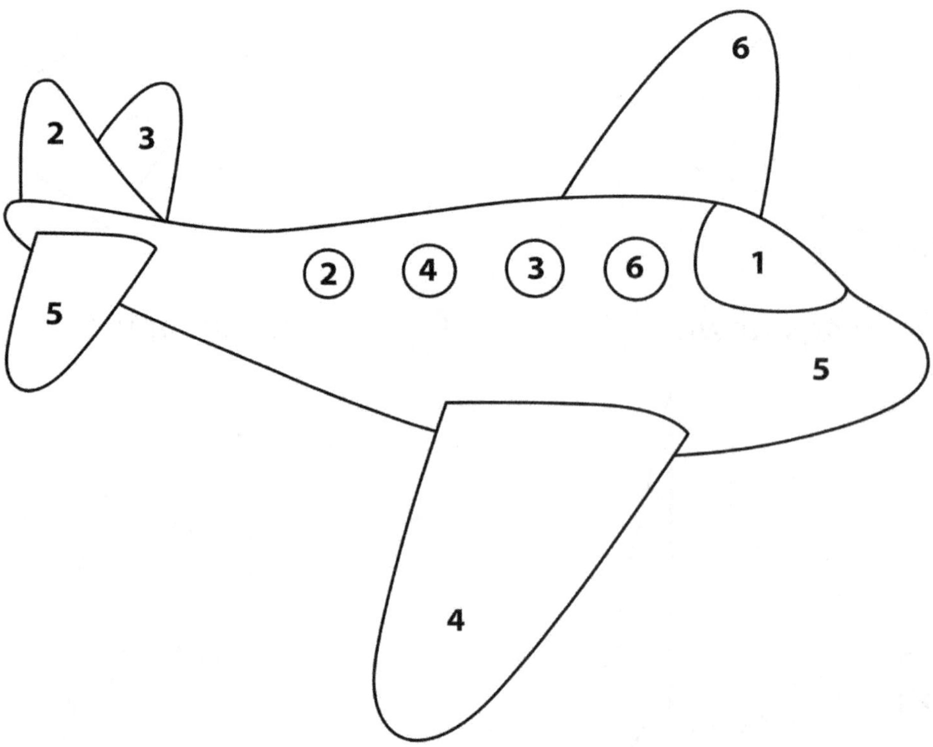

(Topic 7 Unit A, Unit C)

How I feel.

angry

happy

hungry

sad

scared

shy

thirsty

tired

(Topic 7 Unit B)

The Fisherman and the Golden Fish

- Colour the pictures.
- Cut out the pictures.
- Arrange the pictures in the correct order.
- Tell your partner the story.

(Topic 7 Unit C)

Listen and tick (✓) the correct picture.

1. a)  ☐

b)  ☐

2. a)  ☐

b)  ☐

3. a)  ☐

b)  ☐

4. a) 

☐

b)  ☐

5. a)  ☐

b)  ☐

(Topic 8 Unit A)

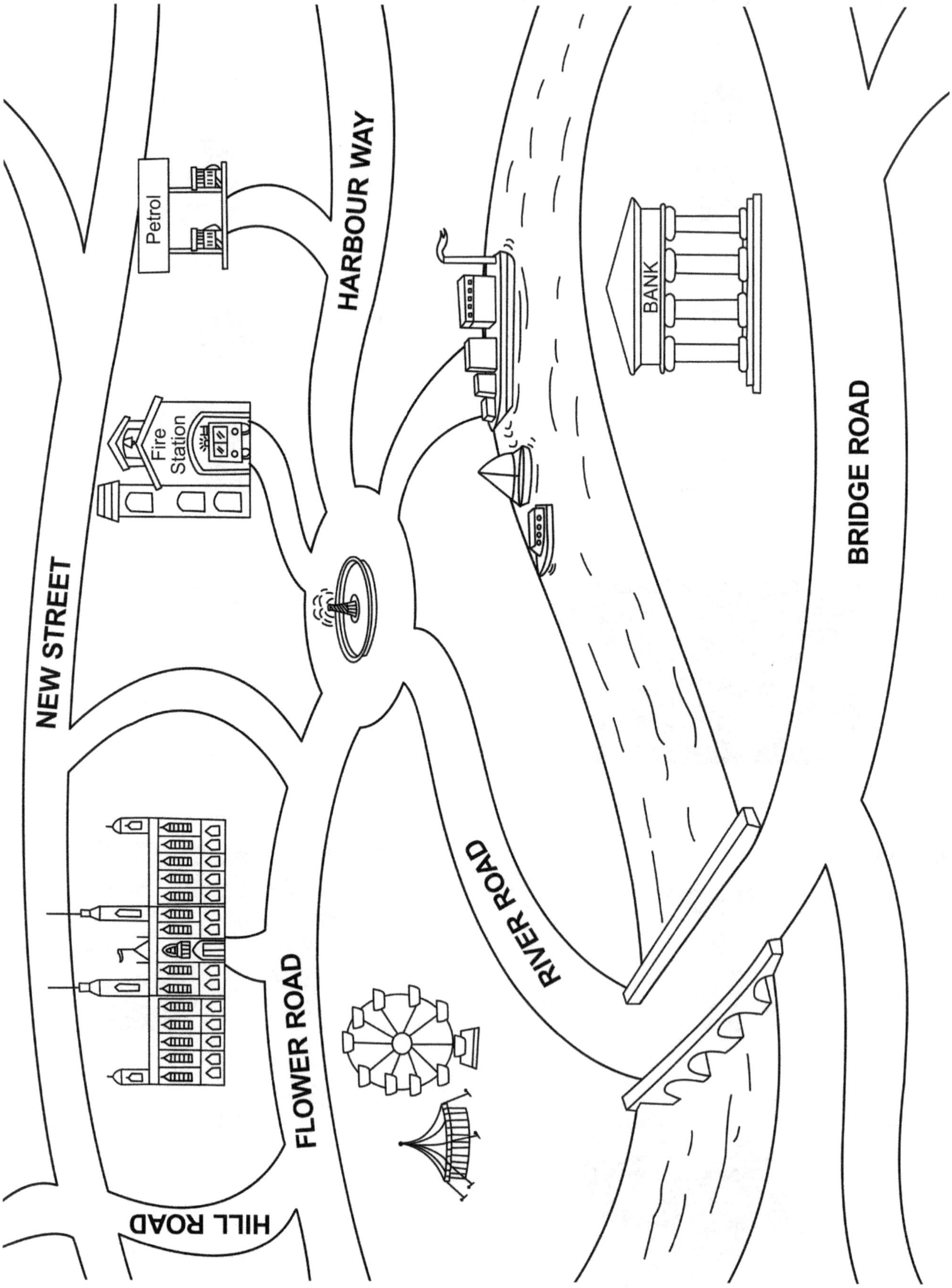

(Topic 8 Unit A)

Listen and tick (✓) the correct picture.

1. a)

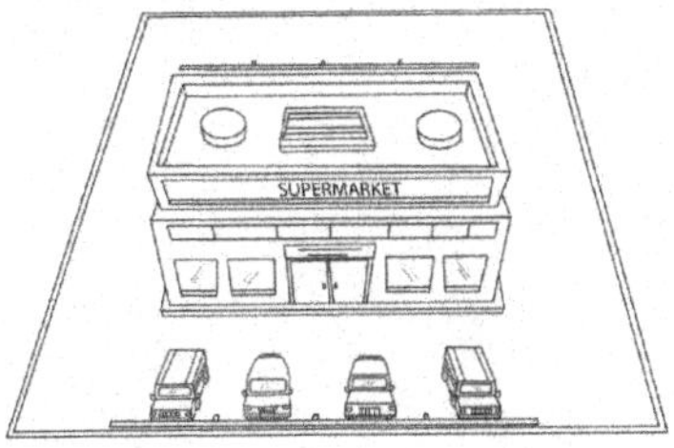

☐

b)

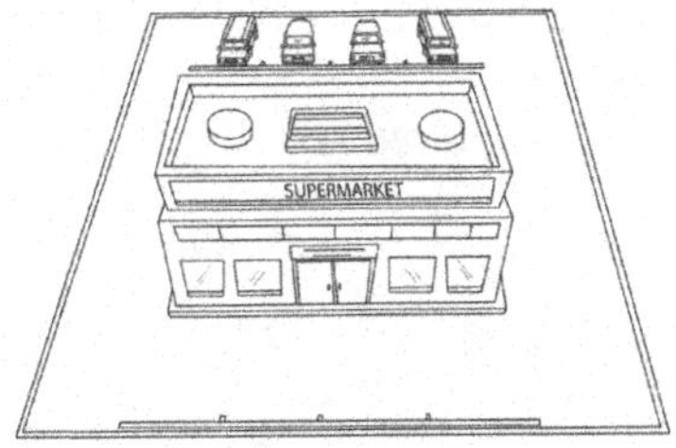

☐

2. a)

☐

b)

☐

3. a)

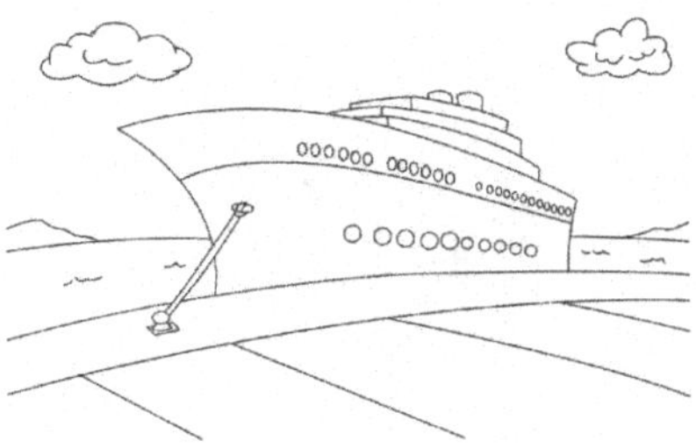

☐

b)

☐

4. a)

☐

b)

☐

5. a)

☐

b)

☐

6. a)

☐

b)

☐

(Topic 8 Unit B)

At the funfair

Cut out the labels and pictures. Match the label with the correct picture.

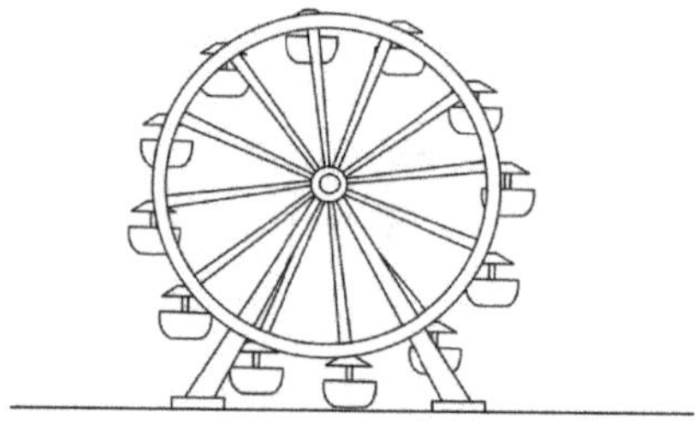

hall of mirrors	roller coaster
ticket office	Ferris wheel
merry-go-round	throwing game
entrance	exit

(Topic 8 Unit C)

Taking the train

Rebecca lives in Green Bay. Help her get to the funfair in Old Town.

1. Look at the timetable.

Train timetable				
	1st train	2nd train	3rd train	4th train
Green Bay	7.00	7.05	7.35	8.00
New River	7.15	-	7.50	8.15
Old Town	7.30	7.25	8.05	-

2. Read the questions. Circle the answer.

a) Which form of transport is Rebecca going to take?

plane   train   car

b) When does the earliest train depart?

7.00   7.05   7.35

c) If she takes the first train, how long will it take for her to get there?

20 minutes   15 minutes   30 minutes

d) Which train won't get her to the funfair?

2nd train   3rd train   4th train

e) If she misses the first train, when is the next train?

7.00   7.05   7.35

f) Which train doesn't stop on the way?

1st train   2nd train   4th train

g) Which train takes the shortest time to get there?

1st train   2nd train   3rd train

(Topic 9 Unit A, Unit B)

Look at the pictures. Use the information on this page to complete activities 3 and 4 on page 146 of your Workbook.

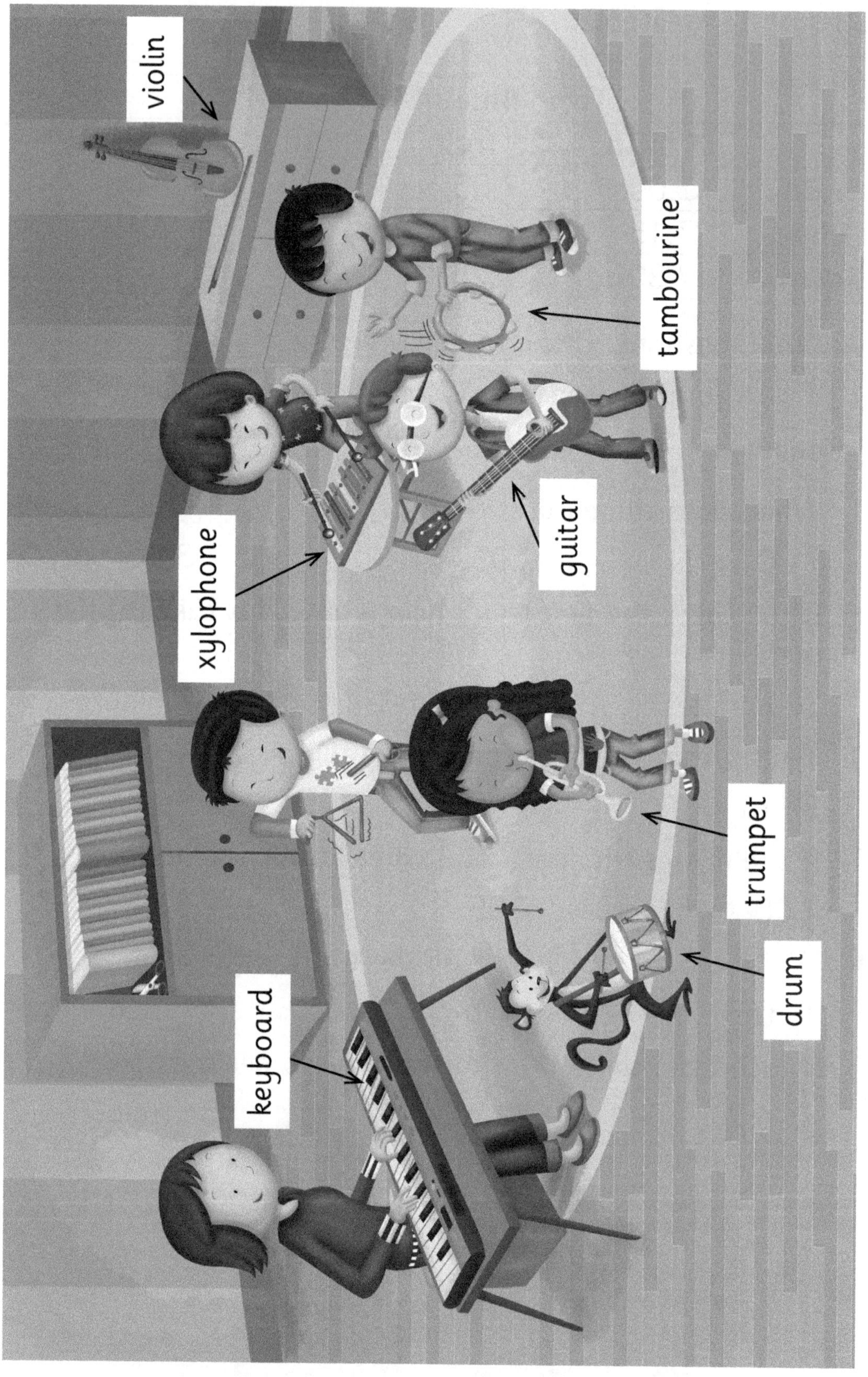

(Topic 9 Unit B)

Make a drum

What you need:

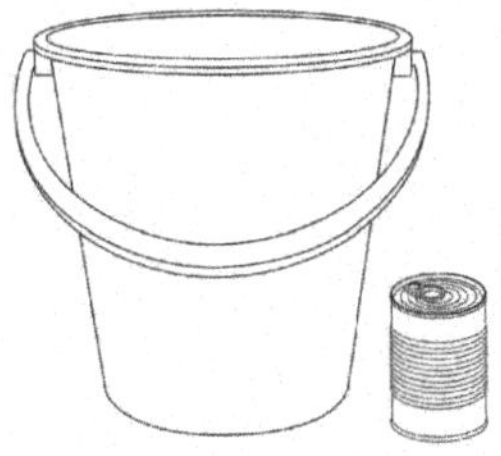 a bucket or a tin	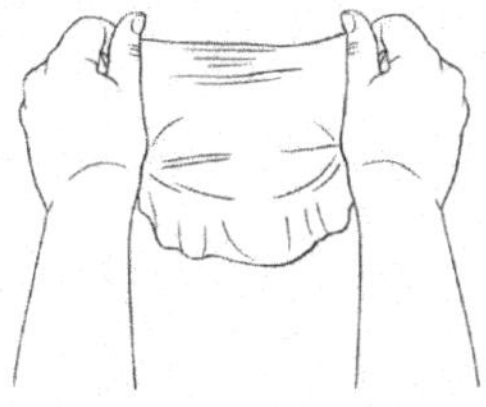 a piece of plastic
 string or elastic	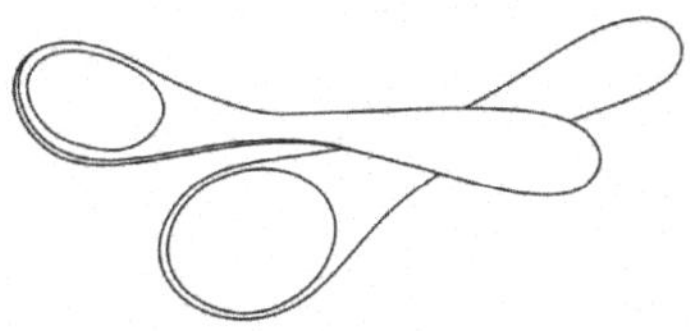 sticks or spoons

Instructions.

1. Cover the top of the bucket with the plastic. Stretch it tightly.

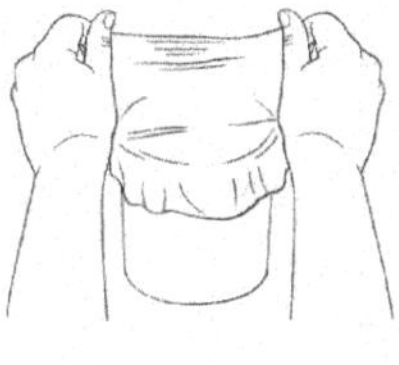

2. Fasten the plastic to the bucket with the string or elastic.

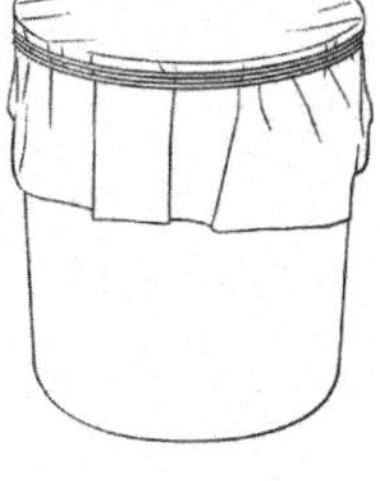

3. Find two sticks or spoons.

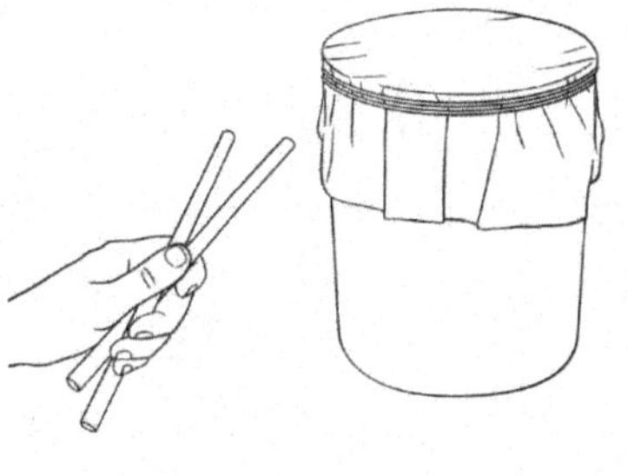

4. Beat your drum.

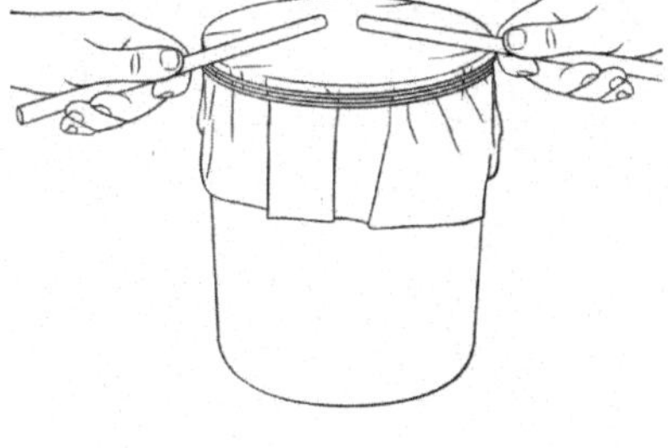

(Topic 9 Unit C)

Musical instruments

Find the instruments in the puzzle.

x	m	n	y	d	r	u	m	s	x
y	v	t	r	i	a	n	g	l	e
l	t	h	k	d	a	y	o	b	n
o	v	b	n	g	u	i	t	a	r
p	s	t	e	e	l	p	a	n	e
h	u	n	s	r	r	t	u	p	c
o	c	b	v	i	o	l	i	n	o
n	u	e	i	d	o	k	n	p	r
e	i	l	n	o	c	v	v	o	d
q	w	l	t	o	a	p	u	n	e
l	o	s	p	o	b	x	t	o	r

Name: ______________________ **Today's date:** ____________

Listening

1. Look at the cover of this book. Circle the correct answer to complete the sentence.

a) The main character is a (girl/boy).

b) The boy's name is (Secret/Bob).

c) The boy looks (sad/happy).

2. Listen to *Bob's Secret Hideaway*. Tick (✓) the things you hear about.

a)  ☐

b)  ☐

c)  ☐

d)  ☐

e)  ☐

3. Listen to the story again. Circle the correct answer.

a) What did Bob climb up to watch?

1) The sun shining. **2)** The moonlight glowing.

b) What did Bob's friends do?

1) They made a noise. **2)** They watched the sun.

c) How did Bob feel when his friends left?

1) Happy **2)** Sad

4. Listen and draw lines. The first one is done for you.

Reading and writing

1. Look at the pictures. Tick (✔) the correct sentences. Cross (✗) the wrong sentences. The first one has been done for you.

a) 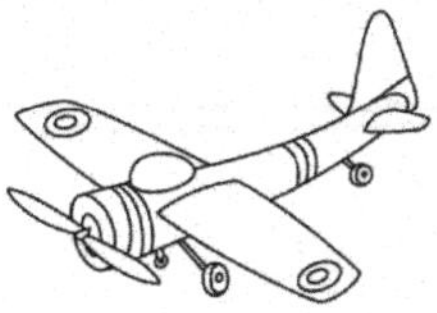

This is an aeroplane. ✔

b) 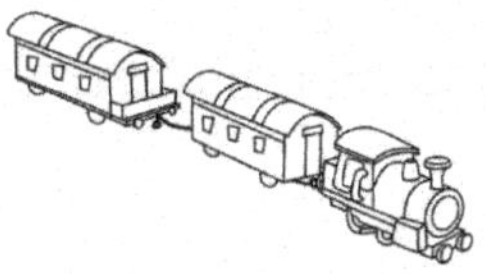

This is a bus. ☐

c) 

This is a car. ☐

d) 

This is a fire engine. ☐

e) 

This is a recorder. ☐

f) 

This is a guitar. ☐

2. Complete the labels.

a) 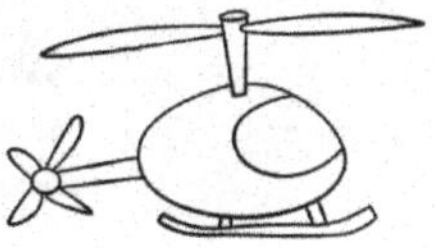

helicopt_ _

b) 

_ _uck

c) 

tr_ _ h _ _ se

d) 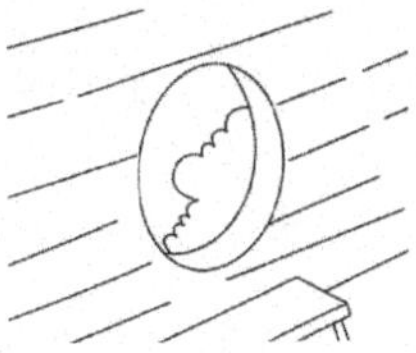

wind_ _

3. Read the sentences. Complete the sentences with words from the box.

a	an	and	but	can	eyes	feathers	wings

Look at me

I am ____________________ bird.

I have two __________ on my head __________ two legs.

I __________ fly because I have two __________.

I have __________, __________

I don't have fur.

Yesterday I sat on __________ elephant's head.

4. Number the sentences in the correct order from 1 to 4.

a)

b)

c)

d)

- ☐ He peeped outside and happily saw that his friends had all come back!
- ☐ So Bob decided not to share his treehouse or his toys.
- ☐ Now Bob was left alone again in his treehouse feeling sad.
- ☐ Bob invited all his friends but all they brought was noise.

5. Look at the last picture. Answer the questions. The first one is done for you.

a) Is Bob playing? No, he isn't.

b) Does Bob have three friends? ____________

c) Can the one boy swing in the tree? ____________

d) Is the girl swinging? ____________

6. Match the sentences to the correct answer.

a) Would you like to come up?	When my friends leave.
b) When do you feel sad?	No, I haven't.
c) Have you ever been inside?	So do I.
d) I like my friends.	Yes, please.

Speaking

Look at the pictures.

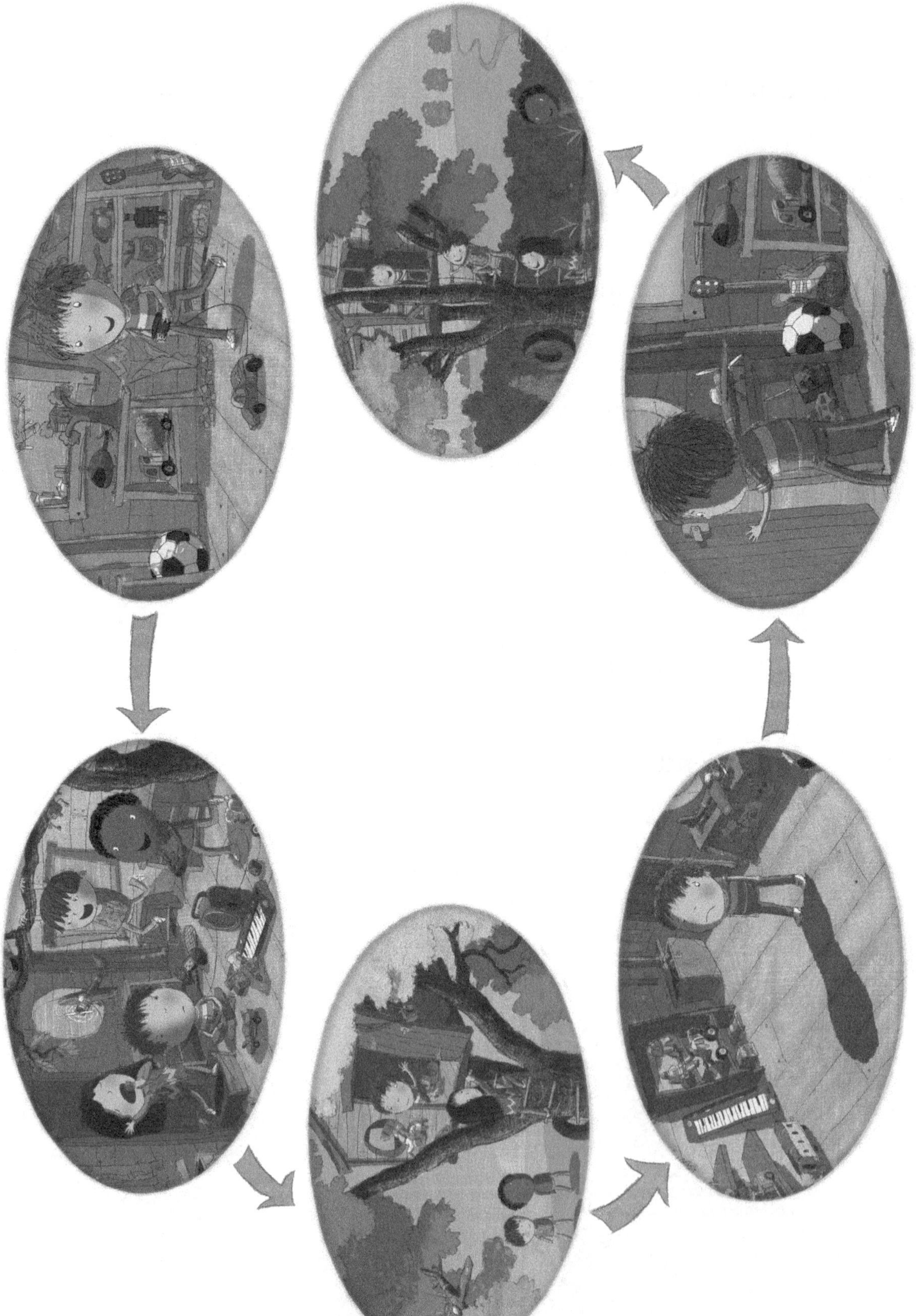

Notes

Notes

Notes